Henry Dry-Bread
THE RICHARD WADE PAPERS

EDITED BY
ROBERT DAWSON

INFORMATION TECHNOLOGY EDITING BY
OWEN DURKIN

ADMINISTERED FROM THE COLLECTION
OF R.A.R. WADE BY
HEATHER SPILLER

PRODUCED BY
DERBYSHIRE GYPSY LIAISON GROUP

Henry Dry-Bread
THE RICHARD WADE PAPERS

EDITED BY
ROBERT DAWSON

INFORMATION TECHNOLOGY EDITING BY
OWEN DURKIN

ADMINISTERED FROM THE COLLECTION
OF R.A.R. WADE BY
HEATHER SPILLER

PRODUCED BY
DERBYSHIRE GYPSY LIAISON GROUP

Published by Robert Dawson
on behalf of Derbyshire Gypsy Liaison Group,
188 Alfreton Road, Blackwell, Alfreton, Derbyshire, DE55 5JH.

ISBN 1-903418-08-9

Printed by 4 Sheets Design & Print Limited
197 Mansfield Road, Nottingham NG1 3FS
Tel (0115) 910 1140

FOREWORD
By His Grace, The Duke of Devonshire

Chatsworth
Bakewell
Derbyshire
DE45 1PP
Baslow 582204

Nov 14ᵗ 2000

Romany people have long been connected with Derbyshire and with Chatsworth in particular. There are records of families both on and near Chatsworth from the late 16th C and there is good evidence to assume that some successfully hid out on the estate during one or other of the persecutions of Gypsies, especially that period extending until the 1780s

Evidence of Gypsy and other poor peoples' graves on the estate has long been known, but the coincidence struck me that the most significant of the Gypsy graves is that of Henry Sherriff's family. His many connections with North Derbyshire are closely linked to the history of Gypsies in this area. The information in this book is of paramount importance to Gypsy studies — even if it is from a man known as a less than truthful rogue. I am, therefore, delighted to commend this book to all keen to learn more about this fascinating and historic way of life.

The Editors extend gratitude to the following:

His Grace, The Duke of Devonshire

Also to the various individuals who contributed
finance to this book.

Local Heritage *initiative*

Heritage
Lottery Fund

Nationwide

The
Countryside
Agency

DERBYSHIRE
GYPSY LIAISON
GROUP

MOVING FORWARD

CONTENTS

ACKNOWLEDGEMENTS

Derbyshire Gypsy Liaison Group, the editors, Dick Wade and Heather Spiller are most grateful to the Countryside Agency for their support in the production of this book. The Group is also grateful for the support of His Grace, the Duke of Devonshire, and to Chesterfield and District CVS (LINKS) for assistance in finding the main funding, as well as to several individual contributors..

As editor, I acknowledge with gratitude the help given me in typing up the original documents by Pauline Duval of Lichfield. Without her help, this project would have been very seriously delayed. My thanks too to Siobhan Spencer for checking and proof reading the whole script; to Molly Hart for acting as 'taxi driver'. My thanks especially go to Henry's son George Henry and his wife Susan and family, and to Arthur Sherriff, Henry's cousin, for their co-operation and invaluable help, and to Bob Lovell, the New Zealand Romanichal folk singer and rokkerer, for his aid.

I must also pay very special tribute to Rom Owen Durkin, a direct descendent of one of the several Boswells who were transported to Australia, and thereby a very distant relative of Henry's. Owen's intense interest in his own forebears, illustrated by his being one of the most distinguished of the members of the Romany Association of Australia, has added significantly to the known history of the journey into exile of the Roma and their subsequent life in Australia. When he agreed to use his computer expertise to take a technical look at the design and layout of the book, I was delighted. Only the very day before he suddenly died, he commented to his wife that all but the index had been thus amended.

Sadly, therefore, he is not here to see this work come to fruition, but this book is dedicated to Owen, his wife Bev and their five children. I hope Owen would be happy with this important, if unusual, addition to our knowledge of English Gypsies of the past.

INTRODUCTION

The overwhelming majority of these papers consist of letters written by one Henry Sherriff, a Romani, to his lawyer friend, Richard ("Dick") Wade, when Henry was in prison. The vast majority – probably all – were written from Leicester prison, and probably also during 1964 and 1965. Henry had been transferred from Dartmoor to Leicester for other hearings, one of which was for his divorce. He had been sentenced to 7 years for bigamy but as he had several other spells in jail for burglary and similar offences, some also in Leicester, the exact date of the letters cannot be ascertained. He also had a brief spell in The Dana prison at Shrewsbury.

About half the Henry Sherriff documents are written on prison notepaper, many of which are marked, "Governor's permission," which Dick Wade seems to have obtained for Henry. One two-page list of 42 Romani words, mainly the names of Counties, has at the end, the words, "Dear Sir, I have Guvernors permission to send this in my letter thank you – G. H. Sherriff 92," and another similar sheet containing parts of verbs and numbers, has "Guvernors permission to send in letter. SHERRIFF 92." A few pages are written in the form of questions in Wade's own handwriting, alongside which are Henry's answers.

Though these documents certainly originated from Leicester prison, 92 was in fact Henry's prison number at Dartmoor. His prisoner number at Leicester was 3010 and at Shrewsbury 1496.A batch of information, mainly vocabulary and family detail, was written in a prison exercise book and sent by post on 9 August to Dick Wade. This is somewhat surprising, as one of the stipulations for the use of the exercise book was, as printed on the front cover, a prohibition on writing about "Your Own Life."

Most of the documents bear no date, and it is often not possible on the lists to tell in which order they were written. From the contexts, it is reasonable to assume that the majority were written in 1965.It is also very often difficult to ascertain a context. For instance, at the bottom of a list of words, Henry writes, "The piece in the paper you sent – it is very interesting and good. It shows how much you like Romani folki." This was presumably something about Wade which he sent to Henry in prison, but there is no clue as to what.

Occasionally, too, a letter refers to something in a previous letter but as a general rule correct order cannot be presumed. Therefore, attempts at chronology have been abandoned (though some idea of this can be presumed from Henry's own use of Romani: this matter will be returned to). For these reasons, the contents of the papers have been 'mixed and matched', and placed in subject order as far as this is possible. The various lists of Romani have been amalgamated into a vocabulary list at the end.

Henry never received a formal school education. He told Dick he had been to 'College' where he learned to read and write, but this is clearly a euphemism for 'prison.' He must have had some good teachers there, though it has to be said he seems to have spent considerable time locked up so, cynically, had a lot of time to learn. He was clearly a highly intelligent man who learned to read and write quickly. There are very few spelling errors indeed and he commonly correctly writes very orthographically complex words, even when it is clear that they must have been unusual words for him.

Henry's writing ability has proved to be especially beneficial in the extensive tracts of Romani. There is a sharp contrast between the various writing styles used by Henry. Whilst some of the time he writes in a chatty way, at others he reverts to pedantic speech as used by late Victorians. Therefore it quickly became clear to me that some of Henry's 'writings' had been taken from other sources, often being lifted verbatim (or nearly so) from other published sources. I have omitted several matters which Henry writes about and which I am convinced are untrue or incorrect, but have left in a number of paragraphs which might, just might, be true. The reader must decide on the veracity of some of Henry's claims.

Richard Wade

Richard was born in 1926. He has three children.

He qualified as a lawyer in the family practice but retired early to follow his painting and writing career. He painted numerous pictures in oils for Romani people, including scenes of horses, vardos, fighting cocks, dogs and scenery. He was also a successful writer and broadcaster.

Early in the 1960s, he was in the Law Courts in London waiting for a case to come up when he found himself standing next to Bombardier Billy Wells, the famous Gypsy striker of the gong for Rank films. Speaking to Billy, he was suddenly struck by the life and hardship of Gypsy people, and wanted to find out more. The same day, he went to Foyles Bookshop and there bought a copy of George Borrow's Romano *Lavo Lil*, from which he learned basic Romani. Thereafter, whenever he took his family camping in Lincolnshire, and happened to see a Gypsy, he approached him or her and spoke Romanes.

He met and became a close friend of Sylvester Gordon Boswell, the illustrious Romani author (in fact, he only ever used the name Gordon) , and as trust grew between the two men, be was made an honorary member of the Boswell family, something which gave him intense pride thereafter. Sylvester told him, "You are a true Romani." He continued to support any Gypsies he could against prejudice or persecution or merely misunderstanding. He earned the deep respect and love of Romani people.

Dick – as everyone knows him – joined the Gypsy Lore Society and for 10 years until the Society folded in 1975, was assistant editor of the Society's highly respected and scholarly Journal, under the editorship of The Rawnie (Dr. Dora Yates). He is unclear how he first met George Henry Sherriff (who he called Henry) but it was probably through his links with Gordon Boswell senior. At some point, he found himself able to assist Henry through his legal know-how. He did so willingly on several occasions. Additionally, he wrote to and visited the prison Governor on behalf of Henry and persuaded him to transfer Henry to Ashwell Open prison. Dick may well therefore have additionally ensured that Henry did not return to Dartmoor.

Each time Henry was released from one of his increasingly prolonged jail terms, he was contrite and promised that he had reformed. But each time he re-offended. At their final meeting, he had allowed Henry to set up camp in the orchard of his home at Deeping St James, Lincolnshire. It is now clear that Henry used to pump information from Ellie Wade, Dick's daughter, who was then about 7 or 8 years old. This may sound unjust to Henry, but Dick is convinced this was the case, and so am I. That said, Henry also had a genuine affection for Ellie.

In a field out of sight of Dick's home, but which Dick owned, Gordon Boswell kept several horses. Henry avoided any contact with Gordon, presumably knowing that Gordon would have no time for him. On the occasion of the final meeting, Henry ascertained from Ellie that Gordon was not in the area and he went to the field to see the horses.

Ellie was incorrect – Gordon was there and Henry had to go into the pub to avoid meeting Gordon. Gordon was a long time with his horses, and Henry had to remain hidden in the pub for about an hour. Whilst there, he used his time to advantage and sold the landlord £20 worth of goods under false pretences.

Thinking Gordon had gone, Henry came out of the pub – and met Gordon face to face.

"What are you doing here?" he asked Henry. Gordon's loyalty to Dick was absolute, and he took Henry on one side and spoke privately to him, apparently saying that Dick was a good man who did not deserve the treatment which Henry was likely to give him. Dick did not hear the conversation, but heard enough to realise that Gordon was saying, "I'm telling you, Dick Wade is an honest man and you come here taking money from his next-door neighbour. Get down that road and don't bother Dick again." As a result, Henry immediately packed up his belongings and left. Dick never heard again from him.

Gordon said to Dick, "Don't have anything else to do with him. We do what we can for people in prison, but have nothing to do with him." I have since discussed Henry with Gordon's son (also Gordon), particularly about this incident. Gordon junior is a distinguished and highly respected Romani. He would say nothing derogatory against Henry Sherriff, but he did remember the man and said his father had no time for him. He believes that his father thought Henry was intending to use Dick in some way.

Dick remembers Henry as being a very intelligent man and wonderful (Dick's word) with his hands. He cited as an example, a superb caravan money box made of matchsticks which Henry made whilst in prison for Ellie, Dick's daughter. Ellie does not know what happened to this caravan.

Significance

Henry claimed to be the last living speaker of puri chib, the old inflected Romani language which had reputedly disappeared from Britain by the early 1960s, though there were still Welsh Romanies who could all-but speak this most beautiful yet highly complex language. By this, I mean that these Gypsies, although they commonly spoke the next phase of Romani – known as Poggadi Chib (broken tongue) – were still able to include chunks of puri chib phrases as a matter of course.

Henry went beyond this. He claimed to still speak the inflected puri chib and thereby to be the last speaker in the country. Such a claim needed investigating very carefully since, if true, much of the evidence about how the language evolved would have to be changed. Not least, it implied that Henry was an isolated speaker of Puri Chib, a sort of last of the Mohecans, and thereby that his brand of Anglo Romani must be the most developed and modern form of the Anglo dialect yet discovered. This, of course, begs the question as to who he must have talked Puri Chib to. Henry explains this by saying that he learned it from his grandparents (who brought him up) and that it was only when he realised that

Dick had a deep knowledge of the language that he was able to resurrect it.

It quickly became apparent that huge chunks of puri chib Anglo Romani were actually lifted, often verbatim, from other books, especially Smart and Crofton (see Bibliography) . In addition, in some of Henry's apparently early letters he does not know some quite basic Romani words which Dick asks him. Yet suddenly, he becomes this fine speaker.

It is now clear that what happened was this. Henry suddenly discovered that Dick was a man with a greater knowledge of Romani than himself. Perhaps he wished to please Dick, who was doing so much to help him, or perhaps he saw an opportunity to use Dick to his advantage. At any rate, he found Smart and Crofton, and regurgitated that, and extracts from other books, for Dick's benefit (and from comments he has pencilled alongside extracts, Dick realised). He appears to have convinced the Romani scholar Fred Huth that he was indeed 'the last of the speakers' but I am inclined to think that Fred, who as a young man had heard English and Welsh Romanes far finer than anything of Henry's, believed it was the truth. That could have been the end of the story of Henry 'Dry-Bread', but something strange happened. Whether it was too much trouble to copy out some very dry chunks of Victorian-flavoured Smart and Crofton's Romani, or more likely he suddenly found he had re-learned his own language, he began using it to write his own letters and to make up his own texts and translate his own stories and songs into Romani. In so doing, he applied Romani to new ideas and facts that had not existed in the past, moulding the language in exactly the sort of ways it must have been used by his forebears when they found new things on their long trek from India.

This point is returned to and expanded in the notes on the text. It is clearly a very important aspect of the papers. Added to that value is the family history, stories and poems and reminiscences of life on the road, all of which add to knowledge of Gypsy people. and almost unique as papers written actually by a Gypsy about English Gypsies, rather than (as has almost always been the case before) by some well-meaning gorjer. Probably the most significant exception to this long history of other people writing about Gypsies is Sylvester Gordon Boswell's own *Book of Boswell* – and a strange irony that the only man to write such a book until then should be the one who warned off the only other major Gypsy writer. Purists may well point to the following previous English Gypsy authors:

- Carew, F.W. No. 747, *Being the Autobiography of a Gypsy*, (c 1890);
- Carew, Bampfylde Moore, *Life and Adventures of Bampfylde Moore Carew, King of the Beggars* (1793);
- Petulengro, Gipsy (Xavier). *A Romany Life* (1937);
- Smith, Cornelius. *The Life Story of Gipsy Cornelius Smith*;
- Smith, Gipsy (Rodney), *Gipsy Smith: His Life and Work* (1901);
- Steggall, John H, *The Suffolk Gipsy* (c 1857).

Of the above, the two Carews were not Gypsies. Cornelius Smith's work was ghosted by a gorjer; Rodney Smith did include some Gypsy information in his autobiography, but the majority of his works are of a religious nature. Though Steggall claims to have been a Gypsy, there is no evidence whatsoever. Gipsy Petulengro also claimed Anglo Romani descent through his father and Continental Romani through his mother. Although the Smith family from which Xavier claims descent is well documented, it has not yet proved possible to place Xavier into it with certainty.

The Discovery of the Papers

Credit for helping to make these papers public has to go primarily to Heather Spiller, an afficionado of and worker with and for Gypsies for many years, especially in the health field. Because of her interest in Gypsies, her son told her of meeting a man who spoke Romani and knew Gypsies and would like to make contact with Heather. She and her family developed a friendship with Dick. Years later, he suffered his first massive stroke – it would have killed a lesser man – and with tremendous courage and determination, Dick defied the doctors' predictions, found himself a council bungalow, and refused to go into a nursing home. His strength of spirit is shown in that once, when Heather visited him in hospital, he was sitting up in bed and playing the mouth organ.

Dick's interest in and knowledge of Gypsies was a treat for Heather, though it quickly became apparent that he had forgotten many things due to the effects of the strokes. Gradually, Dick's trust in Heather increased, and he began to show her some of the extremely interesting papers and photos he had in his possession.

One day, out of the blue, he handed her a large brown envelope and said, "Do something with this." She realised that he sought publication, took the bundle home, and sat and went through it.

Quite early on, Heather contacted me to ask me about the papers, –

several hundred of them – though at that stage I had not realised their significance. Eventually, she asked me if I knew anyone who would be able to take on the papers and write them up and edit them – a colossal task. As she explained more about what they contained, I realised that she had in her stewardship, information about English Gypsies which would be of immense value to sociologists, historians, genealogists and linguists alike. The Romani which Henry used was especially interesting.

Of course I volunteered, and Heather went back to Dick and told him about me. In fact, Dick and I had been in correspondence in 1973 and had bought some of my own collection of books on Gypsies which I was then disposing of. I had joined the Gypsy Lore Society in 1957 at the age of 13 and for a while was the youngest member. Dick learned of my reverence for Dora Yates, 'the Rawni', or "Beebi Dora" (*The lady, Aunt Dora*), an eminent Gypsy scholar and secretary of the Gypsy Lore Society and editor of its journal for many years.

Thankfully, Dick accepted my credentials and allowed Heather to pass photocopies of the papers onto me to work on. It is indeed a great honour to me to have been able to work on them, and I am most grateful to both Dick and Heather. Heather's role has not been easy – Dick's serious illness makes him very forgetful and she often has to go over things with him time after time.

At any rate, I am proud to be involved with Dick and Heather, and thank them for this great privilege.

Orthography

In the following pages, I have used Henry's spelling of Romani throughout. This has inevitably led to some variation, as he was writing it as he thought the English sounded with an English letter system. Therefore, variations in the spelling occur frequently, and especially minor changes, even in the same passage, such as doubling of consonants in one word and not in the next.

Though a system for writing Romani was developed by Dr. John Sampson, of Liverpool University, it is complex and required the use of several Greek letters. Henry could not have come across this, and even if he had, it is difficult to imagine he would have found it helpful. More modern and simpler systems have now been developed on the Continent for writing Romani, but these were not available at the time Henry wrote.

Therefore, enormous credit must go to this Gypsy who had learned to read and write in only a few weeks in prison for managing to record his language so uniformly and successfully. Knowing Romani already, it is difficult for me to judge how a person without Romani experience would naturally speak the words as Henry wrote them, but I imagine that Henry's spelling is usually so logical that it could be accurately spoken with ease and accuracy.

All comments and additions of my own are in italic script. Therefore all text not in such scripts originates from Henry or, in the case of the additional notes in Chapter 10, from Dick Wade.

Abbreviations

BKM – Buckinghamshire

cp – compare

DBY – Derbyshire

HMP – Hampshire

illeg – illegible

LIN – Lincolnshire

NTH – Northamptonshire

NTM – Nottinghamshire

OXF – Oxfordshire

STF – Staffordshire

WKS – Warwickshire

The 1996 Monty Sherriff Tape

In 1996, Siobhan Spencer, secretary of Derbyshire Gypsy Liaison group, and her husband David (then chair of the organization) discovered an elderly Gypsy man living in a small old peoples' bungalow in Leicester. He gave the name Monty Sherriff. They loaned Monty a tape recorder for him to record his memories, of which he taped about 20 minutes' worth. Throughout, he is lucid and it is apparent that his mind is as clear now as when he was a young man.

Subsequently, we realised that this man was in fact the same as Henry Sherriff, also known as George Sherriff and Sherriff Boswell. His reminiscences coincide with incidents described in the papers, but unfortunately there is little brand new information on the tape.

Several matters add to the information in the papers. One especially important one is the proof that Henry remembered Dick with admiration for the work that Dick and Gordon Boswell did (with others) in saving Appleby Fair.

Henry also refers to ancient stopping grounds at Flash Dam, Riber, and Sticker Plantation at Buxton.

Amongst the Gypsies he mentions is Tommy Finney, who Henry says had a particularly fine Reading wagon. Tommy used to hawk pots and baskets which he carried on his head. He refers to the famous Gordon Sylvester Boswell as 'Uncle Gordon Sylvester' and it appears that this was not simply the usual Romani term for an older and respected Gypsy, but seems to imply an actual relationship. It is said by local Gypsies to be a distant one through Reni Boswell, but I cannot link her to Gordon Sylvester's family.

Several Derbyshire Gypsies are mentioned. His aunt Reni lived for some time on land at Renishaw. Denzil Smith became a councillor – Henry is not sure if this might have been Denzil's brother – and Minnie Smith won a £10 bet by kicking a chandelier down in a public house. Scottish 'white heather' came from the moors above Beeley. He lists Ayres, Blairs, Partridges (including Benny), Fred Moss, Calladines as amongst local families and describes how Junky Lee, son of Christmas (and brother of Walter) lived in a hole in the ground in the north of the county and, Henry alleges, smelt so bad that no other Gypsies would go near him. Ezzy and Mushy, sons of Trout Taylor, were two exceptional step dancers in their day. He makes passing mention of Bob and Iza Braddock, Mushy and Iher Toogood and the Wiltshire family. Also Tom and Bob Smith, the Hames family (nicknamed Whistlers), the actual family of Whistlers, and the Booths who mainly travelled Cheshire and the Wirksworth area. He associates Stevens, Whattons and Locks especially with Shropshire and Wales.

Amongst Fighting Men he refers to are Bartley Gormon, brothers Opey and Hughie Burton, Fighting Tommy Lee, Tommy Woodward (son of Kizzy Woodward). Big Tommy Forrest, Little Wry-Necked Robin Winter and Tommy Winter of Leicester, ex-soldier and regimental champion. Henry's grandparents, who brought him up, bought five houses and a field – sadly he does not say where – and settled there in their old age. His grandfather died aged about 90, and Trainette at over 80. At one point Henry says his grandfather never drank in his life, but elsewhere says he was a regular at the Miners Arms in Newbold.

Henry first went hawking at the age of 7 and his grandfather used to send him out a pint of beer and his grandmother half a pint from the pub when the day's hawking was done. At the age of 11, he was out hawking with a grinding barrow when he was arrested at Bakewell. He escaped, retrieved his barrow from the back of the police station, and made a forced march to his aunt's at Buxton where he hid out for a while, before resuming the journey, on foot, to his Uncle Buller at Stockport. Later he moved to Derby.

With Kizzy, his partner during World War 2, he kept largely to the Long Eaton and Sawley areas on the Derbyshire and Nottinghamshire borders, but otherwise he seems to have travelled throughout the East Midlands, though he says he travelled the whole of England, Scotland, Wales, Northern Ireland and the Irish Republic. Kizzy's parents, incidentally, were Black Billy Elliott (or Woodward) and Ellen Smith, daughter of 'Mad' George, this couple being famous for Black Billy's trait of bringing the horse into the kitchen of their house in cold weather, when he used the sink as a manger. Black Billy was also infamous for his whip, which he used regularly on people who offended him. Henry ends the tape on a sad note. He says,

"If anyone would like to come over *(to Leicester)* they can stop as long as they like and bring a typing machine with them and I'll give them a good story, the best story they've ever had among Travellers as long as they jog my memory. I'd love to do that because I'm on my own *(and at this point his voice cracks)* I'm lost, I'm on my kookeroo *(= lonely – voice cracks again)*. So if anybody can come over please let me know. I've been living in this place a few months since I came out of the hospital. So please let me know and you can come over any time you want, just let me know when you're coming and you'd be welcome and I'll give you a story. Moro dadus jivs pre doi kom see tuttis nav, kushti bok." *(Our father who lives up there, hallowed be your name. Good luck.)*

He makes no other mention of Dick, the man who had done so very much for him.

It was only after, when I was researching for this book, that the reason for his intense loneliness emerged. Henry had at least seven female partners, two of whom were legal wives. In each case, he abandoned one woman for another, and that coupled with his frequent prison stays must have made him a thorough nuisance and a potentially dangerous man, in both respects, for every Gypsy he met. Given the very strict taboos about sexual relations, Henry probably proved himself untrustworthy, and also, wherever Henry was to be found, the police were never far away.

The morning he left prison from one of his sentences, he visited his daughter-in-law and gave her a bag containing women's clothes and jewellery, inviting her to help herself. She realised the goods were stolen and did not touch them. A fortnight later the police arrived and would obviously have arrested her had she done as Henry said.

Henry was an unhappy man, as evidenced by his feelings of rejection by his own people. On one occasion in prison, he tried to kill himself by swallowing a fork and had to have emergency surgery.

1. HENRY'S FAMILY AND UPBRINGING

Henry's Descent

Thanks to the research needed for my **The Genealogy of the Romani Boswells**, it is possible to trace Henry Sherriff's Romani roots along one line from the early part of the 17th century. Henry himself mentions his ancestry from Appy Boswell and Appy can be placed with certainty into the Boswell genealogy.

> Francis Boswell, gentleman, wife Ann
> Francis's son Haniel Boswell, King of the Gypsies, baptised 27.10.1583, London, wife Abigail Scott
> Haniel's son, Edward Boswell, King of the Gypsies, wives Elizabeth, Bridget and Alice
> Edward's son, John Boswell, wife Easter
> John's son, also John Boswell, wives Mary Jeffery and Mary Bibby
> John's son, Black Jack Boswell, wife Molly
> Black John's son also John (but Boss), 'The Flaming Tinman', wife Mary Newberry. Married 1780, Nottingham
> The Flaming Tinman's son, Anselo Boss and Phyllis Blewitt
> Anselo's son Absalom (Appy) Boswell and Trainetti Boyling
> Appy's daughter Tresi Boswell, husband William Sherriff
> Tresi's son Hope Sherriff, wife Trainetti Boswell
> Hope's daughter Tienni Sherriff, husband George Boswell
> Tienni's son Henry Sherriff ('Monty').

So Henry has a fine Gypsy ancestry, Haniel and Abigail being the ancestors of three of the seven proven Boswell lines, viz Robert, Edward 1 and Black Jack. It is also likely that another Robert, one of Haniel's brothers, gave rise to a fourth Boswell line, that of the Seth Boswells. Therefore, Henry Sherriff's breed (to use the Gypsy word for lineage) is impeccable.

The Sherriff families themselves became a Gypsy family due to the union of a man whom oral tradition describes as a mumper, William Sherriff, with Tresi Boswell. The word mumper usually means tramp, but William was a grinder by occupation and in this case mumper probably indicates someone whom the Gypsies themselves thought of as socially inferior. Indeed, research of my own makes it clear that there were Romany Sherriffs well before the union of William and Tresi, and that William was probably descended from these.

These Sherriffs remained a Midlands family. To the best of my knowledge, all stopped travelling and went into housing, though it is still unclear as to what happened to all but one of Henry's own children. However, I am not aware of any Sherriffs left on the road today.

In correspondence between the eminent Gypsyologist Fred Huth and Dick Wade, little snippets of information occur. But other than parish records themselves, by far the most valuable information comes from the notebooks of that doyen of English Gypsy researchers, T. W. Thomson. Thomson recorded meeting Trainetti/Trenit, the wife of Hope, who told him that Appy – our Henry's great grandfather – was the result of a brief alliance between a Trainetti Boswell and Black Ambrose Boswell and that he was born on Selston Common, Notts. Later, however, Thomson (rightly) amends this to Anselo (Ambrose's brother) and Phyllis Bluett or Blewitt. The second is unquestionably correct.

Other genealogical information comes from Henry himself, and is presented below almost entirely as he gives it, though with occasional slight editing of punctuation to clarify one or two points. Unfortunately, though Henry names many relatives, it is not always clear from his notes how he was related to them.

An extensive search for Sherriffs in the parish records of the whole of the East Midlands has been undertaken, and the search taken further afield into Counties where the family has been known to travel. Although this has increased knowledge of the family considerably, significant gaps in knowledge remain, and it has to be assumed either that the family were well away from their traditional areas, or that they were using different surnames, a common trait amongst Gypsies of the past.

In the material below, most of the Sherriffs extracted from parish records appear to be Gypsies, gorjers who married Gypsies, people with authenticated and unusual Gypsy forenames, or people regularly associating with Gypsies. Several proven Gypsy surnames appear with them, and the most significant are those relating to the woad fields and parishes along Watling Street.

Less obvious surnames encountered with Sherriffs include Palmer. There was a Palmer amongst Gypsies who were involved in an attack on Squire Nehemiah Parry (1849) after he had dishonoured one of the Shaw girls; several Palmers married Coopers (who also married into Sherriffs) and I have a burial of an apparent Gypsy Palmer at Whitwell, NE Derbyshire, in 1710. By the 1890s, there is ample evidence that the family had become show people.

It is therefore clear that, even if William was technically the first of the Sherriff Romany family, there were plenty of prior Gypsy links. With the following references it is also possible to use baptismal stepping stones into generations pre William and thereby take his own genealogy back with at least 90% certainty.

The Sherriffs' Genealogy

The earliest Sherriffs I have found date from 1608 when a Richard Sherriff had children baptised in both Bedfordshire and Worcestershire. Was this Richard a Gypsy? There is no evidence at all that he was, but having children baptised in diverse places at least indicates vagrancy.

During the remainder of that century, Sherriffs appeared occasionally in Bedfordshire, Worcestershire, Buckinghamshire and Shropshire, though there is no reason to think any were Gypsies, despite the known Gypsy forename of Bettridy appearing once in 1655.

In the early 18th century, Sherriffs occasionally appear in the same counties, plus Lincolnshire, where occurs a marriage of a Sherriff and a Joanna Lovell though, again, there is no evidence that she was a Gypsy.

The earliest Derbyshire reference is at Repton in 1706, and the very fact that these Sherriff entries are so scattered strongly suggests vagrancy. Thereafter, Sherriffs appear much more regularly in all the Counties so far named, including a Mary Sherriffe, daughter of a traveller, baptised Shabbington, BKM, 10.6.1717 and a Frances Sherriffe who married Moses Wood 1.7.1739 Hanbury, STF. Though Moses may well have been a gorjer, the surname Wood and specifically Moses Wood are confirmed as Gypsies of that period, though it is impossible to say that Frances's Moses was a Gypsy.

The first almost certain Gypsy reference is of John and Mary Sherriff, who had children baptised as follows:

John, parents 'two poor travellers', 19.8.1739 Flore, NTH.
William 20.4.1746 Lower Winchendon, BKM.
Thomas 17.0.1749 Lower Winchendon.

The Flore reference is exceptionally interesting. Flore was an 18th century centre for woad and on Watling Street. Other identified Gypsies who appear in the records between 1728 and 1741 are Solomon and Artuly Draper (daughter Elizabeth baptised 1728); William and Elizabeth Boswell (Martha, 1737 and Ann, 1740); Thomas and Mary Smith (Thomas, 1738); William and Mary Blithe (William, 1740: "The father is gone for a soldier, the mother is a travelling woman"), and William Boswell, labourer, buried 1741.

Solomon Draper married Artuly Stanley at Canterbury in 1732 and she was bur at Burford, OXF, in 1745. Solomon and Valentine Draper (?a brother) were convicted of highway robbery at Winchester, HMP, in 1739.

Sadly, William and Elizabeth Boswell cannot be placed in the Boswell tree, but it is worth noting that a later William, born 1780, son of Edward Boswell and Mary Smith, married a Sarah Draper in 1803 at Langar cum Barnston, NTT.)

Obvious vagrant or Gypsy references then become more common:

Joseph son of John Sherif, "a travelor", buried 21.7.1746 at Norton-by-Daventry, NTH – also a woad field area.

John Sheriff married Mary Evins (sic) 20.6.1740 Armitage, STF. (The Evanses were an associate family of the Boswells.) They had children baptised as follows:

James 20.11.1740 Fulstow, LIN.
Elizabeth 18.4.1742 Fulstow.
Mary 14.1.1749 Fulstow.
Thomas 17.9.1749 Lower Winchendon, BKM.

Benjamin, son of Isaac Sherriff and Susannah Wood baptised 25.4.1749 Sydenham, OXF; also son Thomas 28.3.1748 All Saints Church, West Bromwich, STF; daughter Hannah 14.1.1750 All Saints, West Bromwich.

Joseph Sherriff bur West Wycombe, BKM, 6.4.1760. This is probably the same Joseph, wife Elizabeth, who had a son Joseph baptised 18.12.1749 Burton on Trent, STF. Joseph himself was baptised 28.1.1724 at Stoke Poges, BKM, son of Henry and Sarah Sherriff, who appear to have been Gypsies.

Our George Henry's great great grandfather appears in the records as George Sherriff who married Susanna Palmer 16.10.1777 at Ombersley, WOR, and had sons Thomas, Edward and John baptised respectively 13.8.1778, 9.1.1780 and 25.11.1781 Ombersley and Mary Ann, 13.4.1788 St Peter, Worcester, WOR. Their daughter Patience, m. Thomas Boswell at Knowle, WKS. 1.3.1812. This Thomas, nicknamed Hairy Tom, was son of John Boss and Mary Newbury and a grandson of Black Jack and Molly Boswell. Another apparent daughter, Mary, married Ephraim Taylor 12.11.1812 at Handsworth, and again at St. Mary's Church, Handsworth, exactly three years later.)

There is no trace of this George's own roots which in itself, may imply vagrant parents, but Edward, his son, married Mary Hart on 24.8.1807 at Aston Juxta Birmingham, WKS. They had children baptised as follows:

John 24.7.1808 Aston Juxta Birmingham, WKS
Mary Ann 15.6.1810 St Martin, Birmingham, WKS
William 10.2.1812 St Martin, Birmingham, WKS
George 9.5.1814 St Phillips, Birmingham, WKS
Selina, m. Big Frank Heron
Charles m. Elizabeth White 2.8.1827 at Dronfield, DBY and
    16.9.1827 Staveley, DBY.
Joseph, died Sinfin Moor, DBY, buried 1.3.1828 at Chellaston,
    DBY, age 2, as Joseph Sherratt.

It is the William born 1812 who, see below, married Mary Ann Boss to form the officially accepted Romany Sherriffs. But was William a Gypsy? Why was he described as a mumper in oral tradition? Clearly, his father was not a Gypsy. By 1880, there was a small Gypsy family called Hart, whose origins are unsure, though I have been told by Gypsies that they descended from Herons. However, in 1823 a group of Gypsies held for vagrancy in Beccles Gaol, Suffolk, included a Mary Smith and her seven children, Margaret and Hyram Buckley, William Wilson and Lidia Hart. The late 19th century Harts were also associated with the Wilson family. The Lidia Hart reference is the only known one connecting Harts with Gypsies before the 1870s,

If Edward's wife was related to this Lidia Hart, it might explain why their son was regarded as a mumper, since Lidia appears to have been someone associating with Gypsies, and perhaps the partner of William Wilson.

Another Palmer reference is of Isaac Sherriff who married Mary Palmer 13.5.1799 at Aston Juxta Birmingham, WKS and had a daughter Mary Ann baptised 5.6.1800 at Birmingham St Phillips, WKS, the same church where George Sherriff and Susanna Palmer had a child baptised.

Of the myriad of subsequent Sherriff entries, most are of little interest in this context, though several may be of Gypsies. One exception, because of the known link between Gypsy Curtises and Smiths in Buckinghamshire (vide my *The Hanging of Tobias Smith*) , is Robert and Elizabeth Sherriff who had children baptised James Curtis bapt 19.1.1807 Waddesden, and Robert Curtis 12.6.1810 Quainton, both BKM. The name Curtis re-emerges with Sherriffs when a Robert Sherriff and Martha Cooper had a daughter Elizabeth Curtis baptised at Quainton in 1844.

There is also a baptism of an Ambretty Sherriff, dtr of William and Elizabeth Sherriff, at Shipton on Stour, WKS, in 1805, Ambretty (in various forms) being a relatively common forename amongst Boswells of the period.

An important subsequent Gypsy reference is Isaac Sherriff, age 40, who was tried in 1846 with his wife Rebecca Biddle, daughter Mary Ann (Polly) Biddle, James Biddle (?a brother-in-law) and Jacob Skerry (?Scarlott/Scarrett) for murder. Details of crime and location not known. Isaac Sherriff, James Biddle and Jacob Skerry were sentenced to death, but this was commuted to transportation. Isaac later returned to England.

Isaac and Rebecca had children baptised as follows: Esther (at Glympton, OXF, 24.6.1833), Naomi (Enstone, OXF 4.5.1834), Elizabeth (Tredington, WKS, 20.3.1836), Mary (13.5.1838 Stretton on Fosse, GLS), Henry (23.5.1841 Tysoe, WKS and Middle Tysoe, WKS, 23.3.1843).

The following sundry Gypsy Sherriffs are also worthy of mention:

Mary dtr of David and Mary (as Sherratt), potter, baptised 24.10.1819 Brampton, DBY

Elizabeth Sherriff m. Joseph Billing (?Boiling) 28.11.1835 Womburn, STF

Levi Sherriff, b 1860, scissors grinder, accused at Derby Quarter Sessions 27.6.1876 of horse theft at Ashbourne, DBY (two separate counts) and jailed for 9 months with hard labour on each count.

Henry Sherratt (40) labourer, imprisoned at Derby Quarter Sessions January 1905, accused of false pretences at Marston Montgomery, DBY. Henry had 14 previous convictions between July 1888 and 1904 for petty theft.

We now return to our George Henry's great grandfather William, who married Mary/Mary Anne ('Tresi') Boss or Boswell, on 6.8.1832 at Rugeley, STF. William and Tresi travelled Oxfordshire and Buckinghamshire but most of their family settled in Derbyshire.

Their children were:

Tom = 1) Sophia; 2) Genti Boswell. Tom is buried at Gainsborough.

Eldorai = Isaiah Boswell

Uriah baptised 2.11.1846 Endon, STF = Susan Clayton

Hope baptised 28.11.1855 at Mickleover, DBY – father a travelling cutler of Walsall, STF, m. Hettie (Henty or Genti or Trainet or Trenetty – name varies) Boylin 9.6.1874 at Mickleover, DBY: Henry's grandfather.

Loreni baptised 9.44.1864 Mobberley, CHS.

Perun (Perrin), baptised 3.7.1864 Checkley, STF married Raia (Maria) Smith 2.11.1863 Ashbourne, DBY. Henry states that Maria was actually a Clayton. Their children included Lementina baptised 14.5.1865 Norbury, DBY, father a chair bottomer, and

Coralina baptised 5.7.1867 North Wingfield, DBY.

Abraham = 1) Coralina Boswell; 2) Delilah Smith married 9.10.1871 Duffield, DBY

Oati = 1) Edward (Hedji) Heron; 2) Frampton Boswell

Matilda = 1) Lander Boswell; 2) Isaiah Holland

Alfred

William, bapt 31.10.1858 Great Comberton, WOR as Francis William.

Joseph b 1879. Joseph, described as a labourer, appeared at Derby Quarter Sessions on 2.7.1902 accused of stealing a pigeon at Wirksworth, DBY. He had previous convictions for stealing pigeons at Wirksworth (1900), and Longton, STF (1899); for stealing a chicken at Longton (1899); for assault at Ashbourne (1895) and one conviction for drunkenness. Joseph was discharged, having spent the previous (?two) years as a certified patient in a hospital.

Henry, died Sinfin Moor Bridge, DBY, buried Chellaston, DBY, 10.9.1854 as Henry Sherratt, age 11 months

Other possible sons – James, married Caroline Slater 14.1.1884 at All Saints Church, Derby, DBY; Richard baptised 31.10.1858 Great Comberton, WKS.

Henry's grandparents, Hope and Trenetty, had the following children:

Tom

William m Gladys Hough. According to his son Arthur, William was actually born at Bulwell, NTM. William and Gladys's other children were Geoffrey, Malcolm, Esme and Betty.

John

Abraham baptised 4.2.1891 Brailsford, DBY

Eliza (Maria) = George Boswell (but used name Sherriff)

Izia = Rose Loveridge

Uriah

Buller

Naylis = Drusilla Heron

Raini = Arkless Holland (according to Henry, but a Smith according to Henry's cousin Arthur Sherriff.).

Matilda = Ephraim Booth

Victoria

Graveli

Another Raini and the Graveli, above, may have been the wives of two of Uriah, Buller and John. But there was also a Reni Boswell who was the first wife, until her death, of George, before his union with Eliza Sherriff. This Reni has been claimed to me as a sister of Gordon Sylvester Boswell, and thus a daughter of Algar and Athaliah, but the family state this is incorrect and nor do I know of this.

Cornelius (age 25) and John (age 20), with Cornelius Smith (age 23) were accused at Stafford of theft on 27.11.1908. The following year, Cornelius Sherriff was assaulted by Marilda Smith at Malvern, in September. In the same group were James Virgo and Cornelius Holland.

Tom, William and John, above, were arrested in January 1903 for an attack on a policeman, who died as a result, at Burton, STF. None would state who was the actual killer, and all three were jailed. According to Arthur Sherriff, the killer was actually Tom. All three were released early from jail on condition they joined the army: this was a common early-release system used for much of the 19th century and until after World War 1. Another interesting fact to emerge from this generation is that John, then himself elderly and walking with a stick, approached George Henry's mother-in-law (Lily Walker's mother) after the separation, and offered to buy George (Lily's son by George Henry) for £100. The offer was promptly refused.

The children of Eliza (Maria) Sherriff and George Boswell (but used name Sherriff):

Freddy
Hope
Billy
Coraleana, baptised 23.7.1867 at Parwich, DBY, as Camelia, and married James Turnbull, a gorjer, 24.5.1886 at St Alkmund Church, Derby, DBY.
Isabel
Betty
George Henry (Monty)
David
Stillborn girl

The Sherriffs' Nickname

From this point on, Roman type indicates text from the Wade papers, particularly the words of Henry Sherriff; italic type indicates text inserted by the editor.

Question to Henry from Dick: How did the Sherriffs get the nickname "Drybreads"? (Shookamauro)

Many years ago one of my relations gave her boy bread without butter. He said he could not eat it on its own, so she told him to go and sit beside his sister and eat it . She had not mong'd (*begged*) anything the day before. *(Interestingly, a family of Dutch Roma in Australia today have an almost identical explanation of their nickname with the same meaning.)*

My Relatives

Sundry family information from Henry:

Matilda Sherriff and Ephram Booth's children, my cousins: Ephram, Hope, Mathew, Sylvester, Henry, Freddy, Marina, Edna. Marina was married to me before she died of cancer. One of my aunt Matilda's sons lives with Katey Hames. Hope Booth married a Price. Ephram Booth married a Hames.

I have a lot more relations but I don't know much about them as they are scattered, some in America, Australia and Ireland. I have not seen my Uncle Izia since I was very small. He has been in Australia since just after that trouble with the policeman in 1903. He went to Australia in the 1920s. He may be dead now. We don't know.

Meero Folki ta Simensaras (My family and cousins)

Uncles
Thomas Sherriff, Rabi Boswell, Izia Sherriff, Buller Boswell, Uria Sherriff, Hope Sherriff, Kruza Boswell, Buller Sherriff, Sylvester Boswell, John Sherriff, Naylis Sherriff.

Aunts
Minnie Boswell, Raini Sherriff, Teanai Boswell, Matilda Sherriff,
Martha Boswell, Victoria Sherriff, Darkus Boswell, Graveli Sherriff,
Lurayni Boswell.

Uncles and aunts by marriage
Ephram Booth, Matilda Sherriff, Arkless Holland, Raini Sherriff
Rebecca Clayton, Hope Sherriff, Tutti Smith, Buller Boswell, Rose
Loveridge, Izia Sherriff, Naylus Sheriff, Drisila Herne.
Anselo Boswell = Eliza Boswell (*Though Eliza was certainly Anselo's
main partner, as indicated, his first partner, and the mother of Tresi,
was Phyllis Druett.*) William Sherriff = Tresi Boswell.

Appy Boswell = Trenit Boilin (Rebecca Clayton) (*This statement is
incorrect: Trenit was Appy's half-sister, but his wife was certainly Becky
Clayton. See my Genealogy of the Romany Boswells.* Dick Wade trawled
the Journal of the Gypsy Lore Society and found bits of information
about the Boylings, but some of that appearing in the Journal about this
family is incorrect. A full version of its genealogy as relating to Appy
appears in my Boswell genealogy.)

Hope Sherriff = Trenit (Hetty or Henty) Boswell. *Henry's father,
George Boswell, was usually known as Hope and his wife, officially
Eliza, was usually called Trenit.*

Tom Sherriff (*another of the sons of Trenit and George and so Henry's
uncle*) killed in action 1916.

Old Isaac Sherriff and brothers Tom and Ishmael, travelled Warwickshire in 1840s.

Isaac married Rebeeca Biddle.
Anselo Boswell = Eliza Boswell.
William Sherriff = Tresi Boswell.
John Died Dartmoor.
Hope (= Rebeeca Clayton).
Lini.
David (*Henry's youngest brother – see below*) Captain in Royal
Artillery brought up by Carter of Bakewell and bears their name.
(*According to Arthur Sherriff, David was awarded the Victoria Cross for
rescuing a fellow officer and carrying him from danger. I have been
unable to find independent confirmation of this incident.*)
Bill.
George Henry.
Tina.

The King and Queen's 'Cooks'

Uncle Izia Sheriff married one of the cooks of the king and queen. They have been in Australia since about 1920. They have a big farm there. Uncle Joe Sheriff died about 1906-7 in Dartmoor prison, Devon while serving fifteen years for murdering a Policeman in 1903. The other two uncles finished their sentence and joined the army as Guardsmen.These should be easy enough to verify prala *(brother)*. Chesterfield will have all details.

Grandfather's brother my Great Uncle Naylie Sheriff – Grenadier Guards 1900 and before.

Grandfather Hope Sheriff Born Staffordshire.

Grandmother Trainetta Boswell born Derbyshire. Buried Newbold Church near Chesterfield.

My brother David lives near Matlock Derbyshire.

Uncles

Here is something you will be able to check up on from Chesterfield prala:

Thomas Sheriff. Private Coldstream Guards killed in action 1916. Name Regiment and number on Newbold, Chesterfield, War memorial.

Uria Sheriff. Sergeant, Grenadier Guards wounded about 1917 France

Izia Sheriff. Life Guards Corporal

John Sheriff. Coldstream Guards Private

Hope Sheriff. I am not sure which Guards regiment but was in one of them

Grandfather Hope Sheriff. Soldier Boer War, also Big Drummer in the Sherwood Foresters 1914-1918

Cousin Joe Sheriff, Police force for a few years.

My youngest brother Herbert David Sheriff now named Herbert David Carter through adoption at Bakewell after the death of my mother. Herbert David is a captain in the Royal Artillery at present.

Kanna Mandi sas a Tarno Chavo
(When I was a young boy)

In the following account, Henry describes the death of his mother.In about 1995, a former gamekeeper, Mr. Ralph Lord, kindly showed me a wayside grave off a lane near the Baslow-Bakewell road (the A619) near Pilsley, Derbyshire. Mr. Lord told me of local tradition that in about 1910, a Gypsy caravan slipped off a narrow bridge into a tributary of the River Derwent and an adult and child drowned. The two were buried nearby, beside a lane.

Soon afterwards, Siobhan Spencer, secretary of the Derbyshire Gypsy Liaison Group, and her husband David, met an elderly man who called himself Monty Sherriff. Monty – he was, of course, Henry – explained more of the death of the adult and her burial nearby. On his death soon after, he had hoped to have his ashes scattered on his mother's grave, but at the time the two matters were not connected. He was not aware of the death of a child.

In Henry's account which he sent to Richard Wade in about 1962, he has one or two of the facts wrong. The tragedy occurred not at Bakewell Road, Matlock, but off Matlock Road near Bakewell. And it was not the river itself which flooded – though it may well also have – but pump houses on a hill above where the wagon was parked which burst. The hill known as The Dimple is in Matlock itself.

Smedley's Hydro became part of the Matlock Teachers Training College and is now part of the County Council's offices.

David was not the baby who was born following the incident. David was about 4 years old when it happened, and Henry about 7. The baby itself was stillborn. Clearly, this must be the baby buried near Eliza. David's adoptive family, the Carters, according to local Gypsies, were fairground people, or somehow connected with fairs. Subsequently, I traced and met Henry's nephew Arthur Sherriff, in Retford, and Arthur Sherriff confirmed this.

Henry's aunt Matilda, wife of Ephraim Booth, was almost certainly the same woman who camped in a bender tent on a hillock near the site of the tragedy every year for several decades and put flowers on the grave. I have deliberately with-held some of the information I have concerning the burial of Eliza.

When I was a young boy about eleven, we were stopping at Matlock in Derbyshire. My Dadus *(father)* had the contract for reseating the cane and rush chairs at Smedleys Hydro The manager's name was Captain Douglas. We were the only Romani folki that was allowed to camp on the

Bakewell Road Matlock, this was because of my fathers contract with the Hydro. Inspector Kennedy was in charge of the police at the time, he was a friend of my father's. Near where we where atchin *(stopping)* was a steep hill up to the Hydro; at the back of our Bow Topped waggon was the river Derwent.

There was a flood at the time my mother was in bed with confinement. My father stuck the kettle iron as far in the ground as he could, and then fastened a chain to that and the waggon wheel, so as the flood would not move our Vardo *(wagon)*. The pipes at Smedleys Hydro burst, and the water came rushing down the Dimple, that is the name of the hill, the water went over our waggon front board and into the waggon and to bed where my mother was laying.

The Gorgio folki *(local people)* got my mother out of our waggon and they took her to Darley hospital. She had a boy, my youngest brother David. With getting wet through in the flood she had pneumonia. In two days she died. They said it was the flood water that had killed her. We buried my mother and burned the waggon. I went back then to live with my poori folki *(old people)*. My father, who had never drunk a glass of beer in his life, started to drink heavy.

My other brothers and sisters were taken by my different uncles and Aunts, all but one, Hope, he stayed with my Dadus. My Uncle Hope Sherriff and Aunt Rebecca, she was a Clayton, were stopping with their waggon at Ringing Lows. Ringing Lows is just on the moors outside of Sheffield My Uncle Hope had very little money so he walked from Ringing Lows to Matlock and had blisters on his feet. He took to my sister Trainett. My Uncle Uria took to my brother Fred.

My youngest brother David is now a Captain in the Koorramengroes *(soldiers)*, the Royal Artillery. A Bauri Rei ta Rauni *(a great gentleman and lady)* called Carters at Bakewell, Derbyshire had him staying with them as a bitti chavi *(little boy)*. They finally adopted him with my father's consent. He was sent to college and has had a fine Education. He uses the nav *(name)* of the people who brought him up, Herbert David Carter.

If you are ever in Matlock and talk to any of the old folki, you will be able to hear this story as it was talked about a bit.

(At this point, Henry gives further details about the events leading up to the death if his mother. These have been omitted to avoid causing embarrassment to the descendants of other Romani people concerned.. These incidents were a major factor in the death of his mother. My brothers and sisters are all doing well and happily married thank God. My Dadus *(father)* died at eighty-odd years of age.

Patser mandi, meero pooro Dei shumas a latcho Duveleski trashava
monishni. Yoi pend laki monya sorkon rarti katar moro Duvel. Duvel
kom laki sorkon chairus. (*Thankfully, my old mother was a good God-
fearing woman. She said her prayers every night to God. God love her for
ever.*)

Yek Paramish (A Story)

When I was a lad and lived with my Poori Dei *(grandmother)* and Pooro
Dadus *(grandfather)*, we had a Bow Topped waggon and one mare. My
Pooro folki *(grandparents)* did not have much money. My pooro Dadus
had been on a month's drinking and spent it all, only what my Poori Dei
had and that was only a few pounds. We set off one morning from Leek
in Staffordshire to a village called Mayfield near Ashbourne, Derbyshire.
It is very hilly country and when we had got about nine miles on our way
the mare fell down dead in the shafts of the waggon, it had broke its
heart with pulling. We got it out of the shafts the best way we could.

As luck must have it, my Uncle Ephram and Aunt Tilly was travelling
with us. They had a big family, fourteen children. My Pooro Dadus got
in the shafts of our waggon and all my cousins and myself got behind the
waggon and pushed it. My Uncle could not lend us a grei *(horse)* as they
only had the two for to pull two waggons. We pushed our waggon all the
way to Mayfield after resting many times. My Pooro Dadus acted as a
grei and was shouting and chingerin *(quarrelling)* all the way. When we
got to Mayfield he got some money off the old woman and went straight
to the kitchema *(pub)* to get drunk.

We never saw him again for a week. He had set off from the kitchema
at closing time and gone to Stockport. When he came back a week after,
he had two as bonny a horses as I ever saw, one a dapple grey, the other
a coloured mare. My Poori Dei put her hands round his neck and kissed
him. She said to him, 'I knew you would come back with a good grei, but
you have done better, we have two.'

I have seen my Pooro Dadus come home many a time and tell my
poori Dei to get her things out of the waggon as he had sold it. We have
had to make a rod tent for a night or two but you could bet he would finish up buying another twice as good as the one he sold. They loved a
good waggon but never kept one long, always swopping and selling the
ones they had. Always trying to get one better.

I only once in my life called my Pooro Dadus a liar. He tied me to the
back waggon wheel and thrashed me with an Ash plant until I could not

walk. I never back answered him after that. He was as good as gold but would not stand any cheek from anybody.

My Pooro Dei was always known as Trainet The Fast Walker. Uncle Bill will tell you. *(Presumably Bill Hames)*. She could walk faster than any other travelling woman alive and my Pooro Dadus was over six feet tall and as broad as a door. He could fight for fun and so could my Poori Dei. The smallest of my Uncles is six feet tall and all as straight as broom sticks. They was a rough lot at one time and feared nothing or anybody on the drom.

I saw my Pooro Dadus have a fight when he was turned seventy with a young travelling mush. My Pooro Dadus knocked the daylight out of him in two rounds. I used to spar with him and he used to give me a few hard digs in the ribs, he said it was to harden me up a bit. I often sit and think of those days and wish they were back. We worked hard but had plenty of fun, good fun. Singing and dancing around the yog until early hours of morning.

We used to run one another for money and see who could break a grei in first and ride for miles bareback until we were sore. We went poaching nearly every night and have had deer off the Duke of Devonshire's Estate, Chatsworth House, Baslow *(Derbyshire)*. Kushto mas, *(good meat)* venison. In them days I used to mong *(beg)* the Gorjers *(non-Gypsies)* for Shuvories *(sixpences)*.

A Lad at Buxton

Kick-up grinding barrows varied greatly in quality. The most primitive were entirely home made, even the block of stone being painstakingly carved into a circle and a hole put through the middle. Home-made sharpeners of this nature were an indication of great poverty.

More sophisticated ones, whilst still usually home made, had a bought wheel and were fastened into a handcart, often highly decorated and with a sign on to tell people the purpose. There were two basic types, one which leaned against a wall, and the other more recent, free standing. Each had a foot pump rather like that found on old fashioned sewing machines, but the speed of rotation of the grinding wheel was limited to work on scissors and knives.

More recently, a grinding wheel was attached to a bicycle, which was placed on a stand for the sharpening to take place. This was far faster and allowed larger tools to be sharpened. The most modern machines run off petrol grass cutters and can be used for any grinding work. A few modern Gypsies use electric but they are generally not as powerful.

When I was a lad living with my grandparents, we had a Bow Topped wagon and three horses. We were stopping at a place called Sticker Planting just outside of Buxton in Derbyshire. My Aunt and Uncle, Tilly and Ephram Booth, were stopping at the same place. They had a boy older than me, my cousin Matty.

There was an old travelling man came to see us, his name was Silvester Taylor. I called him by his first name Silvester. It was a bad thing to do in them days as we was always made to call anyone older than ourselves uncle or aunt. My Poori Dadas gave me a good hiding with a Ash plant that he always carried with him. I asked my cousin Matty to run away with me, he said he would. My Pooro Dadus told me to Puv o greis *(illegally graze the horses)* about nine o clock while he went to the kitchema *(pub)* with the other folki *(people)*. My cousin and I Puved o greis and when we came back to the tan *(stopping ground)*, we chored my Koko's *(stole my uncle's)* kick up grinding barrow. It was a Rinkeno *(beautiful)* Barrow nearly all brass work on it. We set off in the Kaula Rarti *(darkness)* and made for a place called Moneyash.

When we got there it was very late and we were tired, so we found a hay barn and put the grinding barrow inside, and then made ourselves a woodress *(bed)* for the night. As I said before, my cousin was older than myself, and we started to Rokka *(talk)* about Ghosts. My cousin pen'd *(said)* that the barn was haunted and that a Rakli *(girl)* came every Rarti *(night)* with her head under her arm. He said the reason for this was because the Rakli had been murdered in the barn.

This barn had a bottom and top door and about midnight the wind got up rough. I went to sleep and was awakened by a creaking sound. I nudged my cousin and asked him what it was. He said it was the Ghost of the Rakli coming. The more I listened to the sound the trashier *(more frightened)* I got. He kept on telling me about this Rakli. I thought I dik't *(saw)* her, and made a run for the door. I kept on running and never stopped until I got back to the tan. My folky *(family)* were sitting up waiting to see if we came back.

Other Gypsies Connected or Distantly Related to Henry

Connections of Star Price died May 1965
(This information appears to have originated from Fred Huth.)
Fighting Fred Price = Ellen Taylor.
Sampson Price = Jane Hollow, d. of Old Kradock Price and Emily Slender.
Kradock Price = Polly Price.
Credit (Boggi) = Starina (Star). The journal call her Isabella Cellina (Star).
Had 7 children. Billy died May 1965.
Connections of Sam Price, Owner of Pot Waggon at Appleby Fair.
Kradock Price = Polly Price.
Jack Price = a Reilly. Been in hospital (Divi Kor) *(lunatic asylum)* for years, d. of Saki Finney + Britty Price.
Sam = Maureen Finney; Sam has a sister Beryl + one more sister. Sampson of Bentley near Doncaster. This is the Sam Price who had the pot waggon at Appleby Fair. This is not the Sam who had the waggon at Appleby.
Sam Price, son of Chesi Blackbird Price and Dolly Price.
Black Othea Lee, son of Peron (Brui) Lee + Darkless Price.
Obediah (Opi) Price, son of Kradista + Fee Price = Geraldine daughter of Jack Price.
Children of the above Jack Price and a Reilly:
Billy = Starina (Star); Boggi = Credit; Carole = Sam Price, son of Chesi Blackbird Price; Maureen = Black Othea Lee; Geraldine = Obadiah Price; Berylena (single).

There is a Shoshoi Price who had a daughter "Agness" with old Marjorie Taylor, wife of Adolphus Lovell, This "Agness" first had Dick Price, secondly Dozey Gaskin who she left. But this "Shoshoi Price" must have been an older man than Tootsy. *(The Shoshoi Price here referred to must be a different one, and this must relate to correspondence not retained.)*

Henry's Birth, His Wives and Partners

*There is no firm information about when and where Henry was born,
and his birth does not appear to have been registered. He told Siobhan
Spencer that he was born in 1911. But at his death, his age is recorded
as 'about 80'. He died on April 8th 1998 and his ashes were scattered
in the glade at Gilroes Cemetery, Leicester.*

*He also says that he was 11 when his mother died, and elsewhere 7.
Unfortunately, this does not help either, as there is no firm evidence as
to exactly when Eliza died. Local gorjer tradition has it as 1910, but
this cannot be correct and the favourite year for this is 1919 which fits
well with his own claim of being born in 1911.*

Henry gives little information about his female partners. He says:

In 1936 I met Anna Howard, old Jo Howard's daughter from Lancaster, we were as good as engaged. In 1937 I went out with a young
Gorgio Rackli *(non-Gypsy girl)*, she was sixteen. She came down to our
waggon and tent and told us she was shoobli *(pregnant)*. Miro folki
(my people) wanted to pack up and jal *(go)*. I was young and foolish and
said no. I saw her mother and she asked me to rommer *(marry)* her
daughter, in all fairness I did. This was in 1938. We lived together
travelling for twelve months, and parted by mutual agreement, the
best of friends, and we still are. I divorced her last December the ninth
at Leicester divorce court after being parted twenty-four years.

I lived with my mother's sisters girl, that is my aunt's daughter
Marina Sherriff, for years until she died with cancer of the liver at
Wolverhampton Staffs in 1959.

I then got in with Sarah Lock who is my *monishni* (woman) now. I
intend getting *rumedi* (married) to her proper as soon as I am released
(from) here. I told all this to my lawyer and we asked for the judges
discretion at the court; anyway he gave me my divorce which was
annulled on the 9th March 1965, last March.

Writing to Richard Wade about Sarah Lock, Fred Huth says:

Henry's present wife's antecedents seem pretty clear. He tells me
she is Sarah Lock, daughter of Fiddling Jack. This is how I make it:

Henry Lock or Boswell = ?

Henry's son Mathew Lock = Memberense Boswell (London-side
Boswells).

Matthew's son Ezekiel Lock = Ansey Taylor d. of Edward Tayler
also called "Bill the Barber" and Lucy Lock.

Ezekiel's son Fiddling Jack Lock = Sarah....?

Fiddling Jack Lock's daughter Sarah Lock = Henry Sherriff.

<u>Note:</u> Fiddling Jack Lock had brothers and sisters – Isiah; Enock; William (Winkles) = Priscilla; Florence; Ezekiel; Andrew; Phoebe (died). Priscilla was first married to Reuben Potter. Winkles Lock married her late in life.

When Siobhan Spencer met Henry in his last year, she gained the distinct impression that Henry had other 'wives' than those listed here. Though there is no information about the death of his wife Sarah Lock, it may be that these others were after her. In total, I have only been able to positively identify six, ie:

1. *Anna Howard*
2. *Lily Walker (legal wife, married Chesterfield Registry Office), separated, then divorced 1964).*
3. *Kizzy Woodward/Smith/Everett*
4. *Marina Sherriff (cousin), died of cancer 1959*
5. *Jane Swales, of Middlesborough, married bigamously*
6. *Sarah Lock*
7. *At least one more partner between 6 and 8.*
8. *2nd legal wife – traveller from Leicester*
9. *Possibly one more.*

In his last few years, Henry is known to have had a wife or partner called Dolly, and one called Gladys. In addition, an apparent wife, Elizabeth Mary, was buried at Gilroes Cemetery, Leicester, in March 1996. Presumably these were wives 7, 8 and 9, though the order is not known.

For part of his life, Henry received aid from a Derbyshire man known as John Henry Birks.

Henry's Children

Though Henry states that he had seven children, only three have been identified and only one of these, George Henry, is from a legal marriage, ie that with Lily Walker.

George Henry, b. 1940
Henry, probably b. 1941 or 2 = Rosemary Smith, daughter of Bill
   and Tilly
Tina, probably born 1943 or 4 = Bill Finney, son of Billy
Boy
Boy
Girl
Girl

George Henry junior was brought up initially by his mother and by her partner, Philip Rice. When he died, she lived with William Deakin ('Lofty') but following incidents in the family, he went to live with his aunt, who brought him up.

Arrest and Imprisonment

Henry senior gives little information about the reasons for his own arrest and imprisonment. However, he received 5 years for the bigamy, 4 for another burglary and 7 more for a major burglary. Together with other brief sentences he admits to, he must have received over 21 years so would have served at least 14.

In one prison letter, undated except 1964, and written to Lily, he says, "Well dear, my luck has run out but I have had quite a bit out of it. I have about 50 or 60 different charges of warehouse, shops and housebreaking and carrying firearms so you can see I am in for the high jump."

In another, he reports getting his own back on an army officer. He is clearly trying to impress Lily, and perhaps even warning her not to make life difficult for him in the divorce: "I told him I would get my own back and I did just that ... I burgled his house at 2 o'clock in the morning and took a 12-bore London hand-made gun and cartridges and other stuff. I bet it would make him remember when the police told him who had done it. I have paid quite a few visits to people I had to pay debts to, and I also got a few pounds at the same time. They say us Gypsies never forgets, that is true. I intended doing them wrong just the same as they did me wrong. It has cost me nine years altogether but I can do it with a contented mind knowing I have done what I had to do."

Miro Nogo Tatcho Paramish
(My own true story)

A few years ago my rakli *(girl)* and I was atchin *(stopping)* in Wigan. We were stopping on the car park in the town. I had been grinding one Friday in a district just outside of the town.

A few days after on a Saturday night, we were just getting ready at about ten minutes to six, to go for a drink in the Stanley Arms at six o'clock. A police car pulled on the car park and four detectives got out. They came over to our trailer. One of them said to me, "We are the Police. What is your name?" I told them Sheriff Boswell. He asked me if I had been in a certain district on Friday last week. I told him, yes, I had been there grinding. He searched our trailer. They then told me to get in their car.

I asked what for. He said, "You will find out soon enough." They told my rakli she could not come with me.

They took me to Wigan Police Station and we went into a room where there were two more detectives. These two said they was from Scotland Yard. The other four left the room. These two made me take my clothes off and they searched them. They asked me where I was on the Friday night. I told them in the Stanley Arms with my rakli from six until half-ten. After two and a half hours, they asked me if the landlady would know me again. I told them 'Yes,' as I was singing through the mike and that my rakli and I were people that stood out in a crowd, being what we are.

At quarter to nine four of them told me to get in the car again. I did, and they drove to the Stanley Arms. One of them got out and went inside for about a quarter of an hour. He came out, and said 'Yes, he is telling the truth, he is clear.' They drove me back to the car park.

My rakli was going mad waiting. I said 'Will you please tell me now, what it is all about.' They told me that a little boy had been murdered in that district on the Friday night and with me being there on the Friday, grinding, they thought that it could have been me. The people had told them a Gipsy had been around grinding. I can tell you, Dick, I have never been so trashed *(frightened)* in my life as when they told me what it was for. Murder. My rakli and I went straight to the pub and got a few whiskies down me before half-ten. We left Wigan the next day. They got the man later. His name was Green, and he had killed two boys in Wigan.

Prison

I was first sent to Stariben *(prison)* in 1940 for six months for attempted larceny. This was a trumped-up charge because I was absent from the kooromengroes *(army)*. I was bound over in 1942 for chorin *(stealing)* a bicycle and putting a grinding machine on it. I was sentenced to three months in 1943 at Nottingham for showing the police false discharge papers and identity card, "false representation". I served six months in Leicester in 1948 for false pretences of a carpet. My army discharge was sent to me there.

In 1951 at Leicester Assizes I was sentenced to twenty-one months. I came out and six weeks later got 18 months at Preston Sessions. I finished that and a few weeks after got twelve months at York Assizes. I got into no more trouble until 1956. My oldest son and myself were charged at Chesterfield with selling a piece of lino by giving the wrong length. False representation. My son was found not guilty. I got six months which the Inspector said he would get me. I got *(here, Henry names a Derbyshire firm)* for my lawyer, it was a waste of money. I would have done more myself – he said about three words. *(Henry's son George Henry was with Henry when this incident occurred. He states that on this occasion, Henry was certainly innocent.)*

In 1961 I got two years at Bury St. Edmunds Suffolk. After three months I was transferred to Scotland and got another two years at Edinburgh High Court to start from expiration of my English sentence. I went to Peterhead Prison. I petitioned as my romni *(wife)* Sarah could not read or write and was travelling around Shropshire and I could not read or write. I was transferred to Shrewsbury where I got visits from my romni every month until I came out on 18th December 1963. We went to Ireland in December and came back in January 1964. I was put on probation for two years at Brecon, mid-Wales, in February 1964. I could not get a pedlar's certificate and the probation officer told me to carry on hawking and grinding as I had never had Insurance Cards or been in a Labour Exchange in my life.

Anyway Dick, as you can see I landed up getting five years at Derbyshire Assizes 9th. May 1964. I have a very kushti prison record.

In fact, Henry received the five years not for having no hawker's licence, as he implies, but for a major burglary in which £2000 worth of property was stolen.

Romano Paramush jib (Gypsy chatter)

In the following, Henry seems to be going to great lengths to convince Dick that he likes gorjers more than most Gypsies. Dick would be aware that friendship with a gorjer then, even more than now, was suspect amongst other Gypsies.

'Tatcho' Travellers

Kamlo Prala *(Dear brother)*

I am sure you can travel miles today before you meet a tatcho Romani chal or chei *(a true Gypsy boy or girl)*. I can truthfully say without fear or contradiction that there are no more than a thousand if that, tatcho Romano folki in this country today. The biggest part of the different breeds have inter-married so much. At one time of the day a few years back, this would have been a terrible thing to do. But I am sorry to say it is allowed today. I feel sure in years to come there will be no such thing as a Romano chal or chei.

I have stopped beside different travellers and their ways and doings are no different than a gorgio's. The black-faced-uns, as the travellers call my people, are dying out fast. The biggest part of tatcho Romano folki are good honest working folk. I am just one of the odd ones that has gone off the rails.

I am as a matter of fact the only one out of all my mother's and father's family that has ever been in trouble. I feel sure that with me being in the army had a lot to do with my bad ways. My brothers and sisters think the world of me, but do not like me. I have like a good many of my people, been blamed for things I have not done. I deserved all I got this time and can do my chairus *(time)* with a good heart, knowing that this is one time I was not blamed for something I did not kel *(do – but* Kel *is a much more embracing word than that, the nearest meaning in English really being undertake)*.

My life as a boy was the same as all Romano chavos. If my folki *(family)* decided to send me to school I would go, but the Gorjer chavies *(non-Gypsy children)* used to skit me and call me "Dirty Gypsy". I am certain that my folki and myself were as clean, if not cleaner than the chavies who called me or their parents. I got that way, that I hated Gorgers like poison. I have learned a lot different since I was a lad. Some of my best friends are Gorjer folki.

I would sooner have a Gorjer as a friend, than some of these Posh-Ratveli *(half blooded)* travellers today. I have never classed myself as an

English man and never will. When I was in the army, I had in my pay book where it said nationality "Romany". I have always, all my life, been very thankful for being what I am, a Romano chal. I would not change for all the riches in this world. I have many a time made enemies with people, through telling them what I am, a Gypsy. I have know times for a Romano chal or chei who is ashamed of our race, they should be drowned. There are no more than a thousand, if that, tatcho Romano folki in this country today.

Sutton Lane, Shrewsbury Newspaper Clipping

The reason I sent you the paper clipping of Sutton Lane Shrewsbury was this. I had just come out of Stariben *(prison)* in December 1963. Sarah picked me up at the prison gate, also a few more friends. My things was at the time a Blue Bird trailer which we had in Sutton Lane. When I got home there, was the McCanns, Irish tinkers stopping right near us. They caused no end of bother and after a couple of days the Television men and their cameras came, and took pictures of us, which was on the Television in the end of Dec. 1963. The next thing was the Council and the Police. They pulled us all out of the lane with their lorries and tractors.

When they went and left us on the road, me and Sarah pulled our trailer back right to the other end of the lane near the Golf Course. The house at the far end of the lane where we pulled is a white, four-bedroom house and Billy Roberts the grinder and his wife Dolly Lock and their daughter Janice lives in it. So we was all right for company. No one bothered us after that. It is only because the McCanns and the Wards pulled back there again that they bothered this time. They have never as long as I can remember shifted any Tacho Romani – folki *(Gypsy people)* out of Sutton Lane before. When they move the Tinkers, they must move the 'chals' otherwise it would cause murder as you know. One of the men on the Council told me straight, they had nothing against the Pure Gipsies. Only the "Didikyes" *(half-castes)* was the way he put it. he said if the tinkers had not come, we would not have been moved.

In the Shropshire papers it said there was only one true Romani family stopping in the lane, which was Sarah and myself. You may have seen it on Television December 1963. Reading about Sutton Lane brought back happy memories to me prala *(brother)*. Memories I shall never forget. It was the last lane I stopped in before getting leld *(arrested)*.

Here is something you may know. Every man doing five years or over can, providing he has friends or relations where he can stay, with a fixed address, go there on seven days leave a few months before his discharge. This is a Home Office order and applies to all long-term prisoners. The reason for it, is to give us a chance to get a job ready for our discharge.

I do not know anywhere I could stay so this will not apply to me. The prison pays the expenses for the seven days, board and lodgings etc. This scene was put in force when the Tories were in power about five or six years ago. Men go regular for home leave as it is called, from here, about four or five months before their release. I, like every other long-term prisoner, go in front of a Hostel Board ten months before discharge. People who are lucky enough to get the Hostel are told a week after the Board and are allocated to either Birmingham, Preston, Bristol, Stafford or Leicester.

They mostly wait about three months for a vacancy at the Hostel, they are allocated to. If a man gets this, he does not get Home leave as he can go home or to see his friends different weekends. The Hostel is alright to save a tidy few pounds for a start on release. They mostly save around a hundred pounds, all depends on the wages – some have saved two and three hundred pounds. The Hostel takes about three pounds for board, they give you about thirty shillings to spend and the rest is put away for you on release. "Kushti eh?" If I get to Ashwell, which I am sure now I shall, I shall miss the Hostel Board which I should have in either October or November (I am not certain which month I go out in) August about the last day and should have my interview the month before release. The Board sits every last week in the month. About a third of those that go up get it. The others get Home leave providing they can give an address where they can go to. The Police check the address.

Whether Henry meant this to be a persuasion for Dick Wade to intervene on his behalf or not, Dick did so. He appears to have contacted the Home Office and the Governor and, as a result, Henry was ultimately transferred to Ashwell Open prison. The correspondence then seems to have ceased, though presumably Dick visited him there.

The Prison Governor

At some point, also, Dick Wade must have approached the prisoner governor to arrange for Henry to be given paper and pens and to be allowed to send out what he wrote. Presumably, Dick wrote to Henry to tell him about this, and to praise the governor. The letter was, as usual, marked "Governor's permission." Clearly, the staff did not know the true contents.

Dick remembers the Governor as a very amiable, radical and liberal Governor, who had the best interests of his prisoners at heart and who did not see imprisonment as such as the answer to solve crime.

Despite this, Henry had a different view:
Miro kamlo prala,
Komyer patser mandi. O stariben bauro rye see kek vel sar latcho sar

yov keraw avri yov see. Me shan penehavadas kova pa e door chairus, "dui mui" konaw me jin. Savo sastis me ker "chichi" adray akei Avri rig howli Me wouldasava pukka lesti savo te ker sar lesko-kokero. Duva folki se gozwero me penehava tutti haieva aduva. Me sastis haiavas les mishto les se lenti butti. Me kek-komi sor yaun se. Doi se kek i tukalo yek adray soor. Kanna yaun se sor-ketanay. Yaun sor mutta adray o yek koro. Me kel jin kova, o bauro rai couldela shan keldas lesopray lesko nago. Yov sar bitcherdas mushaw fon akei te kek-pando staribens "Ford" pa yek. Komusti men sastis bitcher yek-awaver lilaw ta me sastis avel ta dik tutti kenna me avel avri akei. Me shan bitti Hopey te rokka te ta yov se kushti malyew pa mandi. Me rokka te lesti dosta e ora. Folki wouldasar peneha me shomas dinglo ifasar yaun shoonella mandi rokkerin te lesti.

My dear brother

Please believe me. The prison governor does not come out as well as he seems. I have known him to be two-faced for a long time. What can I do, nothing in here. Outside I would have told him what to do with himself. I know you will understand that people are sly. I can understand it well, it is their work. I don't like what he is. That is not the to you one in all. (Note: This literal translation is the best I can offer.) *When they are all together, they all urinate in one pot. I do know this, the gentleman could have done this on his own. He has sent men from here to Open Prison, Ford for one. Perhaps we can send books and I can come to see you when I come out of here. I have little Hopey to talk to and he is a good mate for me. I talk to him all the time. People would say I am mad if they heard me talking to him.*

(Piecing together the scattered clues in the correspondence, it is apparent that Dick loaned Henry £3 to buy the bird which Henry called Hopey. It is unclear whether Henry repaid this money.)

Romani Rokkerban

Mandi ghili diosta ghiveliaw katar mi-kokero ta shoonta te o chiriklo sholavin adray meero dikesti-hev. mandi shoonta lendi dosta e ora. Sorbon krukingrus – divvus man jal katar kongri te shoon reshei roker troostal moro Duvel Les see o nevo ta rinkeno kongri. O Rashei see foshano, yov rokerew (?) Troostal Duvel, Keker yov jalaw katar kongri. O Rashei see gozvero gairo sor yov penehavadas troostal see luver patser. Mandi sastis pukka saw yov rokerela. Doi see ken nanei boot adosta.

Mandi yekorus putchova lesti, savo chairus see les. Yov pendas kekerjin vaniso drom totti see jalin kek-kei, soski putch man o chairus. Mandi chingariben pashal lesti. Mandi putchdom lesti, yov sas kek-latcho, ta akova yov sas jaw shootlo ta yov jal katar Bengesko-tan kanna yov mel.

Yov see kuskto pashal mandi kenaw. Yov yekorus putchtas mandi "Sor Romano- chalaw see pensa yek awover lenti pen savo lenti penchava. Sar sastis yek mush pukka mandi "Mandi jal katar Mi-Duvelesko tem." Mandi kom tooti te dik lesti, tooti savaben teero shero, alay. Kumoni chairusaw yov avels te meero bitto kamora tu dikavato Dikomengriaw opre meero misali ta opre meero tov-vast-atch. Yov sorkon chairus penaw "Teeroaw see e latcho jivoben tooti see Duvel's folki."

Mandi Kefi akova bitcharna sas pardel, ajaw mendi sastis shan e latcho roker ta pee katani. Mandi shan tallani dui beshaw te kel kenaw. O chairus see jalin boot-sig. Les kairs o chairus jal delomus opre katar tooti, Mandi dik sorkon divvus pa teero lilesti fon tooti mantchiaw mandi-opre. Righer tooti mishto. Mandi penchava o Duvelesto chairus ov tooti. Tooti see o tatchenoest chal mandi jin. Kek-dosta mushaw wouldasar shan delomdas-oprem katar en churkno Romani-chal adre stariben tooti keldas. Mandi kek-komi-bisser akova. Tooti see e tatcheno pral. Mandi shom booino tooti delomus-opre katar mandi ta tooti e jinomeskro Reio e pukersomengro Mandi kefi tooti sorkon chairus meero prala ta chavoli kei, meero tukali. Duvel parav tooti ta estist mandi sastis kair-posh tooti kanna mandi avel avri akei. "Mandi jin me sastis" adre komodair dromaw nei yek. Variso mandi sastiro kair pa tooti mandi wi. Teero tatcho prala sorkon chairus.

I sing many songs to myself and listen to the bird whistling in my ear. I listen to them much of the time. Every Sunday I go to Chapel to hear the priest preach about God. It is a new and beautiful Chapel. The priest is false. He preaches about God, but he doesn't believe. I can tell that from all he says. He does not know anything like enough to go to church. The priest is a sly Gorjer, all he will speak about is money.

I once asked him, "What time is it?" He said, "I don't know, anyway you are going nowhere, why ask me the time?" I argued with him. I told him, he is no good, and that he is going sour and he is going to hell when he dies. He looks after me now. He once told me , "All Gypsies are like one another, they say what they're thinking." How can one man tell me I am going to heaven? I want you to see him, you will laugh your head off. Some times he comes into my cell and looks at the photos on my table and on my wash basin. He always says, "Yours is the good life, you are God's people."

I would like this sentence pardoned, so we can have a good chat and drink together. I have two years left to serve now. The time is going very quickly. It makes the time go writing to you. Every day I look for correspondence from you to cheer me up. Take care of yourself. I forever think of you. You are the truest mate I know. Not many men would have written to a poor Gypsy lad in prison, (as) you did. I will never forget this. You are a true brother. I am proud you write to me and you are a clever gentleman to talk (Romanes).

I often wish you (were) here, my brother and mate, me (and) you*. God bless you and maybe I can help you when I am released from here. "I know I can" in more ways than one. Anything I can do for you I will. Your true brother for ever.

(*There is doubt about the meaning of the phrase meero tukali, *which translates literally as* 'my to you.')

Literacy in Prison

Here is the proper way to say: What time have you got to stay here in prison? Savo chairus lian te atch akei adre stariben?

I only put the katar in for to as I thought you may misunderstand te for to it makes it awkward for me only learning to read and write in the last three years. I am not well up on verbs and nouns etc. I only wish I could read and write like yourself. You see Dick, I never went to school in my life, so you may understand how awkward it is for me.

The teacher of the class on English in prison said I had done better than anyone he had had on the English class before.

It is learning me to write a lot better by writing you regular, and it is keeping my mind on our own Rokaben Romanes; So please forgive me if I make a few mistakes in my spelling. I write my words as they sound to me when I say them. – Mandi jal yek gaver katar waver. I go one town to another, this is the way we say it. Mandi shan barvalipen ta misto ta kushko bok – I have wealth and gladness and happiness – Too righerdas o tooshni kere.

A lot of chals say thinkasova, we have always said penchava. Which one do you use, Vaniso — penchava, some say Vaniso — thinkasova wantasova; these are Gorjikanes words with asova; lots put asar on the end of different words; willasar this is Kek – latcho. "Don't you think so."

Meero kamelo prala

Here is a few things that I think will be alright for you to send for the next edition of the "Journal" anyway prala you will know better than I when you have read them I hope that they are what you want. The paramish about the Beng *(see page 63)* happened to my grandfather when I was only a young boy, he swore blind he saw the Beng and my uncles swore blind they saw the footprints.

The folki that were at my aunt's bedside just before she died all said my Aunt's face lighted up when she was talking to the angels. My Grandmother and my Grandad always believed that my Aunt sent the

Devil through the Angels to trash my Grandad through his heavy drinking and falling out with my Grandmother.

One Day Soon...

Yek divvus aglal door mandi ti gilli sor kolli giveliavo kateni adray komeni bitti kitchema poshay teero bitti gav. Palano rarti me mong mi-Duvel pa bicherin tooti te mandi. Parikerava totti pa chirikler hoben. Pesserava totti pawlay yek divvus sig prala. Komyerdo muk mandi jin ifasar o paramishaw se kushti pa teero kimbra*. O Romani Lil. Mi Duvel parav Prala.

One day before long I will sing all these songs at the same time (lit. together) in some little pub near your village. Every night I pray to God for sending you to me. Thank you for the bird food. I will pay you back one day soon brother. I want you to let me know if the stories are good for your forthcoming Gypsy Journal.

God bless you brother.

**The word* kambra *here is interesting. It is clearly Anglo Romani* kambri *meaning pregnant, but is here intended to indicate forthcoming or pending. Interestingly, the word does not appear in Smart and Crofton but is known in the form* kambri *by almost all elderly English Gypsies today. In* Henry on His Release *(page 26) the word appears in the form* kimba, *with the meaning of list or preparation..*

Henry in Prison

Yek Divvus adray stariben *(A day in prison)*

Posh tchave atch opre, kair wudrus, shan e tov; Efta-oro or gairo pirivaw o wudar, mendi keker adre les miro muter kova; posh tschowe hoben adre moro kamora, wuder pandado apopli ta klisindes; Ochto oro mandi jal te booti; Desta dui opro mendi avel pauli kali stariben. Shan moro hoben adre moro komoro wudar pandado ta klisindas; Yek-oro pauli te booti; Pantsch oro pauli katar stariben, hoben adre moro kamerio, wudar pandadivo. Mendi atch adre moro kamoro's ti ovavo saulo. Muterimengri pensa parni due chairusaw e divvus. Hoben keker del jukel. Wafedi.

Half six get up, make bed, have a wash; Seven o'clock the warden opens the door, we (have) not urinated in the urine pot. Half-cold food in our cells, door closed again and locked eight o'clock I go to work twelve o'clock we come back (to the) sombre prison.

Have my food in my room, door closed and locked; one o'clock back to work; five o'clock back to prison, eat in my cell, door closed. We stay in our

*cell till next morning. Tea like water twice a day. Food you wouldn't give
to a dog. Awful.*

The Singer

Mandi shoonaw a mush koliko krookingrus divvus giliv opre o divio
mokta, yov keld mandi rov. Yov giliod, Divvus posh divvus. Les see a
kushtiest giveli mandi shan shoonaw for dosta dosta bershaw.

*I heard a man singing last Sunday week in the psychiatric cell. He made
me cry. He sang, day after day. It was the best singing I have heard for
many years.*

Hopey the Talking Bird

Kamlo prala *(Dear brother)*, I am very glad to tell you my Rinkeni bitti
Rokerin chiriklo *(beautiful little talking bird)* has just come. It is a young
blue one and a chrome chiriklesti-kair *(bird cage)*. I wish you could dik les,
it is Rinkeno *(see it, beautiful)*. I have budgie seed and grit and also millet
and tydisan for the cage floor, little steps and a bell. I shall call it Hopey.
I will rokka *(tell)* you about it next chairus *(time)*. Latcho Rarto Bor *(good
night friend)*.

The Home Office

Yek ov o bauri reiaw pukkerdas mandi te rokkrass tutti from opre te o
kairi kamora adre Lundrum o baurider gav. O rei rokkerd mandi duvva
tutti couldasar lel mandi te Ash-parni-hev kair adre bitti-tem pa mandi te
ker sor meero chairus. Pukka o keri- kamora-mush duva me shan sorkon-
chairus vel kushti adray stariben. O bauriest bitcherma me shan keld
aglal sas dui-beshaw. Pukka o rei adray Lundrum Soskies duva tutti wouldasar kom te di k mandi e kushti dosta chairusaw ta rokka mandi. Me
penchava tutti jin savo te delom opre fetadair na mandi. I bauri rei adray
Lundrum wi lel komeni veen ov utti na mandi. O rei pukkerd mandi pendas les wi vel kushti. Me shouldasar dik tutti kon kanna tutti kom to avel
ta dik mandi. Vaniso chairus tutti kom. Shoon te mandi Romani chalaw
beshin adray o puv troostal o yog. Mandi penaw mendi drab o baulo kosko
kosko saulo mendi jalaw te Drabengro kair trin-oro hol *(word illeg.)* E
drab mendi lalaw kon te sweti paulay mendi jalaw.

*One of the senior warders told me to tell you what the Home Office .in
London, the capital city, said. The gentleman told me that you could take*

me to Ashwell Prison in Rutland for me to do all my time. Tell the Home
Secretary that I am always well behaved in prison. The biggest sentence I
have been given is two years. Tell the gentleman in London the reason that
you would like to see me, the good opportunities to talk to me. I think that
you know how to do it better than me. The Home Secretary in London will
take more notice of you than me. The Governor told me to say it will be OK.
I should see you whenever you want to come to see me. Any time you like.
Listen to me, Gypsies sitting in the field round about the fire. I say we poi-
son the pig. Very well, morning we go to the Doctor's surgery (?chemist's).
Three o'clock Eat ... The poison we administer works after we have gone.

(Henry's idea for the last paragraph probably comes from another source.
Although most Gypsies born before about 1940 are aware of the old system of
Drabbing the bawlor – *poisoning a pig for the meat* – *I know of no evidence*
that it was still happening in the 1960s, except that once when archaeologi-
cally examining an ancient stopping ground near Worksop, I did find a
large quantity of the bones of a young pig, which a professional archaeolo-
gist said constituted most of the animal's bones, but with the head missing.
The probability is that it was many years old, but even if not, the absence of
the head makes me suspect it was not a drabbed bawlor. Although the head
of a drabbed bawlor were not eaten, as it was believed that the poison affected
the brain, I would still have expected to find it there.)

Henry on His Release

Kanna mandi jals paulay tei Chumba Kalesko Tem, mandi penchava
aduva mandi will lel kommeni kek tei lav a Kimba ov Romanes for tooti
te del opre te o Gypsy Lore Society. Latcho folki. Komova tooti te lav a
Kimba for mandi. Mandi will bitcher tooti o paramish te chiv adre les.
Mandi penchava les a latcho kova te kair. O Romani chals savo sastis Del
opre o kimba ta lel o Romani lavs pawlay adre lenti shero, kair tooti penchava mendi sastis kair les. If ajaw lel-kustoben bitcher mandi lav pawlay
adre tooti lil. Mandi keka chiv Gaujokones lav's adray o Kimba, kon Gau-
jos keka jin savo o lavs shan or vanmiso-kumeni but a Romani chal or chei
jins.

When I go back to Derbyshire, I think that I will not make a book list of
Romani words for you to give to the Gypsy Lore Society. *Good people. I*
want you to prepare a book for me. I will send you the stories to put in it. I
think it is a good thing to do. The Gypsies can create the book to give the
Gypsy words back in his head, do you think we can do it? If so, please send
me word back in your letter. I will not put gorjer words in the book, there-
fore Gorjers will not know what the words are or anything else but a Gypsy
man or woman will know.

Henry's Letters to Lily (nee Walker)

Henry also wrote several letters at about the same time, to Lily (his first legal wife). Several of these contain very personal matters but they also cast light on the character of Henry and about his thoughts and feelings. What emerges is that Henry retained a soft spot for Lily. He excuses his frequent prison stays as the result of his drinking but, in one letter, is convinced that marriage to Jane Swales will keep him on an even keel. (It didn't.)

I am grateful to Mr. G.H. Sherriff for access to these. Information from these letters has been incorporated into the relevant part of the text.

In Memory of

THOMAS SHERIFF

**Private
24245
2nd Bn., Lancashire Fusiliers
who died on
Saturday, 1st July 1916. Age 24.**

| **Additional Information:** | Son of Hope and Franeette Sheriff, of Littlemoor, Newbold, Chesterfield. |

Commemorative Information

Memorial:	THIEPVAL MEMORIAL, Somme, France
Grave Reference/ Panel Number:	Pier and Face 3 C and 3 D
Location:	The Thiepval Memorial will be found on the D73, off the main Bapaume to Albert road (D929).

Display Record of Commemoration

Extract from Commonwealth War Graves Commission Records of Commemoration

2. HENRY'S REMINISCENCES

Rocky Price

There is a true story about "Rocky Price" at Ipswich I can tell you.

At nearly the end of the last war, I was stopping with Black Billy Woodward, Everett Elliott and Bessy Woodward's son. There was Black Billy and his woman Ellen Smith (old Gipsy George's or Mad George Smith's as some called him's daughter), Black Billy's sisters Leena and Kizie. They were twin sisters, you could not tell them apart. It was Leena's place we were all stopping at.

One night we were all in the Raleigh public house. Kizie said to me, "You know I lost my man at Dunkirk. When are you going to ask me to be your Romni?"

Now Kizie and Leena were like Black Billy, very dark and rinkeni. They were twenty two years of age. I hit the table where we were sitting, and said, "Listen Billy, I'm having your sister Kizie. If you want to stop me, try now."

He laughed and said, "She told me this morning she was going to ask you, prala. I wish you both luck. Drink up."

When we got home that night, Kizie said to Ellen, "Make the supper while I go and fix the bed." In the early hours of next morning, Kizie said to me in bed, "How much money have you?" I got up and counted my money. One hundred and forty three pounds. She got up and went to a cupboard and counted her money. Nearly two hundred pounds. "Put that with yours," she said, "And buy us a waggon and horse."

That same day me and Billy went into Nottingham Market. At opening time we went in the Market Tavern and who should be in there but Rocky Price, Spider Bennett and other travellers. After a while I asked Rocky if he knew who had an old waggon for sale. He said Harley Burly had got one. At closing time, we all went to a field at Breaston near Beeston, Long Eaton.

They were stopping in the corner of the field. Rocky had a big heavy waggon. Burly had a Bill Wright's Bow Topped wagon and a bender tent. He showed me his Bill Wright. It was full of carved work and well painted, a lovely waggon, but old and a bit of rot in the wheel hubs. We settled at 65 pounds and a pound back for luck, sixty-four pounds. I paid him and gave Rocky two pounds for getting me the deal. I knew I had paid plenty but nothing is dear when you want it badly.

Me and Billy went back home to Nottingham. I said to Kizzy, "Get your things packed in the morning. I've got a waggon."

We hired a man to drive us and our things to Breaston the next morning.

Billy and Ellen went with us. When Kizzy saw the wagon, she liked it. Burly's wife had left the curtains in for luck. I borrowed a mare from Nayliss Lee and pulled half a mile up an old lane at the side of Spidey Bennett and Stuttering Jarv Lee.

Me and Black Billy were hawking lino together and he came every morning to pick me up. One day he said to Spidey who had a nice Bow Top waggon, "How much for your waggon, Spidey? Let's go to the public and have a drink."

Black Billy finished up giving Spidey forty-three pounds for the waggon and a pound back for luck. I lent Billy twenty pounds towards it. The next morning Billy went over to get his waggon. It had been scrubbed out spic and span by Pearl, Spidey's wife. It turned out to be buggy.

A few days after I bought a brown mare from Fighting Big Tom Lee for forty-two pounds and a set of harness from Jarv Lee for six pounds. The next day Kizzy and me, Black Billy and Ellen pulled away to Sawley Lane.

Fighting

Meeri Pooro Dadus merdas sare yogenghi naflopen. Yov shamas posha yekshel. Beshaw's Pooro yov ta meero Poori Dei pukerdas mandi sor o Romanes me jinaw. Yon jindas sorkon lav adre Romanes. Moro Pooro Dadas sorkon-chairus rokerdas adre Romanes te moro Poori Dei ta mandi. Yov sorkon-chairus pendas aduva les sas o feterdair jib adray o Duvelestochairus. Me penehava ajaw kair totti Me shan e dikomengri si lesti adray o Koonus oi meero komora.

Yov shomas e latcho kooromengro ta koordem komeni boot latcho mushaw ta koordas len sorkon-chairus. Yov shomas kek-komi koordno adray leskjo jivoben. Tooti putch koko Bill Hames, me penchava yov jins. Sor meero Pooro Dadusaw chavies meero kokoaw 'Koor pa peias'.

Me shomas latcho, kanna me shomas Tarnodar katar ((te) pooro kenaw. 'Jaldas see o latcho koor kon jal adray o kitchema ketane, ta shom e piaben lel moto ketane te risser vastus. Kanna me penchava pauli te o pooro divvusaw, me jin mandi shamas bootodair bahtali. Parano chairusaw see latcho chairusaw. Me shan jaldas kishli sar penchavadas troostal o latcho divvusaw me shan diktas opre o drom ta kenaw jalin divio adray akei. Me shom bongo adray meero shero, me shouldasa bi grei choopnied.

My grandfather died of a burning fever. He was nearly a hundred years old. He and my grandmother told me all the Romani I know. He knew all the words in Romani. My grandfather always talked in Romani to my grandmother and I. He always said it was the best language throughout eternity. I think so, do you? I have his picture in the corner of my cell.

He was a very good Boxer and he fought some very good men and beat

*them every time. He was never beaten in his life. You ask Uncle Bill Hames.
I think he knows. All my grandfather's children, my uncles, 'fought and
drank'*

*I was good when I was younger. I am too old now. Whenever we had a
good fight, we went into the pub together and we had drink, got drunk
together and shook hands. When I think back to the old days, I know I was
much more fortunate. Old times are good times. I have gone wandering with
thoughts about the good days I have seen travelling and now (I) am going
mad in here.*

I am wrong in my head. I should be horse-whipped.

Bill Finney and Mi Kokero (Myself)

*Gypsies are very resourceful and will turn their hands to anything. Dur-
ing the 1950s, as the economy recovered from the ravages of the war,
linoleum came into fashion and people wanted bits to put down in their
rooms. Gypsies often bought up the off-cuts from rolls which had been used
in the homes of the wealthier people.*

In 1960 I was working partners with Bill Finney. We had a 1958
Comma Van. We were hawking lino and carpets. We were paying a man
from Hanley, his name was Bob Blewer and he had been a taxi driver. We
paid him three pounds a day and all his beer we paid for.

One day (it was a Saturday) Bill said he did not feel very well. I told him
to have a day in bed and whatever I earned I would split fifty-fifty. Every
time I got a flash with a piece of lino, Bob Blewer came in the house with
me just to hold it up as I opened it to show the people. I had six quick deals
and after giving Bob his three pounds driving money, I had forty-three
pounds profit to split up between Bill and myself. Bob pulled up at a
kitchema *(pub)* in Newport, Shropshire.

We got talking and he said I was a fool to give Bill half. I spent the odd
pound, leaving forty two, twenty one pounds a piece for Bill and myself.
When Bob and I got back to Abbey Hulton near Stoke where we were stopping, Bob left me with the van and he caught the bus home. I found Bill
in the Werrington at Buckley. I told him what Bob had said. He said to
me, "He is getting too big for his shoes, we will sack him."

Bob came down on the Monday morning as usual. We went and bought
our gear from old Tinsleys shop. We decided to go to Shropshire again,
Ironbridge and Dawley. I thought Bob had forgotten what I told him on
the Saturday. As soon as we got to Dringington, Bill said to Bob, pull in at
the White House public. As soon as we got in the public, Bill ordered double whiskeys, a thing he had never done before we started hawking before.
I would not have whiskey. Bill and Bob kept on double whiskeys until

5pm. I would not let Bob drive. I drove our van myself because he was too
drunk.

Bill started on about Saturday. He shouted to me, "Pull up." He chal-
lenged Bob out to fight. They were falling over one another. I said, "Get
back in for Gods sake. You're both useless." We never hawked and at 5.30
pulled in at a public called the Blacksmiths arms at Loppington, Salop.
Bill ordered whiskies again. They had that much money the landlady told
them to buy a bottle it would be cheaper. Well Dick, I never laughed so
much in my life. We finished up having a deal with the landlord and landlady with a carpet, a Belgian 4 by 3½, and twenty square yards of Super-
linoleum. I must have pulled up forty times for them two to fight before
we landed back to Abbey Hilton. The next morning we gave Bob Blewer
the sack. He came back wanting to drive again, but I drove myself. It
saved us three pounds a day and beer money. I saved over three hundred
pounds in three months – that was apart from beer money etc, so you can
tell we were having some tidy deals. I finally finished getting fined
twenty-five pounds at Brecon, Wales for a driving offence. I was drunk but
did not show it, otherwise I don't know what would have happened.

Selling a Wife

Here is a true story, Dick. I have not put the travellers' surnames in as it
would not be fair to their children.

*(I have heard similar stories over several years and can imagine them to
be authentic. The Bold Rodney yard, which Henry mentions, was a major
and very regular winter stopping place. The pub no longer exists. One local
Gypsy family does have a family secret which they will not disclose. Two of
their forbears were called by the names Henry here quotes.)*

I was stopping in the Bold Rodney yard at Chesterfield. The yard was full
of travellers – the Finneys, Smiths, Spencers, Cartridges and some of my
own family. The yard belonged to the landlord of the public house just
outside the entrance. The public was the same name as the yard, The Bold
Rodney.

There was a few of us inside the public house one dinner time having a
drink. A traveller by the name of Jim came in. He asked Tom Finney to
buy him a drink, which Tom did.

Jim sat down and started to talk. He asked, "Is there anyone who would
buy a living for life for the price of two pints of beer?"

One traveller, who's name was also Jim, asked him what the living was.
Jim said to him, "God strike me dead mush, it is a good living and you will

have to buy it sight unseen."

The other Jim said, "Alright mush, I will buy it. Drink up and have another pint". He gave him five shillings and said, "There you are, there is a bit extra for luck ".

We all sat drinking until nearly closing time.

About half an hour before the pub closed, Jim went out. He came back about quarter of an hour later. He had his wife Tutti and their two children with him. He said to the other Jim, "There you are, mush, she is all yours, chavies as well, she can earn you two or three pounds every day hawking. She is a living for life."

They shook hands, and Jim, who had bought the living, took Tutti and her two children out and to his waggon. That is a few years ago. The same couple are still together and have a family of their own and also the other Jim's two children.

They are as happy as the day is long and if you ever say anything to them about how they got together, Jim will say, "Yes mush, the best two pints I ever paid for". The Christian names are theirs, also the juvel's Tutti. They have some good things today and as I said are as happy as any two travellers on the road.

Uncle Bill will know the Herringtons and Quintons. Ask him if he know Harry Quinton or George Dedman and his brother Tidli Dedman, or Silvester Taylor known as old Trout, the best skewer maker amongst gypsies.

An Evil Policeman

In the 1950s, we, that is Mushy Toogood and his brother Iher, Bob Braddock, Ezi Evans and my juvel *(wife)* and myself, were stopping at a place called Llanomonak in between Oswestry and Welshpool, Shropshire and Montgomery border. We were all on Dutch Barns painting. We had a few contracts to finish around about this area. We all had good motors and trailers. Iher Toogood's trailer, a Coventry and all steel, cost him two thousand two hundred pounds. I had a very nice Berkeley and Bob Braddock had a Willerby. Early one morning we had just got up and lit a fire outside, as we always did. We were just going to have our breakfast when the Gavamush *(policeman)* came on a bike. He came like a bulldog. "Get packed up and move on", he said. We told him we would shift as soon as we had our breakfast. He would not have this, he insisted that we move right away.

Bob Braddock asked him if he and his family had had their breakfast. The policeman said, "What's that got to do with you?"

Bob said "Well, let us have ours in peace, then we will go."

The gava said, "If you don't move now, I will fetch some more to shift you all."

Bob said, "If you don't shift, I will soon shift you". The gava kept on, anyway, Bob up and hit him. He finished up putting the gava and his bike in the hedge bottom. The gava got up and went away. We all packed up quick and drove away.

We did not get far, before we were stopped with police cars. They took us to the police station, where the gavamush picked Bob out as the man that del'd *(hit)* him. Bob was taken to court, and explained everything. The judge would not believe him. He said, "All you Gypsies are alike, all liars". He gave Bob six months for assault on the police.

Tatcho Paramush Troostal Meero Biveli Reini (True story about my fortunate aunt Reini)

The disaster which Henry describes below occurred at Creswell Colliery, DBY, on 26th September 1950 and not, as he states, before the War. It was a most horrendous disaster. A belt rubbing against a roller is believed to have started a fire. The fire spread rapidly as the coal itself caught fire. Eighty men were trapped in the pit and the bodies of 47 recovered on the same day as the disaster. All had died from carbon monoxide poisoning from the burning coal.

To prevent the fire spreading, the remaining men had to be sealed into the pit. It was assumed they were dead, but there was no certainty. The pit was accessed again on 25th March 1951 and a further 27 bodies recovered, the remaining six being found on 11th August in the same year.

The coal faces concerned were not restarted until 1962.

It is worth noting that the widow of one of the dead men, remarried – he was another miner who moved pits – very soon after, exactly as Henry has described.

I am obliged to Coun. Ian Whyles of Whitwell for this information.

Before the war, my aunt Reini and myself were hawking in the Bolsover area. I called at a house and the woman gave me two pairs of scissors to sharpen. When I took them back the lady asked me in to have a cup of tea. She asked me if my mother or anybody was with me who could tell fortunes. I told her that my aunt was with me, and that she was a good fortune teller. She asked me if my aunt would tell her fortune. I said "Yes, madam if you pay her." She said, "Would you like to fetch her to me?"

This I did. My Aunt told me after, that the woman's husband worked down the pit on night shifts, and that the woman had a lover who used to spend nights with her while her rom *(husband)* was working. She had asked my aunt if she thought anything could happen to her rom as she was sick of him. My aunt told her there would be a big disaster in the pit and her rom would get killed in it. She had given my aunt two pounds, and told her if this came true she would give her ten pounds if ever she was around Bolsover again. We said what a wafedi *(wicked)* woman she was. We forgot all about this in a few days.

About ten months later there was a big pit disaster at Creswell coal mine. About three weeks after this disaster, we were calling Bolsover again. There was my aunt, my romni *(wife)* and myself. My aunt was missing for about an hour and then came and told us a woman had made some tea for us.

We all went in the house, and it was the same woman that my aunt had read her fortune. This woman had left her house and her and the man she had been seeing while her husband had been working had bought this one. She had already told my aunt how her husband had been killed in Creswell pit disaster. The woman had given my aunt ten pounds and she put us a bundle of nice clothes up to take with us.

My aunt said when we got outside. "I hope she drops dead, the mairus *(blaggard)*." On my chavies *(child's)* life, Dick, within a fortnight the woman had died. I have often wondered if my aunt was a witch. She seemed to know everything that any of us did without being there with us.

She told me once I was going into a big building to stay for a bit. Sure enough a week after I got six months. I went into a big building – Leicester Prison.

Gypsy Law

As you may know there are secrets amongst my race that will never be known, only amongst the Romani-folki *(Gypsy people)* and when my race dies out, the secrets will die with them. I feel sure you have noticed, that choose how much an outsider is accepted, there are lots of things that the Romani folki will never talk about in front of them. When you are talking to a chal *(Gypsy boy)*, always watch his romniaw *(wife's)* eyes or who ever is with him. You will see them talk with their eyes. I have done it thousands of times, so have my folki *(family)*. It is a thing we learn as chavies *(children)*.

A Romani-chal will only tell you what he wants you to know and will always change the subject to suit himself. Even when a Romani chal marries a Gorgio woman, he never tells her certain things, that is the same the other way round if a Romani-Chai *(Gypsy girl)* marries a Gorgio mush *(non-Gypsy man)*. I jin *(know)* lots of people who have been very friendly with Romani folki and they would swear they knew all the secrets. This is wrong, for no Romani-chal or Chai would tell them. There is one thing for certain, they would always take a friend's part if in trouble, and a tatcho chal *(true Gypsy)* would never let a tatcho friend down or do him any wrong, choose what.

Old Cradock Price was upset about Gaskin getting in trouble and using Price's nav *(name)*. If it had been the likes of me that had been talking to him he would not have said that, as you may know. That was because it was you he was talking to. I should have told Craddock he had been a lucky man not ever been leld *(arrested)*, and he would have known it was the truth.

Please believe me prala, Romani chalaw can always put a front on when need be. I am telling you this because you have always been the best friend I ever had when in need of one. I shall tell you a lot, if lucky enough to get to Ashwell to see you. Things I would never write on paper. Just between me and you.

Please ask Rockey Price at Ipswich how his brother "Archer Douglas" (nick name – Big Harry Price) at Walsall is going on. Big Harry married a young Gorgio rakli *(housedweller girl)* old *(illeg.)* seaachs daughter, a log dealer at Gloucester. Big Harry Price had a fight with his brother-in-law who is also Rocky's brother in law, "Mandy the Black". He married Rocky and Big Harry's sister. Mandy the Black stuck a peg knife into Big Harry and just missed his heart. Big Harry, who can fight, would have beaten him otherwise. Ask Rocky about it, he will tell you or Phyllis that it happened at Gloucester a few year back. Big Harry has a son named after Rocky. Big Harry's first wife was a Policeman's daughter at Walsall. Harry lives at Guild Avenue, Blakewell Estate, Bloxwich, Walsall. He is proper blond headed person.

Anyway prala *(brother)* I am living in hopes at being able to have a good talk with you before very long. As I have said before we can rokka *(talk)* about things that we would not write in lil *(a letter)*

Have you ever seen Romani Cheiaw gets pieces of dead bark off an old oak tree and put perfume on the pieces? This is sold as Indian bark to put in your pocket or in the wardrobe. Never loses its scent, also lucky.

We will have a good laugh together when I see you I can promise you that and a cup of mutermongri *(tea)*, that is allowed in all staribens *(prisons)* now on visits.

Don't forget prala, ask Rocky about the fight between Big Harry and his brother-in-law, Mandy the Black. Harry would have mord *(killed)* Mandy if Mandy had not stabbed him.

Note: *The pieces of dead bark, or semi rotted pieces of trunk, soaked in this*

way are called fonkum or funkum (this Cant word means smell). Contrary
to what Henry says, they do lose their scent.

My Grandparents – and modern Gypsies

My pooro Dadus *(grandfather)* and pooro Dei *(grandmother)* were as black
as the Ace of Spades and you could not tell when they had washed their
faces. I loved every hair of their head and many a time sit and think about
them. and the good old days. We made our own entertainment around our
stick fires in those days. Good singing and step dancing and different kinds
of music. We used to tell a lot of paramush *(folk tales)* until very late at
night.

The only thing that three parts of the travellers can do today, is sit in
their fancy trailers watching television. Every Sunday we used to go coursing with our dogs. We would bet on which dog could kill a hare the first. We
also always had Bantams and Game Cocks. We used to carry them in the
Pan pox under the back of the waggon, and sometimes in the pans at the
sides of the waggon. The real old chals used to take their shoes and shirts
off and put a silk Dikla *(neckerchief)* around their waist and fight one
another for money and to see who was the best man. I have seen many a
time a brother and sister fight another brother and sister of a different
breed.

These things have nearly died out today and also hundreds of other
things that were part of our life. The only time you will see a bit of the real
old Romani ways is at a fair like Appleby. Even that has changed a bit. Some
chals today look down on others who are not so well off. This was a thing
that was never heard of in days gone by, and as a matter of fact is not today
with the tatcho Romano folki *(proper Gypsy people)*.

We were always taught to call anybody older than ourselves Uncle or
Aunt and anybody around our own age brother or sister. Even this is dying
out today – I have always respected the traditions of my folki, two of which
is, Never chor *(steal)* from another Chal *(Gypsy)* and never chor from a
friend. Also, always help another chal in need. I have been a bad one, but
can truthfully say, I have never broken the old and true traditions of my
people, which I was taught from being a boy. I love and respect all tatcho
chals and Cheis and all Tatcho Romano folki with all meero zee *(my heart)*,
but the Posh-breedopen *(half castes)* I have no time for. I think you will
agree with me prala that the real Poori Tatcho Romano folki are dying out
fast

Kanna Mandi Shomas Nevoli Romedi
(When I was newly married)

Many years ago we were stopping at a place called Sticker Planting, just outside of Buxton, Derbyshire. The nearest house was about two and a half miles away. It was the farmer's house who owned the fields around us. It was just before Christmas and the weather was very bad. The only tent my juvel *(wife)* and I had was one made out of nine willow rod benders. We had an old horse and flat cart to carry our things on. There were a few more rod tents and a couple of Bow Topped waggons.

One day it started to snow heavens hard. We had used every bit of wood that we could find and we had no fire. One of the chals, Jim Worrel, said, "I will get some wood." He went over to a five-barred gate and lifted it of the hinges. We broke it up and made a good fire. We had just got the kettles and pots around the fire when the farmer came.

He said "How do, it is bad weather for your children." He went away and about one hour after the police came. They asked who had stolen the gate and burned it. No one knew, so they took us all to the police station. They was going to charge us all, but Jim Worrel said, "No, I stole the gate. Mother's mouth do you think I was going to let my children sit there in the cold when there was wood about?" They let us all go bar Jim.

He went at the front of the magistrate next morning. They asked him had he any thing to say. He said "Yes sir, would you have let your dear little children starve in the cold if there was a wooden gate to make a fire with?

The justice said, "That's nothing to do with it. You can not go about the country burning gates. You will go to prison for three months."

Before we left Sticker Planting there were eleven gates missing

Romanes Paramish (Gypsy tale) – Doovel Taylor

Dosta bershaw palla, mendi shamas atchin adre o posh-hori ta hori opuv adre Bauri Lon Gav adre Kalesko-tem. Yek simensa katar mandi shomas atchin opre o puv, ta dosta bootodair Romani chals. Meero simensa putchklo mandi katar jal katar o kitchema pashal lesti. Ghiom katar o kitchema shamas odi shomas kumeni ghili. Meero simensa pendas choomoni troostal yek of o Romani chals, Doovel Taylor. Doovel Shoondas meero Simensa ta putchtas lesti katar koor. Doovel deled meero simensa moker. Yov kon pukedi mandi duva mandi shomas yek of o waver mushaw folki ta koorelas ta mandi deld lesti. Kanna mendi jal pauli katar o puv Dooval korus avel-avri ta koor sor toot koorin mushaw yov tei pendas mandi satsis del toot sor o latcho deldaw. Meero prala Kaulo Billy del lesti wi kavvi-sastra. Mendi chiv moro greiaw adre moro vardas ta ghiom adrom. Leski folkii nor meero folkii shan rokerd katar yek waver fon duvva divvus katar kova divvus. Mendi kek-komi yek waver pensa drab.

Many years ago, we were stopping in the Halfpenny and Penny field in Northwich, Cheshire. One of my cousins and I were staying in the field, and many more Gypsies. My cousin asked me to go to the pub with him. We went to the pub, while we were there, we were singing some songs. My cousin said something about one of the Gypsies, Doovel Taylor. Doovel heard my cousin and asked him to fight. Doovel struck my cousin below the belt. He then told me that I was one of the other man's people, and we fought and I hit him. When we went back to the field, Doovel shouted, "Come out, come out and fight, all you fighting men." He also said, "I can give you all a good seeing to." My brother Black Billy hit him with a kettle iron. We put our horses to our wagons and took to the road. Neither his people nor my people have spoken to one another from that day to this. We avoid each other like poison.

Beeston Castle

In 1960 my juvel *(wife)* and I were stopping in an old lane in Loppington, Shropshire. It is a small village with two public houses in it.

We were in one of them, The Blacksmiths Arms. I was half-drunk and was singing About nine o'clock, a big black Humber car pulled up outside. A lady and a gentleman got out and came into the inn. They ordered a whisky and gin.

They both sat down at the side of my juvel. They asked her, "Are you Gypsies?"

My juvel told them, "Yes, we are." I came and sat down and the Rei *(gentleman)* started to talk to me.

He said "I like you people". He asked us to have a drink. I said to him, "Please sing us a good old song". He got up and sang a song. He was a terrible singer, but we all praised him and said what a good singer he was.

He asked me what I did for a living. I told him I was a grinder. He said to me, "I can find you some work, please give me a call on Monday, here is my card with my name and address on it." I could not read then, so I put the card in my putsi *(pocket)*. On Sunday, we were in the same public house and I asked the landlady if she would read the name and address for me. I gave her the card and she read it for me. The Rei was the gentleman from Beeston Castle in Cheshire.

My juvel and I went on the Monday. The castle was up a long drive. I called at the door and a servant came out and asked me what I wanted.

I told her I had called for the grinding. She said they do not want any-thing grinding there. I told her to go and ask the lady or gentleman of the house as I had been asked to come. Anyway the Rawni *(lady)* heard us talking and came to the door. She said to the servant, "Who is the boss here, you or me? When anyone comes here, please let me know. I asked these people to call."

She fetched the Rei and he found us enough grinding to last us three days. He told us that we could stop on his land anytime we wanted and nobody could shift us. I always call when I am around there. He is a good Rei.

A Buggy Wagon

Gypsies frequently traded – chopped – wagons with each other. One of the common problems was ending up with a wagon which had lice or fleas, and even though cleaned thoroughly on the inside, ordinary washing did not destroy all the bugs. Certain families were renowned for having lice or fleas – or both – and trading with them was avoided. But it was not always possible to know a wagon's previous history and it was easy to be caught out.

My brother and his wife and myself and my wife were stopping in Sawley Lane at Sawley, near Long Eaton, Notts. My brother had a Bow Topped waggon that he had bought from Burly Price. It was a buggy. He had paid eighty-four pounds for it and was told it was good and clean.

His wife Helen stopped him from burning it. Stopping a bit further down the lane was Jack Two-Wives, Old Woodbine Smith's boy. His two wives are sisters Kizie and Priciler. The one that earns the most money hawking in a day sleeps with him that night. Anyway, he had a little square bowed Open Lot, what we called a rasher. We all got together in the kitchema *(pub)* in Long Eaton, called The Corner Pin.

My brother told him, "I have a good big bow topped waggon, it is too big for me and my wife."

Jack Smith jumped at it, and said, "My Open Lot is too small for me and my two juvels and chavies *(wives and children)*, can we have a swop?"

My brother asked him twenty-five pounds to swop. At the same time my brother would have given him twenty five pounds to swop, as with his waggon being buggy, it was no good. Anyway, Jack said, "I have only twelve pound in the world. I will give you that." My brother finished up drawing fourteen pounds to swop.

We went back down the lane, and Jack Smith got his things out of his Open Lot and put his horse in and brought it down to our Billy's place.

My brother Bill got his things out of his waggon and they exchanged. Jack put his horse in the one he had swopped for. The next night, his two wives came down to our place. We were in bed. They shouted to my brother, "Please fetch the waggon back, as we cannot sleep in it. There are too many bugs."

My brother shouted, "Go back home. I was done with it, and now you are."

The next day the police came. They asked my brother if any money changed hands. My brother told them he had drawn fourteen pounds to swop. They said they could do nothing, but if it had been a straight swop without money changing hands, they could have made my brother swop back.

So Jack Two-Wives was left with the buggy waggon.

Wartime

The Chals' whistle consists of two notes, the first long, and the second, lower, shorter. It is very distinctive. All Gypsies appear to know of it, though not all use it. Some families claim only they have it – the Welsh/Midlands Taylors spring to mind – but that is not so. I was once in a large shopping centre where I knew Gypsies regularly went and used the whistle as an experiment. Sure enough, within a few moments two burly men appeared in the vicinity. I did not make myself known.

Gypsy people have always considered helping each other when in trouble to be an essential feature of life. Numerous Gypsies have told me of instances when they have hidden other people, or adopted them into the family. A great many stories of times when Gypsies have also adopted gorjers are told, and I have authenticated or personally witnessed several of these.

When the war was on in 1942 there was a lot of us stopping in Findern Lane near Derby. There was old Mandrew Price, Tom Price, Fighting Tom Lee, Rocky Price, George Gaskin, Ezie Roberts, Jack Smith, Woodbine Smith, some of the Dedmans, one of the Cunninghams, old Sofia Lee, Nelson Lee, Peter Lovell, some of the Hearns and a few more that I did not know.

I was at that time *prarsterin avri o kooromengroes (had deserted from the army).* I thought that I was the only one. We had all just come back from the *kitchema (pub)* and were talking around the fires. Just before midnight we saw motor headlights coming down the lane. The first words that were said were, "Muskras, jal" *(Police, scram).* I ran and as I looked around half of the other chals *(Gypsy boys)* were also running. I got away into a wood. After a few minutes there were about six or seven of us all sat down together in the wood. We stopped there for about an hour and then made our way back to camp very quietly.

We saw that the Muskraw *(police)* had gone, so we went right up to our places. Nearly all of us packed up our things and moved away there and then. Three of us with waggons and horses made for Burton on Trent, which is over the Derbyshire border. We pulled in an old lane just outside of Burton. It was breaking daylight so we made a fire and our women made some breakfast.

I said to Credi Price that I thought I was the only one prarsterin *(on the run).*

He laughed and said, "I think everyone is".

We were left alone there for a few days, then one night we were just having some supper when all of a sudden four motors were right upon us. The police got out and they was all around the place.

I got under the bottom bed in the waggon. The Muskras came in the waggon but did not see me. They took Credi away. The other chal and myself told our juvels *(wives)* what to do, and we left on foot. We walked for miles until we came to our meeting point, which was Tamworth in Warwickshire. We knew it would take a while for our wives to get there with the waggons and they would keep going round about roads, so as the Muskras could not follow them, we knew they would.

We waited and waited until night, and decided to find a place to sooti *(sleep)* for the night. We got down in an old barn with some straw in it.

Early next morning we were up and out. We mong'd *(begged)* a jug of tea from a kair *(house)* and then went to our meeting place. Our juvvels landed with our things around dinnertime. They told us they had pulled out for the night, as the Muskras had followed them. We settled down and made a good stick fire, and started our hoben *(food).*

We saw the Muskras coming a good distance away. The two of us jumped up and set off across the puv *(field).*

We made for Loughborough, that is where we told our juvels to bring the things to. We had arranged to meet them in Slash Lane just outside of the town. We got to Slash Lane and slept in the bottom bed of Johnnie Squires's Bow Topped waggon. The next day we sat in the lane waiting for our juvels. They did not come. The next morning we set off to meet them. We got about twelve miles out and we saw our waggons in a field just at the back of the hedge. We gave a Chal's whistle, and my juvel came to us.

She told me, that while they were travelling, the horse had pulled up quick and a motor had hit the back cratch and kettle box. We went into the puv and when I looked at our waggon the back cratch and kettle box was smashed in. She told me the Muskras had taken particulars and would be coming back again. She said, "Better if you jal *(go)* and wait in

Slash Lane or Pigeon Lane." I told her Pigeon Lane was the best. I took a tent sheet out of the Vardo *(wagon)*, and away we went.

We got to Pigeon Lane and cut some willow rods and made a tan *(bender)*. The two of us waited a couple of days until our juvels landed with the things. The next morning we set off about five o'clock and we made our horses go as fast as ever they could. Every time we spotted a Muskra, my wife took the reigns and I got back in the Vardo. We kept going until we were right unto Leicestershire.

When we pulled out at night our horses were dead beat. We puv'd *(illegally grazed)* them in a good field where there was plenty for them to hol *(eat)*. We were not bothered by anyone for days. This gave our horses time to get fit again. Us two men were making wooden flowers and pegs etc. and our juvels were going out hawking with them.. They used to bring us our tuvla *(tobacco)* back with them. We used to go to a nice quiet little kitchema *(pub)* in the village nearby. Anyway prala *(brother)* we went on like this for nearly two years.

When I was lel'd *(arrested)*, it was from Findern Tip, Derby. We had pulled on the day before. Stopping near us was Old Trout Taylor and his wife Amelia. One of their lads, Ezi, was on the prasta *(run)* like myself. The muskras came and I hid under Spidey Price's bottom bed in his waggon. They arrested Ezi and old Amelia started shouting, "You have my son, there is more here, look under the bottom beds." The muskras looked under and found me. They took us all to the police station at Derby to await escorts back to the kooromengroes *(army)*.

The escort got me as far as London. I ditched them on the tube station. I made my way North to the first camp I could find. The Romani chals and cheis fixed me up with luver *(money)* etc and I made my way back to where I had always told my juvel to be if I got lel'd. When they finally got me a long while after, they sent me to Egypt in the brig of the *Leopold Anvis*, a Belgian ship. After a few months in Egypt, Syria, and Palestine, they sent me back to Belsdyke Military Hospital at Larbert Falkirk, Scotland.

I nashedi *(escaped)* from there and never saw the army again until they sent me my discharge to Leicester Prison in 1948. I always said I would never koor *(fight)* for the country because of the life we had led, moved from pillar to post. Maybe I did wrong, in my own mind I think I did right. I was like a lot more Romani chals, bitter about the way we were treated. You see, Dick, you are one out of a thousand. Lots of Gorjers hate Roman folki. I wish there was more like you.

In a separate letter to his wife, Henry says that following his arrest by military police, he was put in Aldershot Military Prison. A Col. Jackson had him taken from prison in handcuffs and sent to Egypt. He subsequently burgled Col. Jackson's home in retaliation.

The Ghost

When I was a bit of a lad, my people and I were atchin *(stopping)* in an old lane just outside of Bakewell. This old lane was supposed to be haunted. One day my cousin Mart *(?Matt)* Booth said to me, " I will have a bit of Piva Terarty *(have some fun tonight)*." At about eleven o'clock that same night, we were all sat around a stick fire beside the wall. All of a sudden there was a white thing ran across the field. My folki swore blind it was the Beng *(devil)*. It came back across the field again. It was pure white and just as big and the shape of a man or woman.

My folki were trasht *(frightened)* to death. Some of them said, "It must be the Rakli *(girl)* who was murdered here," others said it must be the Beng. The place was in an uproar, some of the chavies *(children)* ran off. One of my uncles, Hope, said 'I'll soon find out if it is the Beng." He went to his ledge sided waggon and got his yoga (gun) from under the bottom bed. He came out with it. We waited a bit and the white thing came into the field again. My uncle Hope shot at it. He missed and was going to have another shot, when THE THING screamed out, "Don't shoot, it is me, Matty".

We all went into the puv *(field)* and sure enough it was my cousin. He had got hold of a white sheet and cut two eye holes in it. He had put it over his shero *(head)* and with it being night and dark it looked real. He was a very lucky mush *(man)* to have not been dead. My uncle is not a bad shot. It was only with it being dark that saved him.

Anyway there was a bit of a fight with my brother and cousin Matt over my cousin frightening our folki. My uncle Ephram gave Matt a good beating with an ash plant after. So you can see Dick, it was a dear bit of fun. My cousin Matt never played any more tricks while he was stopping beside us.

Uncle Bill Booth has atched *(stopped)* in the same lane, the long lane at Bakewell, Derbyshire. Please ask him if he knows where Sticker Planting, Buxton and Flash Dam at Matlock are. They have been two of our stopping places for years. Also Ringing Low outside of Sheffield. Ask him if he knows old Bob Smith who has stopped at Ambergate with his waggons for years. And his son young Bob Smith and Sier Abbott. They are two brothers, horse dealers, at Brackenfield not far from Clay Cross. They have a public house in Brackenfield.

The Tramp

A few years ago my wife and I were stopping just outside of Oswestry Shropshire. It was about eight-o-clock one morning and we had set out to go out hawking. We got to a place four miles outside of Oswestry called Queens Head. There are only a couple of public houses and a shop and cafe in Queens Head. We said we would have a cup of tea in the cafe before we started to hawk the odd house.

Just before we went in the cafe a tramp came along. We asked him if he would like a cup of tea and a bite to eat. He said, "Yes thank you." We all three went into the cafe. I ordered three teas and a breakfast. The lady of the cafe kept on looking at the tramp, and asked me if he was with us. I told her we had asked him in for a drink.

She said to me, "You don't know who or what he is."

I said to her, "I don't care Mrs, he is as good as us, choose what he is."

Anyway she decided to serve me with his tea and breakfast. He asked us where we were going. I told him we was going to hawk all the odd houses on the way to Ellsmere and back home. He said he was making for Ellsmere, did we mind if he came along with us. I told him we did not mind as long as he did not let the people at the houses see him with us, as it would make it bad for our trade. We set off.

After we had been hawking for about an hour and a half, we asked a lady at a house to make us a jug of tea. The woman made us a jug full and my juvel gave her some pegs for it.

We got into Ellsmere about half past twelve time. The tramp asked if my wife and I would like a glass of beer. I said, "Yes, let us go in and have one." I paid for the first couple of rounds. The tramp then got up and asked the landlord to fill them up again and to have one for himself. The landlord looked gone out at him. Anyway the tramp pulled a roll of £5 and £1 notes from his inside jacket pocket. The landlord filled the drinks up and one for himself.

At closing time the man asked the landlord to fill us a big bag of bottles to take out with us. He bought fifty shillings worth. We got outside and were carrying the bottles in a couple of bags, one bag a piece. All of a sudden three police came right up to us.

One of the police said, "I know these two, they are Gypsies – Boswell."

They asked the man who he was. He pulled some papers out of his pocket and showed them to the police. The sergeant had a good look at the papers. He gave them back to the man, and said, "I am very sorry to trouble you, Sir, but we was told that a tramp and two Gypsies were spending a lot of money in the pub. I would not have bothered you if I had known who you were.

The man said to us, "Blast the people, they cannot mind their own business, let us sit down and have a drink." We sat down and had a tidy few drinks. He then put his hand in his pocket and pulled two five pound notes out. He turned around and said to my wife, "Here you are madam, this will repay you for losing time hawking." We said we did not want it. He said to us, "Please take it. I have plenty and a tidy few houses of my own. I am just travelling the country as a tramp so as I can write a book about it. I shall be sure and put in it about the friendly Gypsies I met at the Queen's Head."

I think his name was Davies. Anyway Dick, I could tell as soon as he opened his mouth that he was a pure Rei. I have never seen him again from that day to this, but have often thought about him and wondered if he ever wrote his book. When we parted we shook hands as the best of pals. He said he would always remember us and would always tell people how kind and good he found the Gypsy people he had met on his travels. It's a funny thing Dick, we had talked to one another at first, that is the wife and I, about giving him a few shillings when we left him, and it turned out as he finished up giving us a few pounds. It goes to show, you can't judge a book by its cover. I think you will agree with me

I am dubious about the authenticity of this account. I wish I did believe it. Henry's implication is that this man was W.H. Davies, author of Diary of a Supertramp. *There is an account in the book of just such a meeting, but as it is clear that by this point Henry had access not only to the very rare Gypsy book,* Dialect of the English Gypsies *(Smart and Crofton) and the even rarer* English Gypsy Songs in Romany *(Leland, Tuckey and Palmer), W.H. Davies's best seller book would be easy to find.*

However, the incident would have happened at the right time for it to have been the Irish writer Jim Phelan.

3. ENCOUNTERS WITH OTHER GYPSIES

The following section incorporates Henry's encounters and interactions with other Gypsy people.

Murder of Everett Elliot by Farmer at Stanground

A few years ago Everett Elliot and his wife Bessi Woodward and their three children, William and twin girls Kizzy and Leena, were stopping with their waggons on the Stanground at Peterborough. Bessie was meeting a farmer on the sly. Everett found out about this and went to see the farmer. They had a bit of a fight, anyway the farmer went in his place and came out with a gun. He shot Everett and killed him.

Bessie Woodward is living in Nottingham with a gorgio *(non-Gypsy)* man called *(omitted — ed)*. They have a boarding house and also go out hawking peppermint. Romani chals will not bother with them, because of Bessy being the cause of Everett Elliot's death.

You may have heard of or read about Everett. I think that Bill Hames can tell you about it. If you don't know, all the Romani chals cried shame on Bessie.

A Fight

In 1937 we were stopping with a Beverley trailer and a 19.8 Chrysler in a yard on Whittington Moor, Chesterfield. Little Izaac Winter was stopping with his Eccles trailer at the side of us.

It was old year's night and we had all gone to the kitchema for a sing-song. Isaac Winter's uncle, James Crosby, had driven from Wigan to see us and was drinking with us all in the kitchen. He said to his nephew Isaac, "They tell me you can fight. I intend trying you out before morning". We all went back to the yard and put the motors with the headlights shining inwards.

Jimmy and Isaac took their shirts off, tied their trousers up with their dicklers *(neckerchiefs)* and got in the centre so as the motor lights shone on them. I handled Izaac and another traveller handled Jimmy. They started to fight , and were fighting when the bells were ringing the old year out and the New Year in.

Old Jim was beaten by his nephew Izaac. He blamed the beer and said, "If I had been sober I would have beaten you." Every time Jimmy Crosby and I meet we always talk about him fighting the old year out and New Year in. Little Izaac Winter is dead now. He died with cancer in Nottingham St. Annes Well Road. He had many a fight and never lost one, he beat and broke the best fighter in Chesterfield's jaw. His father and mother were Andrew and Annie Winter. She was Anna Crosby, James Crosby's sister before she was married. You may have heard of them. They have plenty of money.

Some News of Travellers

Although Henry has laid this out in prose, it is clearly intended as a poem. The list is interesting in that it presumably a list of Travellers whom Henry knew. The implication is therefore that all of them travelled the Midlands in the 1930s-60s. They include several families which are normally regarded as from Southern England, such as Scamps and Butlers and Brazils; from Wales, such as Othey Burton, as well as some people with names which have not previously been classed as Gypsy. Perhaps these people were dealers – 'widoes' as they are called in the Northern Midlands. The Jack Two Wives referred to is Johnny Two Wives Smith, who used to 'honour' whichever wife was most successful at hawking, whilst the other had to sleep in a bender. If a genuine personal recollection by Henry, there must have been two Johnny Two-Wives, as this one must have been too young to be synonymous with the Johnny mentioned in JGLS..

There's the Mulverdines and Calladines and Bartley Gorman too. They are fighting with the women, they have nothing else to do. There's the Smiths and the Sherriffs and Ria Small you know, they always get moved from atchin *(stopping)* wherever they go.

There's the Tapsalls and the Winters and Ezi Roberts there. They are sick and tired of travelling, they are going to take a kair *(house)*. There's little Mattie Loveridge, he's going to have a fight, he's got to meet Jack Burnside at five o'clock tonight.

There's old Drusila Elliot, she's known to be a witch, and old Tienni Penfold, when she's drunk, she finishes in a ditch. There's little Johnnie Buckland and Big Dave Gray; they are going to the public house and there they should stay.

There's old Tutti Worrel, a *(omitted — ed)* as you know, she's chasing after Peter Lock where ever he may go. There's old Riley Lovel and his aunt Trainett too; they are looking for Sampson Butler to have a word or two.

There's old Izek Crosby and Mary Wilson there, they're dikin for old Trout Taylor to find Micky Mair. There's old Pol Gaskin and Johnie Gaskin too, they are going to see Rosemary Edwards to sell their waggon to.

There's Levi Wiltshire and Beckie Wiltshire there and also old George Deadman who has not got a care. There's the Lees and the Prices who are all one breed; and the Williams and the Jones who know nout but greed.

There is Othey Burton a fighting man you know, who has fought different travellers where ever he may go. There's some of the Boswells and Broadways too, they are making for the country – it's the best place to go.

There's some of the Tarns and Swales and Higgs; they're travelling the country and looking for digs. There's Darkus Quinton and Harry Quinton too, they are looking for Naylie Toogood to bikin *(sell)* their barrow to.

There's another man you all know; he has done very well; his name is Jack Weaver – he is not very slow. There's the fighting man amongst travellers, Nighti Scamp's his name; he is not worth a farthing but still he is game.

There's old Victoria Stevens, the pride of them all; she should have had Hope Holland; he would have shown her how to call. Here's a dukkera *(fortune teller)* amongst travellers, Mary Cunningham is her name; she could not durik *(tell fortunes)* to keep herself warm, but still it is a shame.

There's Sujer Heath and Bob Booth and Little Nattie James, they're always winning luva *(money)* at playing different games. There's old Noah Pinfold who takes after his dad, he's always been a boozin mush *(man)* since he was a lad.

There's old Walter Haselhurst and old Bob Hinds, they are going out selling oilcloth for shillings and dimes. There's young Seuly Brazil and Nenti Brazil too, they are travelling the kalesko-tem *(Black Country)* to find some bikin *(hawking)* too.

There's the Egertons and Herringtons; also the Knowles; Big Amos Braddeck who carries on so. There's Tatti Trainette; Gravelenni and Isabel Smith, they are all relations to Iziah Smith. Theres the man with two wives: they call him Jack Big Head; his father's name was Woodbine, but he is now dead.

There's old Trafalger Loveridge and Buller Lovell too; one of their kin married a Finney, she had nothing better to do. There's some of the Poshrats; they are stopping in Slash Lane; they are badly liked by the gorgios , because they are always choring game *(poaching)*. Well here ends my ditty, I hope you don't mind; so please forgive my insults as these are all kind. (Henry.)

Please ask Uncle Bill *(Hames)* if he knew Chichi from Bung – some called him Chitti from Bung, and ask him did he know 'Half-a-Twid'. They call him half a twid because he cannot say half a quid. Also Stuttering Jarv Lee.

These are three chals I feel sure he will know – Chitti from Bung, Half-a-Twid and Stuttering Jarv. Also ask him if he knows Mandi the Black, who married Big Harry Price's Sister. They are atchin over the bridge in Gloucester. Mick Mares is old Pol Gaskin's husband

Some Derbyshire Gypsies

Please ask Uncle Bill Hames if he can remember his brother Peter courting Lizzie Sherriff when they were young and his lot and my lot used to stop together in Derbyshire and Staffordshire. Ammy *(Annie or Army?)* Hames was with them then. The Whistlers always stopped with my lot and some of the Heaps. Ask him if he knows any of the Herringtons, Derbyshire Travellers. Bob Herrington is settled down at Wirksworth now in a council house. He sometimes goes out grinding, also young Peter Hames who lives at Matlock, goes out grinding with a bicycle barrow. Old Bill will be his uncle. Please tell him that my aunt Tilly Sherriff's husband, my uncle Ephraim Booth died a couple of years ago at Swadlincote near Burton on Trent. I had his kick-up barrow grinding machine, my Aunt Tilly gave it me. It was my uncle Ephraim's wish that I should have it when he died. He was a right old man.

Tutti Worrel

Old Tutti Worrel and her rom Jim was stopping outside of Leek in Staffordshire. They were atchin *(stopping)* with some more travellers. Amongst these other travellers was a man called Quinton, a grinder, who was in his twenties, Tutti was a woman nearer forty. Jim came back from hawking one day and found the lot gone – Waggon, horse and Tutti. He went looking for his romni, and when he found her at Tideswell Derbyshire, she had Quinton stopping with her.

Jim called him a ring-tail and everything else. There was a fight. The one that won was to have Tutti. Quinton won. Tutti made a great mistake, every time she bought a horse or waggon, her fancy man would go into a kitchema and sell it. He always made sure he drew the money. He would spend every penny on drink. When he got skint, he always came back to poor Tutti. She is a very old woman today and is atchin in a Bow Topped waggon at Wirksworth, Derbyshire. She is still with Quinton and he still goes away for weeks at a time and spends her hard earned money.

Her son Jim is married and lives and works in Wirksworth. He is working in Shaws Quarry. He sometimes does a bit of grinding with young Peter Hames from Matlock. Last time I saw young Peter Hames they were living in Riber Castle, Matlock, near Peter Smith at Tansley.

Walter Lee

Old Christmas Lee had a few sons, two of these sons were named Chunki
and Walter Lee. Chunki was older than Walter. Chunki married a rikeni
Romani Chei *(beautiful Gypsy girl)*. Walter was courting a travelling girl
– her name was Lizer Partridge. She could fight like a man, and lift an old
washing mangle on her cart all by herself. I was going out grinding with
Walter: This was two or three years before the war, just after poor Christmas had died.

I went down to Whittington Moor one morning as usual, poor Chunki
was sat around his stick fire crying. I asked him what was wrong. He told
me his brother Walter and Peron and himself had come back from the
kitchema *(pub)* last night and Walter and his wife Mary was not there.
This morning when he got up, his wife had lit the fire outside and left the
kettle on. We searched the country for Walter and Mary. Lizer Partridge
said she would kel him *(sort him out)* if ever she got hold of him. Mary and
Walter were not found until years after. They are still together at Burton
on Trent in a council house, and have a nice family. That was the reason
we did not find them, as they got a house right away. Poor old Chunki
never looked up after she had left him.

Walter Lee has worked in a factory all those years grinding barrow. I
bought it off Peron, his other brother. I sold it a few months after to
Ephraim Holland at the Cambridge ground, Penistone Road, Sheffield.

Did You Know ...?

Did you ever know Jimmy and Tutti Worrel or Tin Tack Smiths, Annie
Sludge. The Mammies and Daddies? Ask Uncle Bill if he jins any of them.

I bet he jins *(knows)* old Mandrew Price and his wife, she was a school
teacher when he married her, now she can bikin *(hawk)* a gross of pegs as
good as any chei *(Gypsy girl)*. That is her daughter Pearly who married
Spidey Price. He is the best peg knife waggon maker I know.

He would know old Peggy Smith, two of her daughters, Kizzy and
Pricey, are married to Jack Two-Wives, old Woodbine Smith's son. He has
chavvies with the two of them. The one who earns the most in a day hawking sleeps with him that rarti *(night)*. Ask him if he knows Herbert Bax-
ter who travels around Coalville. He has two romnies *(wives)*. He has two
nice Bill Wright Waggons and about twenty-odd horses. He deals a lot
with Jack Toon of Coalville. Jack Toon sells greis *(horses)* to lots of
Romani – chals *(Gypsies)*. He is a good mush *(person)* to have a straight
deal with.

4. HENRY'S MUSINGS

Henry's Comments on an Unnamed Gypsy

Henry must here have been responding to comments by Dick about an unnamed Gypsy. I disassociate myself totally from these comments, which if anything illustrate Henry's contempt for people who lived honest and worthy lives.

Boot gorjakana[1] folki see le konaw kin (?) Posh rattvali. O bauriest kotor si o Romani chals tedivvus see booinelopus troostal o luva yon shan. Isi (?) yon see aladj si lenti breedopen. Si tooti putchtas. Yek ov len si lesti's. Mei a door chairus pauli mongadi hoben pa lesti. Yov wouldasava pen kek, Kekkomi tooti jin ta me jin aduva poshali sor meero monunshni's jaldas avri bikinin ta mongin. Odoi see yek e trin tedivvus savo kel pensa lenti pooro divvussaw shomas akein apopli. O Romani chals ta cheis shamas latcho ta tatchi ta wouldasar akir-posh yek waver. O chalaw tedivvus yekino savaben kanna lenti dik e chuveno tatchi pooro Romani mush. Me wouldasova chungar opre len yon see yekino[2] posh breedopen Romani chals. O dromaw pa de Romani chal tedivvus see paradas. Yon kel kek roker pensa o pooro chalaw. Yon opensa te sa gorjified. Mandi mi kokero wouldasar kek-komi pura meero jivomus oprem o drom sa sor o filisinaw adre sar o bauri temeskiaw. Les see latcho te besh tale o bauri kosht yok wi de koro of zimen ta o kushti soong avri les. Les wi bi kushti kanna me sastuis kel les apopli. Me shom mongin pa aduva divvus te avel.

Many gorjer people are therefore half-caste. The greatest proportion of the Gypsies today are boastful about the money they have. They are a disgrace to their race. As you asked, one of them is his (ie him). A long time ago I begged food for him. He would not ask, never. You know and I know that after all my wife always went out hawking and begging. There are one or two today who carry on like the old days were here again. The Gypsy boys and girls were good and true and would help one another. The boys today only laugh when they see a good old poor Gypsy man. I would spit on them. They are only half-Gypsies. The ways of today's Gypsies are changing. They don't speak like the old boys. They think they are gorjified. I myself would never change my life on the road for all the castles in all the great countries. It is good to sit under a signpost with a pot of soup and a good smell from it. It will be good when I can do it again. I am longing for that day to come.

---

[1]Underneath the word gorjakana, Dick has written *strangers*.
[2]Underneath the word yekino, Dick has written *first*.

Beduin Folki

When I was on the run from the army in Egypt for four months, I lived with the Beduins in the Desert. George Lee was also with me. I have never seen a race of people so much like the Romanies.

They like gold coins and coloured clothes. Some of the women go out duckerin *(telling fortunes)*. Some of the men have a grinding machine which they carry on their backs. They are a small square wooden machine, very light in weight. Some make and sell rinkeno *(beautiful)* carpets.

Their tents are beautiful inside. They are also good dealers. They have very good ways and respect their laws. Biggest part of them are pretty well off. I learned to speak a lot of Arabic while living with them. Their ways are just like our own, they go and do what ever they think best. A very free people prala *(brother)*.

I liked them and their ways very much and would not have left them, only for getting picked up by the British Red Corps *(ie military police)*. I have often thought and feel sure that the Beduin and the Romanies are from the same race of people. I often asked different Beduin folki *(people)* but never could find out for sure.

I also met an Italian Romani chal *(Gypsy)* in Elepo, in Syria. We could understand a few of the Romani words that him and me spoke to one another. He was also on the run from the Italian army and was living with some Armenians in Elepo. I used to go with him and have tea or coffee with his Armenian friends, very nice people they were and very religious.

Kris – 1

Henry's claim to have been tried by a kris is very dubious. The English kris system – Gypsy courts trying Gypsy people – had almost entirely died out by the latter part of the 19th century. Occasional reminiscences of it remained – I saw something of the sort amongst Northern Lees in Skipton in 1962 and I convinced myself it was a kris, but it was much more like a large family gathering and discussion. There was no formality. Similarly, I can well imagine that Henry's association with a gorjer girl – Lily Walker – must have caused great displeasure amongst the very orthodox Gypsy people who were looking after him, but kris is far too strong a word to describe this. Henry says he remained a year with the gorjer girl before meeting Marina Sherriff.

In one of his letters to Lily, he makes reference to his claim that he was banished from his race by his association with her.

I was tried by a Kris in 1938 for marrying a gorgio rackli *(housedweller girl)*. I was made an outcast until such times as I left her, and got a chei from my own race of people. I was taken back within twelve months because I broke the bond between me and my gorgio woman. I was on our marriage forbidden to go near any of my people and my people never spoke to me or my woman for twelve months. That was when we parted. They never did or ever have spoken to her. Thank God I was taken back after parting from her. It was terrible ladjin *(utterly degrading)*.

This, Dick, would not happen today as travellers are marrying gorgios regularly. Things were different before the war. My people stuck to our traditions and were very keen on them. I had my "Kris" at Chesterfield in 1938 and was taken back at the end of 1939. Not a serious crime, but if I had stopped with her, I would have been finished with my folki forever.

Kris – 2

The same comments about the dubiousness of this account apply as under Kris 1. However, sexual crime against anyone has always been considered very serious amongst Gypsies, probably more so than murder. Sexual crime against other Gypsies was considered especially serious and there are oral traditions of Gypsies being killed by their compatriots for this. Prostitution amongst Gypsy women was also always considered very shocking and both it and infidelity were liable to severe punishment. As Henry indicates, theft from gorjers was acceptable, but theft from Gypsies was considered a disgrace. Sadly, the latter is no longer the case amongst younger Gypsies.

It would seem that Henry had promised to get some earrings made from dollars – silver or gold – for Dick's daughter Ellie.

Yes Prala I have been to a few Romani Krisaw *(courts)*. It is a fair trial Prala *(brother)* , but a very hard sentence if guilty. I thank God I have never broken any of our unwritten laws, and can truthfully say I would sooner kill myself than break them. To be outcast from your race and more so your own folki is a terrible thing apart from whatever punishment the 'kris' puts upon you.

One of old *(details omitted — ed)*, sons, raped a woman a few years ago, she was a Gorgio *(non-Gypsy)* so Romani 'kris' had nothing to do with it. He was tried by an English court and got five years. No Romani will ever talk to him again as long as he lives. He did not break a Romani law but all families of girls and wives etc, they would never trust him amongst our people after doing that. As you know, prala "Rape" is a thing not known amongst our people. A man would be killed for doing such a thing to a

Romani-chei.

A Romani-chei lubni *(Gypsy prostitute)*, which is another thing not known, would be 'burned on her minj' *(private parts)*, to put her out of business, and outcasted for life. To steal from a Gorgio is not a crime or to sell him stolen property. But prala I don't think and would bet my life, that there is not many Tatcho-Romani-chals *(true Gypsies)* who would steal from another or biken *(sell)* him chordo *(stolen)* stuff.

As for getting another one 'leld' *(arrested)*, I have never heard of it. I could not imagine it ever happening, choose how big enemies they were. If a Romani-chal ever got another one 'leld', he would need police to protect him, they would kill him and chuck him in the river somewhere. To neglect a chavi *(child)* is a very bad thing I have only ever seen or heard of one. Believe me prala *(brother)* you should have seen the state of both him and her after they had been dealt with. They could not walk for weeks after, the chavi, a little girl, was taken over by relations. This couple would have been better off if they had been done by muskras *(police)* – they would have only got prison which is not a punishment compared to "Kris" punishment.

As I have said before, prala, I intend and shall tell you a lot of things that I am sure you don't know as soon as we can have a talk together. And I can promise you this, Little Nell will have the "Dollar" earings if I have to buy them myself as soon as I come out. If I do hear from my romni *(wife)*, I shall be able to get them from her. But I promised prala and you shall have them choose what.

A Chal *(Gypsy)*, prala *(brother)*, wants some weighing up, he will call and fight another one and maybe three parts kill him, but there is always that bond between them, they are and always will be Brothers.

I have seen two of my cousins nearly killing one another, a Gorgio mush *(man)* stepped in to help one of them, they both set about the Gorgio mush and told him to mind his own business. They finished up getting drunk and singing and dancing together. I call many a chal but at the same time I should be one of the first to take his part and have done many times. Blood is thicker than water and as you know nearly all Romani folki *(Gypsies)* are relations one way or another, through marriage mostly. I have been talking many a time to strange travellers, and after talking about our folki, have found out we were relations. This happens regular You mention an old uncle or aunt or great uncle and the next thing afore you know is that they were some relation to the people's mother or father or someone in their family and before you know you are talking to a cousin or some relations.

A Letter About Gypsy Ways

The word chiveno in the penultimate sentence is probably a mis- spelling for churello, meaning poor. If it is not, I cannot identify the word, but in that case presume it derives from chiv, *to cut.)*

Miro kamlo Prala,

Me nestissa parikaw tutti disl' (?) adray lavaw pa sor tutti shan keldossa pa mandi. Kekkomi bisserava tutti saw door sar jivava. Yek divvus pesewressa pauley ti mandi. Penessa adray teero koliko lil trustal booino Romani-folki, ladj opray lendi. Pukkerava tutti dosta, kana me dikessa tut. Sor trustal o Posh-rats ta kek kushti folki opray-o drom tedivvus.Pariker- ava mi-Duvel me sastis <u>bonek</u> meero shero opre <u>torro</u> sorkon-chairus adray vaniso tatcho Romani tan. Morava aglal del vaniso Romani-chal-or chei avree te muskero. A Romani chal savo delaw avava Romani-chal avree te muskero shouldesar se chiv opray yog ta katcherdas jivo. Bershaw ghias kova Romani kris kel. Tutti sastis ghinya o tatcho Romani folki opray yek- vast tedivvus. Sor o waveraw si posh-beeno-Gorjers, sar tutti jin, kek tatcho. O poorokono folko shan jaldas pa sorkon-cheirus. Doi se yek ti dui tatcho Romani-folki mooklo kanaw, nai-dosta, les se e ladj O Romani-folki shomas boot booino ofaser lenti breedopen, nanei ajaw dosta bershaw pauli. Konaw sor opensa Gorjers. Jafri folki se kek-kushti pukker sorkon-truppos so trustal Romani dromaw. Les kairs mandi koeni sorkon chairus me peneher (?pencher) Trustal meero folki tedivvus. Kek mong chavi mong tedivvus, poshali sor shan dosta luver. Kek chairus pa chiveno Romani folki. Me paz- eriben tutti komi aglal vaniso Romani folki tedivvus.

My dear brother,

I cannot thank you enough in words for all you have done for me.

I will never forget you for as long as live. One day I will pay you back. Write in your historical book about boastful Gypsy people, shame upon them. I will tell you plenty when I see you. All about the half-Gypsies and other no good people on the road today. I thank God I can hold my head up high, always in any true Gypsy camp. I would die before giving any Gypsy boy or gel away to the police. A Gypsy who gives away a Gypsy to the police should be set on fire and burned alive. It is many years ago since the Gypsy court acted. You can count the true Gypsy people on one hand today. All the other half-born gorjers are, as you know, no good. The old people were nomadic all the time. There are one or two true Gypsy people left now, not many, it is a shame. The Gypsy people were also very proud of their breed, not so many years ago. Now all are like gorjers. Such people are no good to tell every body about what are Gypsy ways. It makes me angry all the time I speak (?think) about my people today. Don't ask children to beg today, nearly all have a lot of money. No time for poor Gypsy people I believe. I am indebted to you before any Gypsy people today.

Here and There and Always Here

Henry's reference here to the Government is probably the weak Conservative Government of 1963-4 under Sir Alec Douglas-Home. The word kimba *occurs here and there throughout Henry's Romani texts. It is not a word I can identify and to the best of my knowledge has not previously been heard in Anglo Romani. In the text below, it appears to have the meaning of* oath, *but this is a provisional translation only.*

Salava kanna paenchava trustal savo o Romani-folki se avelin te. Yawn se lelin <u>shoovlo</u> shero, yek-divvus yawn ti se tugno. O Bauro Reiaw sevo (?savo) dik-palal kova temeskeri ti lel luver fon lendi ta ker lendi atch adray yek tan. Romani-folki kek dikerina kova avelin. Kek-pesser vaniso-kova temeskri-bauro-raiaw kek-kom. Komenna folki savo del luver tre ledni, ajaw saw yawn sastis ewooser les avree-opray divio kovaws. Temeskri bauro raiaw koliko-cheirus kanna adray rusliopen shomas fetadair sor-ketani. Kova yek kek kushti te Romani folki na vaniso-yek, kushti te lendi-kokero duva se sor. Estist ifasor bokalo vaver bauro-raiaw lel-adray te dik palal temeskrim ifasar ajaw kushti. Tutti pendas adray teero kaliko-lik, tutti dikessa mandi aglal kova bersh see avree. "Sar" "Komyer mook mandi jin." Vonka komava te dikessa boot boot, tutti si latcho ta tatcho, kek Romani-folki shomas sorkon-cheirus vaniso-fetadair na si kushti si tutti, adray meero shero. Yek-divvus aglal door mendi dik-yek-avavar, mendi sastis shan kushti rokker ketani "Kon". Sastisava pukkeressa dosta tatcho. Me sastis sulverkon opray kova, opray mi-Duvelaw-kimba.

Kei ta doi ta sorkon-kei o jivermus (?) ofaser o Romani, yek gav te avaver soi-dromaw sas tas sor-dromaw ti se, kek-yek, kek-komi atch les. Les se e kushtio jivermius. Komava les te dromaw

I laugh when I think about what Gypsy people are coming to. They are getting <u>swollen</u> *headed, one day they will be sorry. The great Lords (ie Parliament) who look after this country and take money from them and will make them stay in one place. Gypsy people don't see this coming. The Parliament hates the fact that they don't pay anything. They want people to give money in to them, so they can throw it away on foolish things. When the Government was strong in the past it was better altogether.*

This one isn't any good for Romani people or anyone but it is good to themselves, that is all. Maybe if we're lucky other Ministers will take-on looking after the country if that was any good. You say in your last letter you will see me before this year is out./ How? Please let me know when. What I want is for us to see very many (?Gypsy people), you are good and true, no Gypsy people were ever better how good you are (I think) in my head. One day before long we can see one another, we can have a good talk together, then when I can come, I will tell much. That is true. I can swear upon this, upon God's oath. Here and there and always here is the life of all the Gypsies, one town to another all roads were yours, all roads yours, no- one can never stop it. It is a good life. I long for the roads.

Changing Names

You once said about Romano-chals taking their mother's name. I do as
you know. The reason for this is the Romani-Romeroben As you know, the
biggest part of the tatcho Romano folki always got married in true
Romani fashion. This was and still is, not classed as a true marriage in
this country, so the chavies had to take their mother's name. This is not
so today as the law altered it. You will find scores of Romani folki who
have no marriage lines but I truly married in the proper Romani-drom.

*Henry's implication that marriage Romani-style resulted in children
taking the mother's name is not born out by fact. Though there are certainly instances where this occurred, the lack of a gorjer marriage was not
the reason. What decided it was other family reasons, eg the status of a
family or the strength of will of the mother.*

The Dulcimoor

Dorya boshteenus – dulcimoor, a small box with a hole in the centre. The
box is shaped like a harp and the strings are more or less the same as a
harp. I had one as a boy but could never learn to play it. This is what it is
called in Romanes – Dorya Boshteenus, some chals call it Doryo
boshamengro baro.

Henry on his Gramophone Records

There was a Columbia record that I used to play on a gramophone with a
brass horn on it about 1925-6 time, it was called either *The Poacher* or
The Poacher's Son. I am not certain which now. But it was a real Traveller's record. One of the sayings on it was:

'My father got six months for finding a rope with a horse tried to the
end. Us Gypsies lead a funny life, our roaming is never done. Every time
we pitch our camp, the Police say move on, move on.'

If you ask Uncle Bill, he may remember the record, all the Travellers
had it around the 1925-30s time. My Aunt Matilda Booth gave it to me as
a present when I was living with my puro parents. Maybe you could write
away and get a record of it. It was a twelve-inch Columbia record, cost
about half a crown when I had it.

I also had two Columbia records at the same time called, 'Miria Martin's in the red barn'. There were four sides all about Miria Martin's murder.

Here is a list of some of the records I had at the same time. You will know all these:

- O Solo Mio – Beneath the Window
- Like A Golden Dream (sung by Caruso)
- Little Valley. When the Moon Comes Over the Mountain
- Little White Lies / Springtime in the Rockies
- Hills of Colorado / Blue Danube / Up for the Cup
- Marta / Marta Rambling Rose of the Wild Wood
- Little Grey House in the West
- Waggon Wheels / the Ring My Mother Wore
- Gilded Cage / Music Hall / Pal of My Cradle Days
- Fallen by the Wayside / Mother Loves A Blessing
- I'll Take You Home Again Kathleen
- When You Played the Organ / Tiptoe Through the Tulips
- Meet Me in My Dreams / When I Leave the World Behind
- Old Rusty Bridge by the Mill / Shanty Town
- Will the Angels Play Their Harps for Me.

These are just a few of the records I had 1925-30 time.

Henry on George Borrow

Page 160 in *Lavengro* has these words:

Canna marcel o manus chivios ande puv ta rovel pa leste o chavo ta romni.

When dies the man put into field and cries for him the child and wife.

They have put it this way:

When a man dies he is cast into the earth and his wife and child sorrow over him.

Marcel means 'die' in real old Romanes. Manus is man. Ande is into. Rovel is cry. This is the best bit of Romanes in the book. Some Chals even say 'mard' for die today. This is from the word marcel. There is some real old tatcho Romani lavaws in the book.

This man Borrow could without a doubt speaki Romanes. I feel sure he has put some words wrong to mislead Gorgio folki. He has heard 'parraco tute,' 'rikkeni kekaubi'. These are tatcho words. These are on page 365. He has gillie, luripen, dukkerin, hokkerpen, lachipen, tatchipen. Sor tatcho. He has spelt a lot wrong on purpose. He has put jukel as juggel, poknees plastermengro, Bow Street Runners. A lot call Police Plastermengros even today.

This man George Borrow I think must have been a Romani chal. He puts his words like one. It is the first Romani Kimba I have read, and I like it. It is very good. I shall treasure it. I have read it three times up to now.

George Borrow deliberately, it seems, placed occasional bogus or manipulated Romani words to trip up the unsuspecting gorjer. Marcel is either one of these, or a misprint.

Dick Wade later edited Henry's words, and they appeared in the Journal of the Gypsy Lore Society, with the heading A Gypsy's Views on Lavengro.

Elsewhere, Henry quotes a short rhyme which appeared in Borrow, but gives no indication of its source. Henry has amended the Romanes slightly, perhaps to disguise its origin but more likely to put it into the Romanes register in which he writes.

O Romani chal	*The Gypsy boy*
Ta Romani chei	*And a Gypsy girl*
Shall jaw tasaula	*Will go tomorrow*
Katar drab o baula	*To poison the pig*
Ta dook o grei	*And bewitch the horse*
Of o ghivengro Rei	*Of the gentleman farmer*
O Romane chal	*The Gypsy boy*
Ta o Romani chei	*And the Gypsy girl*
Kom luripen	*Love thieving*
Ta dukkeripen	*And fortune telling*
Ta hokkeripen	*And lying*
Ta sorkon pen	*And everything*
Ki latchipen	*But goodness*
Ta tatchipen	*And truth*

Henry on Snobbery

Dear Dick, Please send me a biggish note book and I will write it full of paramish *(stories)* both about my 'folki *(people)* – other chals and chies *(Gypsy boys and girls)*and also my juvel *(wife)* and myself and chavies *(children)* . I know some of the tales, which will be tatchi *(true)*, you will have a good laugh at. You see, Dick I have travelled every county in England, Ireland, Scotland and Wales. I was in Egypt, Syria, Palestine and some of my relations are now travelling on the Continent and some in America and my Uncle Isia is in Australia.

Mandi's folki *(My people)* are not short of luvva *(money)* but are tatchi Romany folki *(true Gypsy people)* and are proud of it, they will make anybody welcome, even a needi pek *(low status Gypsy)*. I know a lot of chals who are stuck up today and will not own up to what they are. I have no time for them, it is a poor mush *(man)* that is ashamed of being a Romanichal *(Gypsy)*. Thank God all my folki are proud of what they are and would not change for anything or anybody. We would die first. It is surprising how money goes to some people's heads. We call them bori shero *(big head)*. I can take an oath on my mother's life, I have had as much if not more than three parts of the stuck-up Travellers. Thank God there are still a lot who are themselves.

Fred Huth

Fred Huth was an eminent Anglo Gypsy scholar and member of the Gypsy Lore Society. Though ill-educated himself, he had accrued a colossal knowledge of Gypsies and spoke Anglo Romani better than any Gypsy of his day. Gypsies who knew him thought very highly of him: one of his particular friends was Peter Ingram, the Hampshire Gypsy wagon restorer and historian.

Fred Huth, prala *(brother)* is a tatcho puro *(true old)* travelling man, a real dealer. He has travelled and been hawking with people I know very well. He had some very good waggons in his time. He once had one of the best Reading waggons that ever travelled the roads. I know the same vardo well. It finished up in Sutton in Ashfield, Notts. Fred Moss had it, he sold it to a Gaskin, a very pretty waggon.

Making a Grinding Barrow

For a brief description of grinding barrows, see the note on page 3. Henry must have agreed to make a grinding barrow for Dick.

I think I shall be able to make the manriders complete without you sending any parts. As I said before, the only difference will be wooden stones instead of sandstones. The place in Penistone Road, Sheffield, where they used to make cranks and spindles is pulled down now. I told old Fred, I don't think there is anywhere else in Sheffield who makes them. Any blacksmith can make them if you give him details. I have made kick-ups complete myself, the cranks etc I made myself by heating the iron in the fire.

Dora Yates

Dora Yates was the dearly loved and respected secretary of the Gypsy Lore Society, based at Liverpool University, and editor of its Journal for many years. She had studied Gypsies under the scholar John Sampson. She was always known as The Rawni, *the female equivalent of being a Romany Rai or Gypsy Gentleman, a title to which many GLS members aspired. In Dora Yates's case, however, the word Rawni was prefixed with The. To all Gypsies she was The Gypsy lady; to people more familiar with her, as were many older Gypsies, she was Bibbi* (Aunt) *Dora.*

Members of some families, especially the Locks and Griffiths, regarded her as a full-blood Gypsy sister. Commonly, Gypsies visited her specially on or near her birthday in order to take her presents. She was welcomed in any caravan and was probably the most loved GLS member ever.

I have read the book written by Miss Dora Yates. "The Rawni.", 'My Gipsy days'. This book prala *(brother)* is a work of art. Miss Yates is a Gipsy at heart, there is no getting away from that. Her sayings and ways are tatcho *(true)*. She must have spent years amongst my race to know the Locks and other breeds as well as she does. I would love to meet her. I could never imagine another person in the country, who could write such a true to life book about "Kawlay" *(Gypsies – lit. Blacks)* as she has done. I wish her kushti Bok *(good luck)* and a Door jivermus *(long life)*, and sincerely hope she keeps up the good work she is doing. May God bless her always.

A tacho Romani chal *(proper Gypsy)*

Henry on Hedgehogs

A great deal of fiction has been written on how hedgehogs are cooked. I have never found any evidence that they were ever wrapped in clay, which is what most books claim. But I do know several Gypsies who claim that relatives of theirs told gorjers this way to deliberately mislead. Usually, the hedgehog was put on a spit, which removed the need to shave it, otherwise it was cooked in a pot. Some families part cooked it on the spit and then transferred it to the pot.

Some families kept small dogs specially trained to find hedgehogs. There is a particular dog cross-bred from a Norfolk terrier and another terrier – I am not sure which – and this animal seems especially efficient at it.

Hedgehog meat is very fatty and tasty: young children were often given a leg to suck, like a lollipop.

Hedgehogs are still eaten, but some families now consider it a sign of poverty.)

Dikova talla o hotchiwichi, mandi latchova yek, maurova lesti ta morov lesti, yoosherova lesti, chirova lesti kater yog ta kerav lesti ta hova les mongi. Akova see chumoni mandi jin tooti kom ta dik kanna sorkoncheerus pen tooti shan opre o drom. A mandi kek-komi dikt Romani chal keravaw a hotchiwichi vaniso penchava opre a kosht yog.

I will look for the hedgehog, I will find one, kill it and shave it clean. I will put it to the fire, and cook it and eat it myself. This is something I know you say you want to see when eventually you are on the road. Myself, I never saw a Gypsy cook a hedgehog other than on a good fire.

Pot and other Waggons

A felly, below, is a segment from the outer circle of a wooden wheel, under the iron tyre.

The Pot Waggon, prala *(brother)* is made on the tatcho *(proper)* pot cart or dray, whichever you call a four-wheel lorry. There are still a few Pot Waggons about. I have an Aunt Annie who has had one for years. Some kawlay *(Gypsies)* call them a Brush Waggon. They used to hawk brushes from the Brush or Pot Lorry, whichever you like to call it. Bill Wright made a few, but it is well over seventy years, since the last Pot Waggon was made. They are all boat-shaped and spindled sides. They weigh about thirty hundredweights, to be certain between twenty-five and thirty hundredweights. They are a pretty Bow Top and well-shaped. Very good "Warner" wheels, two big ones, two small ones. They all have the Flying Horse over the back window. Every Bill Wright's waggon has.

The prettiest waggon on the road or ever has been is a ledge-sided Swinefleet waggon. I have a big photo of one when Jim Berry had just painted it. There are ten lions heads on it with water spouts in the mouths for the water to run out, There are pretty pens on the sides just over the front wheels up the ledge. They reach from the front S to the beginning of the window shutter in length, there are about twenty carved wooden spindles on each pen, five of these open together. There are three brass S's on each side between floor weather board and the ledge board, one front, one middle, one end of waggon. The back cratch is all spindled and carved. Brass lamp brackets, brass handles underneath, lamp brackets and real cut glass door knobs.

You will like this waggon very much when I give you the photo. The photo is the same size as the two big ones you sent me of you and the family. Any way you shall have it at the first opportunity meeting. There is also one of a Welsh Open Lot with some of my folki *(people)* sat on the front board and steps. Even the jukels *(dogs)* are on it.

Anyway prala *(brother)*, coming back to the Pot or Brush waggon it must be at least a hundred years old. So you can see it has been well looked after.

The Warner bell hub wheels are very good wheels. I bet they have never had a felly put in them since new. I like the colours the vardo *(waggon)* is painted, they stand out. My colours are a green waggon, red on the butterfly chamfers lined with yellow. Yellow underworks, yellow wheels with red lining.

The lighter the paint is on a waggon, the lighter in weight the waggon looks, if the underworks were painted with a dark colour, the vardo would look heavy. even if it was not. The same applies to a trailer. A maroon or dark red painted trailer looks heavier than one painted either a straw or light blue etc.

The colour *(Fred)* Walker has his Reading waggon makes it look heavy. Red and yellow and a dark red. You look at the photo you sent me of the Bow-topped waggon, the one with the door open and your little Nell playing under the front axle. That is painted brown, it looks a heavier waggon than the Pot Waggon but it is not, it is a lighter waggon, but the brown colour makes it look heavier. A nice Pea-green with post office red scrolls and lined with a nice daffodil yellow looks nice and light. A green-painted waggon with a green sheeted top is not as noticeable in a lane with green edges.

Your caravanette is super, a wonderful job and a very nice colour. It is as good a caravannette as I have ever seen prala. Ideal for travelling and can carry stuff for hawking in it at the same time as travelling. Better than a trailer, prala.

Herbal and other Remedies

Before the days of the National Health, few Gypsies could afford doctors. About the only easily available treatments were traditional cures, using plants or, sometimes, less obvious matters – even cow dung and cooked dormice. I have myself recorded over 400 such remedies.

The Gordon referred to below is Gordon Boswell, Dick's Romany friend. Some of the list of cures in alphabetical order may have been gleaned by Henry from a published source. Notice especially the use of the archaic word easeth *in the paragraph on couch. However, in some, he makes errors of spelling which make it seem likely that they are not copied, namely elder flower pancake, hazel bread and bishopweed.*

My Poori Dei *(grandmother)* once called a house where the rawni *(lady)* was suffering from sugar diabetes. My poori Dei told her to get some ivy leaves and boil them, and drink the water as hot as she could. As you know Dick Ivy leaves are poison. Anyway my poori Dei called again about twelve months after. The rawni had done what she told her and sure enough it had cured her. Whether it was just an isolated case or not I do not know. My poori Dei always said that the poison in the ivy leaves killed the other sugar diabetes. Anyway Dick, just ask Gordon and see if he knows about ivy leaves

My folki *(family)* always swallowed a frog a few days old, once a year. This takes the badness out of your stomach. As you know, frogs take the badness out of bad water. When the bitti *(little)* frog dies in your stomach, it comes out when you go to the toilet.

We always use bees or nettles stings for rheumatism. If it is the arms, just put the arm in a beehive and let them sting you. When the blisters bust, you can bet the pain has gone. If it is the legs or back, get someone to beat you with nice young nettles – that is just as good.

Comfrey we use for sprains. Hedgehog oil for the hair. Goose grease for colds, when you rub it on the chest and eat a bit at the same time. Hog fat is all right, but it is not so penetrating as Goose grease. Dandelion leaves in bread and butter are better than lettuce, they purify the blood, also nettle tea does. Sour grass is good for an upset stomach. You will see a dog eat it when poorly. Your own urine is best for chilblains. Smoke from a tree wood stick fire is good for eyesight. The smoke clears the back of your eyes when they run. A bark of a tree is the best toothpaste there is. Burn it black on the fire and then rub your teeth with it. Charcoal chewed is a very good thing for heartburn. Molasses is what they put in silage and is the best thing in the world for constipation.

I am sure you will know these things and, like myself, hundreds more. Every thing that grows is a herb. There is one that will cure cancer if only it could be found. Maybe some day it will be. I hope.

Remedies used by the Gypsies

ADDERS TONGUE. Some of this fern boiled with Olive Oil made into an ointment and rubbed on fresh wounds, is the only herb that will cure an adder's bite.

COMFREY FRITTERS. Strip the leaves of the plant, dip in cold water then in batter. Put them in a frying pan that is on the sizzle. Do them until they are like green and golden colour, then eat. They are tasty and you will like them and they are good for you. Just try one, prala *(brother)*.

COUCH is very good for the liver or Gall troubles, also for Urine trouble and also easeth pains in the Belly. Good for worms in dogs etc.

DANDELIONS leaves washed make a nice salad. Put between bread and butter like lettuce – good for blood troubles and gives a good appetite to anyone who cannot eat.

DEW from the ground first thing in the morning is one of the finest things in the world for eyes. Take the dew from off the top of Fennel or

Greater Celandine plants in May and rub it around your eyes. A good plant to get dew from is Lady's Mantle. The drops of dew collect in the angled cup of its green leaves, also Sundew.

ELDER MILK. Take two corms or clusters of Elder blossom, strip the flowers off. Simmer them for about ten minutes in a quart of milk, Then add a spoonful of semolina beat up with sugar, a little salt two yolks of an egg. Pour the milk into a bowl and float on the top. When it is cold, little icebergs of the white of egg are beaten up with the sugar. Last of all sprinkle sugar and cinnamon on the Elder milk. This milk then will have a delicate and chilly flavour.

ELDER FLOWER PANCAKE. Take the corms of Elder blossom by the stalk, dip them in batter and fry them, pick them up again by the stalk and eat. These are very good for bowels, loosening yourself.

HAZEL BREAD. Pick hazel nuts before they are brown ripe. Take a cupfull of nuts chopped up not too small. Mix them with twice the quantity of flour, half the quantity of sugar, a little salt, two teaspoonfuls of baking powder. Beat an egg up with milk and mix. Knead and shape the mixture into a small cottage loaf and bake in oven for about forty-five to fifty minutes tap the loaf and if it rings hollow it is done. Be sure the nuts are milky when you put them in before baking everything depends on this. The loaf will be very appetizing when finished.

MOONWORT. This is used for helping women to give birth easy, also for abortions. Also for making cows want bulling.

BISHOPWEED and GOOD KING HENRY are used as Spinach, also nettle tops and Fat Hens.

BISTORT is used to make puddings.

BATH ASPARAGUS and HOP SHOOTS make nice salads and are very good for your stomach.

LIME BLOSSOM TEA. CAMOMILE TEA PEPPERMINT TEA. These teas are all very good remedies. Peppermint grows wild in lots of gardens as you will know.

Henry on Dick's Romani

The word mized *in the third paragraph may be a mis-writing for* mixed, *but may also be from the cant word – originally Shelta – mizzle, which amongst several meanings can mean* confuse. *Henry's flattery of Dick is more than a little patronising.*

Henry's comment on Fred Huth's Romani indicates Henry's own lack of knowledge. Fred was the finest Anglo Romani speaker of his day – perhaps the finest gorjer speaker ever – and his knowledge of the language was vast. Whilst Fred certainly knew plenty of such cant, he did not use it in his letters. (I have several of them.)

Dick, I can truthfully say I have never met or heard a Romani-Chal or Chei *(Gypsy man or woman)* who knows as much tatcho Romany jib *(correct Romani language)* as you do. Every word you write in Romanes is pure. It is years since I heard anything near as tatcho Romanes as you write. I always classed myself, as one of the very few today that knows tatcho Romanes. I take my stardi *(hat)* off to you.

You said Dora Yates can Rokka *(talk Romani)* better than you. This wants some believing. I should say without a doubt you are as good a jinomeskro of Romanes *(Romani scholar)* as any living person in this country today. Believe me Dick, I know what I am talking about. I have talked to hundreds of my own race, Gypsies, and not one of them could come anywhere near you in Romanes.

When I first started to write to you I would never have believed it, but now I know. I have even mized *(see Introduction to this piece)* my Romanes up on purpose to see how much you jindas *(knew)*. That was the first few weeks we started writing. As you know, we are a very untrusting race, until we get to know folki *(people)*. I don't think you can blame us for being this way. To me, now, you are more of a tatcho Romany chal *(proper Gypsy)* than three parts of the Romanes today. You have Romany ways. That is something that is dying out. I can truthfully say on my chavies *(children's)* lives. I would kair *(do)* anything for you and your folki.

Even old Fred Huth puts a lot of 'cant' words in his letters to mandi *(me)*. The cant words he uses would be classed as Romani-jib now, but not by the pooro *(old)* Romani folki. The tatcho words have not and will not ever change. Lots of words have had to be added as motors, trains, aeroplanes etc have come out, since Romanes was first spoken.

Romanes Jib *(The Gypsy tongue)*

This is very typically Henry's Romani. Where he does not know a word, he improvises, as in wishtas *and* couldasar, *by adding a Romani ending to an English word. This is still a trait in modern day Anglo Romanes, though not as common as Henry's examples.*

Me hopesar toot kel penchava mandi wafedi pootchin toot te mook me trin bar. Me sastis del les pallla katar toot, kanna me jal avri akei. Toot see o firstadair gairo me avel te diktan as sig as me avel avri akei les wouldasava bi boot latcho te shan (si) a bitti rokerin rinkeni chirikla ta chirklesti kair adre meero bitta kamora.

Me shan kek komi adre sor meero jiviben shoondad diktas vaniso-yek delom opre adre Romanes jib pensa toot. Tooti shan (see) o kushtodar jinomengro adre kova temeskri. Les see boot latcho te de opre teero Romanes lavaw yon see tatcho. Me yekino wishtas me couldesava delom opre pensa totti. Me jin sor moro Romanes lavaw ta sastis roker len. Me kek te latcho delomusn opre len. Me mayaser lel feterdair adre chairus. Delomus opre kjata tooti handaw sor meero Romanes jib palla katar mandi. Atchin akei ta kek-komeni te roker te adre Romanes see keklatcho komeni chairus me si ta penchava a chairus aglas me sastis chiv les adre mi shero. Me kek bisser konaw, teero lilaw see sorkon kolli katar mandi. Posh rig tooti kel mandi boot bahtali wi teero kushtomus ta komelomus. Tooti wouldasar kek-komi shan thoughtasava doova mendi shamas gajikanaw a bitti chairus palla.

I hope you don't think me bad for asking you give me £3. I can give it back to you when I leave here. You are the first person I will come to see as soon as I leave here. It would be very good to have a pretty little talking bird and a cage in my little cell. I have never before in all my life heard or seen anyone use the Romani language like you. You are the best scholar in all this land.

It is very good to read your Romani words, they are good. I once wished I could have read like you. I know all my Romani words and can talk them. I am not good at reading it. I may get better in time. Writing to you brings all my Romani language back to me. Staying here and no-one to talk to in Romani is not good. Sometimes I find myself thinking of times past before I had learned them, when I was not sending them. Your letters are everything to me. Besides, you bring me good luck with your goodness and kindness. You would never have thought that we were strangers a little while ago.

5. HENRY'S TRADITIONAL STORIES

In the days before TV, Gypsy folk tales played an important part in the life of the Gypsy community. They had multiple purposes, as well as the obvious one of entertainment. Some were intended to explain about aspects of the travelling life, or the reasons for it; others emphasised the need for unity in the community against the many hands turned against them; still more explained matters of morality or essential facets of humanity.

There were many outstanding story-tellers though some families seemed to have particular claim to be amongst the best. When families gathered round the fire, all adults were expected to contribute towards the evening's entertainment, and whilst some told stories, others sang or fiddled – or danced. The traditional pictures showing Gypsies dancing round the fire with the tambourine waving may have been crude Victorian fiction, but there is nevertheless some evidence that dancing did occur in pre-Victorian times, Such dances are more often correctly associated with Kalderash Gypsies than with English Romanichals.

Without wishing to sound too sceptical, Henry's descent from Happy Boswell (Absalom), most famous of the English Gypsy Munchausens, may go some way to explaining his ability to put over some of his other claims.

You have asked if I know the paramish off by heart and who learned it me. Yes, I do know it by heart and my poori dadrus and dei learned me. I was brought up by my grandparents, Hope and Trainette Sherriff, and loved every hair on their head. *It is not clear here to which story Henry is here referring.*

Tacho Paramish (True story)

In Dick Wade's hand is added here, "Published in JGLS 1967." *Wade has crossed out Henry's first three words and written in* "My Puro dadrus was given to drinking, which was a great trouble to my puri dai, and one night he ..." *Wade has also crossed out the sentence* "My puro dadrus had been drinking all day."

Accounts of face to face meetings with the devil are common features of English Gypsy stories.

My Puro Dadrus *(grandfather)* was drinking in a public house in a place called Brook-Bottom. The public house was called the Fox Inn. Brook Bottom is down an old rough road just outside of New Mills in the Peaks of

Derbyshire. There is just the public and seven houses. My puro dadrus had been drinking all day.

A stranger walked into the public house, he had a cap pulled down over his face. When my puro dadrus looked down, the stranger had two clubbed feet. The stranger did not order a drink, he just walked to the bar, turned round and went out again. It was as if my puro dadrus had to follow him. My puro dadrus followed him to the end of the old road.

The stranger stopped near a field gate. My puro dadrus went up to him and asked him for the time. The stranger never answered him, only pulled his cap up from over his eyes. My puro dadrus shook with fright. He looked at the stranger's face, and he was the spit image of my puro dadrus. He waved my puro dadrus on. When he tried to move he could not, it was as if he was stuck to the ground. The stranger made a funny laugh and walked away, laughing all the time.

He kept on saying, "Come on Gypsy, follow me," until he had vanished altogether. My puro dadrus went back to my puro dai *(grandmother)*, who was set around the camp fire. He was trembling, and was as white as a ghost. He told my puri dai he had just seen the beng *(devil)*. She laughed at him and said, "You are drunk, go to bed." My puro dadrus never went to bed that night.

Early next morning, he took two of my uncles with him. When they got to the gate where my puro dadrus had seen the beng, sure enough there were the club feet footprints. My folki packed up straight away and left.

Two days later, they were told that their daughter, my aunt Victoria, was dead. She had died at the same time as the stranger had gone into the public house. The beng had warned my puro dadrus of my aunt Victoria's death.

Just before my aunt died, she was talking to two angels at the end of the bed. They told her they had come to take her home. The other travellers were in the wagon at her bedside (but) never saw a thing, but they told my puri dai that my aunt was talking to the angels for a long time, and she was laughing all the time. They said that the waggon lit up as if the sun was inside of it.

My puro dadrus and my aunt Victoria had quarrelled at their last meeting, and she had said to my puro dadrus, "You are like the beng, no good. You will die in hell." My puro dadrus always said that my aunt Victoria had sent the beng to him as she was dying.

This prala *(brother)*, is a true paramish which I swear on my mother's life truly happened. My puro dadrus was not drunk at the time it happened nor was he imagining things. It was the gospel truth. My aunt had wished the devil upon him as she lay dying. My aunt died with a smile on her face.

Gippin a Tit Away (or The Old Iron Pot)

Tacho Paramishus

This has proved an extremely problematic piece to translate, and it has not always been possible to make perfect sense of it due to the presence of several obscure Romani words. For that reason, I am suspicious that it may not be original material.

I am grateful to Bob Lovell, of New Zealand, for his assistance and advice in translating this very problematic piece.

Mery Kanav Baur. Java may te pena tooki bita paramishus.

Yek divvus shomas Lee Velgora, dui graiengeray sas odio sas-len puro grai to komenas te biknen chi-na-mola dova yek graingero penelas ke vaver graingero, "Dova toot bish bar i puray grieski." Naw naw notay. Vaver graiengero o lovo se kushto dosta tar nas biknava meero grai ke graiengero, kova mo grai te jal kushtay taneski."

O graingero kar pendas to delas bish bar i graieski dikas mush te vartaselas len velas ke o mush tar pendas leski." Dikan dova dinlo puro mush nar biknela lesko grai mango odoleski may shom graiengero kin o grai mangi tar dova toot dui bar te kokoveski tar maw day leski booteder bar bish bar dikava toot aray kitchema akai tor peserava toot."

Gias o graingero chin aray kitchema tar chin avree o palano vudar tar prastias. O mush thoughtasas te lelas due bar sig chickeski gias ke vaver graingero ka sas rivdo jaw-sar puro vlijakero tar dias leski bish bar avree leski nogi pochi tar kindas a puro grai. Sar sig sar o graingero, "Yas o lovo oprastias. O mush te kindas a grai gias aray i kitchema te rodel o graingero te lel leski bish bar pawlay tar dui bar pawpalay. Dikas koi-ta-koi tar nar dikelas o graingero, noiano sas lo tar gias i muskerengi boot sig o tan sas pardo muskeray.

Achaws may poshay kitchema tar mi chukni talay mi muski tar mi swigla aray mo mui kerdomas may chee to dova se mo dir duvelesko tachiben vias o vago mush parl i muskerendi ke may tar pendas, "Tuya jines chomoni trustal kava. Lay kowa mush pendas ke vaver muskero tar o vaver muskero tildas man tar lias man sor talay 'rol o gav ke o muskerengo tan. Kana o hulano i kitchemati shundas teb shomas lini gias sig ke o sherno-muskero tar opendas -m Lian o wromngo mush jinava dova tarno mush mishto muk jinava dova tarno mush mishto muk les teb jel nai-lo uzlo kek. Tar o Sherno muskero bishadas lav lengri te anden man pawlay tar mukday man peero. O dui graingeray te kerday o luriben prastilay opray i jalimangeri te kekas sas linay. Kova sas trustal 1959.

Kova feeno hokiben sas jindilo ke o Bristol graiengeray as The Old Iron Pot (but why I don't know). Vaver foki karena les, "Giping a tit away."

Sastis toot haiavesa kova rokkerben prala?

My alert friend, I am going to tell you a little story.

One day I was at Lee Gap Fair, two horse dealers were there and they had an old horse which they wanted to sell, all but dead. One horse dealer said to the other horse dealer, "I'll give you £20 for the old mare. "No, no way,"the other dealer (Thought), the money is very good but I can't sell my horse to this dealer, my horse will go to a better place. The dealer went, he said I'll get £20 for the mare. Look for a man to watch out then come to the man and say to him, See that stupid old man over there, he won't sell his horse to me. I am a horse dealer who wants to buy that horse worth £2 which was my uncle's and won't let me give him more £20. I will see you in the pub here to pay you.

The dealer went to settle the deal in the pub and share out the booty and run. The man who thought to take £2 quickly for nothing he went to the other dealer who was dressed to go. All of the old villagers gave him £20 from their own pocket and he bought the old horse. As quick as the dealer, the money ran off. The man who bought the horse went into the pub to look for the dealer to take his £20 back and £2 besides. He looked here and there and did not see the dealer. He was angry and went quickly to the police station, over the road.

Thus was I near the pub and my whip under my arm and my pipe in my mouth. I made nothing from it, that is my dear God's truth. The police came over to me and said, "You know something about the matter." "Take this man," he told the other policeman and the other policeman held me and took me straight down to the town to the police station. When the landlord of the pub heard how I was taken, he went quickly to the senior police officer and said, "You've got the wrong man, I know that young man well. Let him go, it is not him, he's clean." And the senior police officer sent word to them and they brought me up and left me to walk. The two horse dealers who had taken the money ran off up the footpath before they could be taken. That was about 1959.

That fine trick was known to the Bristol horse dealers as The Old Iron Pot. Other people called it Gipping a tit away.

Can you understand that Romani, brother?

(At the bottom of the pages, in Richard Wade's hand, are the words Chi-na-mola, odoleski, ulyuakero, noano, muski, bago, uzlo *and* sherno.)

Petelengro Paramush (Smith's Story)

Introducing this story, Henry writes, 'Pooro Romani paramush pookadas
ki miro pooro folki kanna me sas en bitti chavi. Me penchava totti wi kom
les – *(an old Gypsy tale told to my people when I was a little child. I think
you will like it). In fact it is a straight lift from Smart and Crofton – see
page 186 – and so omitted, though it is a very fine old story, containing as
it does, the famous Gypsy joke:*
In the morning, Petelengro's old wife said, "I want to go to heaven
when I die." God looked in her mouth. He said, "Don't worry, you can't
go to hell. There is wailing and gnashing of teeth there. You have no teeth
at all. You will go to my house."

A Boot Pooro Romani Paramish

Rokkerd Posh Meero Pooro Dadus

At the top of the page is written, "Here is a tale that my folki have told for
years. I hope you like it Dick. It is a real old Romanes tale. *In the margin,
Dick Wade has written,* See S/C 212. *Dick Wade has marked the section
beginning,* "Sar see tooti roozho puv, see tooti rosheo's rinkeno ... " *to the
end of the passage* " te nasher opre, yon dik latcho." *with the words* Quite
original *and the final section from* "O latcho doosta bershor palla" *to* "te
yoi shan sorkon dikt" *he has marked,* Original.
*As Dick has indicated, this piece is heavily dependent upon Smart and
Croftons' version and, fine tale though it is, I have omitted it.)*

An Unusual Fortune Telling

*Henry's mention below of hawking with his mother should probably read
grandmother. His mother died when he was about seven, or perhaps even
younger, and though children in arms and toddlers commonly went hawking, at seven he would not have been telling someone's fortune.*
Sar-see tooti roozho-puv, see tooti rosheo's rinkeno. Mandi kom
rosheo's mandi penchava toot tei kom roshev's see les o bauri roozho puv
toot si komeni divvus mandi estist bokala doosta katar dik loes. Mandi si
sorkon cheerus varted at sorkon roozho puv. Kanna mandi shan jeld avri
biknin akova stariben shan bauri rinkeno roozlo puvs ta sorkon rosheo
toot sastis penchava troostal. Mandi shan kairdo tushnies katar chiv

Rosheo's adray ta nasher opre, yon dik latcho.

A latcho doosta bershor palla, mendi shamas atchin at Buxton adray Chumba-kalesko-tem. Meero dei ta mandi shomas avri biknin gad-kosht, Mandi bikend komeni gad-kosht katar a rauni at a bauri ker. O rauni putchd mandi, "See toot a tatchi Romani chal."

Mandi pensas "Ourly". O bauri rauni putchd mandi katar puka yoi dukeriben. Mandi pendas kek at firstadair, a bitti chairus palla mandi pendas "Ourli". Mandi pukd o rauni adoova yoi rom shomas adre kom sar awaver gairo.

O rauni pendas "Mandi maw patsaben totti." Mand pendas keka pesa mandi kon, O rauni kek-komi pesadi mandi.

O bershaw palla mandi korendi o raunies ker apopli. Yov pendas avel adrey. Yoi rokadi mandi duvel savo mandi pendas yoi aglal shommas o tatchipen. Yoi del mandi luva ta pendas "Toot shan o kushtiest dukriben pukera te yoi shan sorkon dikt."

How is your flower garden? Are your flowers pretty? I like flowers, I think you also like flowers. Is it a big garden you have? Some day I if I am fortunate I may see it. I am always looking at every garden when I have gone hawking. This prison has a very beautiful flower garden with every flower you can think of. I have made baskets to put flowers in to hang up. They look good.

A good many years ago, we were stopping at Buxton in Derbyshire. My mother and I went out hawking clothes pegs. I sold some clothes-pegs to a lady at a big house. The lady asked me, "Are you a true Gypsy?" I said, "Yes."

The great lady asked me to tell her fortune I said no at first, a little while after I said. "Yes." I told the lady that her husband was in love with another man.

The lady said, "I do not believe you." I said, "Pay no money then." The lady did not pay me.

The following year, I called at the lady's house again. She said, "Come in." She told me that what I had told her before was the truth. She gave me money and said, "You are the best fortune teller that I have (lit. She had) ever seen."

Kova See A Boot Pooro Paramish

Beside this text, Wade has written, 'See S/C p. 217', proving that Dick was aware that this is a straight lift from Smart and Crofton's book. It is the old story of the miller and the fairies at Kellingworth Castle, Warwick.

After the story, Henry writes:

Meero Pooro Dadus sikloo te besh tale dosta ora's pukkerin mandi sor o pooro paramish duva lesko Dadus putchadas lesti. Tooti sastis dik prala duva adoi see shookar a koosi ow o pooro Romanes jib mooklo adre mendi. Kova see hokkabon mandi wi kek-komi bisser as door as me jiv.

My grandad used to sit down for hours telling me all the old stories that his father told him. You can see, brother, that there is still a little of the old Gypsy tongue left in me. I will never tell you lies as long as I may live.

Tuttus

This account may be loosely based upon Esmeralda Lock, who married the Gypsy Lore Society member Hubert Smith and later ran off with, and married, Francis Hindes Groome. Smith took Esmeralda and two of her brothers with him to Norway, where they walked around and lived in tents. Tent Life with English Gypsies in Norway *(London, 1873), which Smith wrote to commemorate the saga, is very typical of its era: The Gypsies are all seen as servants of the Great White Hunter, even Esmeralda, and it is a vivid illustration of paternalistic Victorian attitudes to Gypsies.*

Later, Esmeralda would say little about her relationship with Smith, and was very loyal to him. But it is clear that the marriage could not have lasted, no matter how hard Esmeralda must have tried.

The marriage to Groome did not last, either. Once again, Esmeralda stayed loyal and would say nothing against Groome. Evidence found by myself, and now included within my papers at Reading University, shows that Groome was homosexual. This must have been desperately shocking and shaming to Esmeralda. The proof of Groome's sexual nature is in a poem written about him in deepest Romani by the Rev. D.M.M. Bartlett.

Yek pa o Locks Rom romadi e barvalo gorgio rei.

Yekrus opre e chairus doi sas e Romani chei, yoi sas e rinkeni rakli. Lati dei sas e wafedi monishni, sorkon-cheirus lelin motto. Lati dadus see avree sar awaver monishni.

Yek divvus, Tuttus (akova sas lesti nav) sas avri bikenin driz. Yoi jeldas te a bauri kair, a poori rauni aveld te o wudda ta putched Tuttus adray o kair. O rawni pendas te Tuttus, "Toot see e rinkeni rakli, Sar pooro see toot?" Tuttus pukerdas lati O rawni deldas Tuttus desh balanser ta pukerdas lati te vel apopli adre e koorokiaw chairus.

E kooroki palal, Tuttus jaldas pauli te o kair apopli, akova chairus e

tarno rei veldas te o wudda. "Vel adray," yov pendas katar Tuttus. Tuttus sas atrasht. "See tiro dei adray?" Tuttus puchtas o rei. Yov pendas
avli, "Vel adray." Tuttus penchavadest savo e kushti dikin mush o tarno
rai sas. O poori rauni jeldas adray o komora ta pendas, "Kushti divvus,
meero kamlo, besh tale. Kek toot kom meero chavo?" Tuttus pendas
"Yov dikaw kushti dosta soski." O tarno rei pendas "Me penchava toot
see rinkeni shan toot vaniso komi penyaw.

Tuttus pendas kek me see o yekino yek. Vaniso-drom. Tuttus leld
rumedi adray kongri, Yoi jald keri te lati dei Yoi pukerdas lati dei e gorgios jiveben sas kek kushti. Les sas e bauri kel. Palal dui beshaw Tuttus
chingerdas lati rom.. Lati rom avel te righer lati pauli. Yoi pendas te
lesti, "Kek, me shom atchin ti meero nogo folki."

Troostal efta shunaw palal, Tuttus diktas e Romani chal. Yoi jeldas
avree ti lesti. Yawn shan chavies kon see sor bauri konaw. Akova
Romany-chei Tuttus sas yek pa o Locks. O bauri rei yoi rumedi sas fon
posh-rig Welshpool adray Lavines Tem. O reiaw folki shamas ghiven-
groes te yawn shamas boot barvalo

Tuttus sas meero romni's beebi. Yoi see jivin tedivvus adray Heversham. Yoti ta lati mush booti adray o puvaw sor o beshaw ta shan keldas pa o door chairus. Me kel kek jin vaniso Romanies kon shan rumedi
avri fon lenti nogo folki te see bahtali, les kek booti avri. Me jin yek e dui
kon shan kaird les, yawn see kek bahtali.

Me shom delomus opre teero ghiveli avri ta bitcher len kanna kairdas
boot pooro ghiveliaw, lel-kushtoben fordel mandi pa kek bitcherin len
aglal.

Latcho rarti fon shooka moires.

Henry

One of the Gypsy Locks married a wealthy housedweller.

*Once upon a time, there was a Gypsy, she was a beautiful girl. Her
mother was a wicked woman, for ever getting drunk. Her father had run
off with another woman.*

*One day, Tuttus (that was her name) was out hawking lace. She went
to a mansion, an old lady came to the door and invited Tuttus in. The
lady said to Tuttus, "You're a beautiful girl, how old are you?" Tuttus
told her. The lady gave Tuttus ten gold sovereigns and told her to come
again in a week's time.*

*A week later, Tuttus returned to the house, this time a young gentle-
man came to the door. "Come in," he said to Tuttus. Tuttus was afraid.
"Is your mother in?" Tuttus asked the gentleman. He replied, "Come in."
Tuttus realised what a handsome young man he was. The old lady came
into the room and said, "Hello, my pretty one, sit down. Don't you like*

my son?" Tuttus said "Why, he's very handsome." The young gentleman said, "I must say, you are prettier than anybody's sisters."

Tuttus asked if she was the first one. Anyway, Tuttus was married in church. There was a big reception. After two years, Tuttus quarrelled with her husband. She went back to her mother. She told her mother that the housedweller life was awful.

Her husband went to get her back. She said to him, "No, I am staying with my own people."

About seven months after, Tuttus met a Gypsy. She went off with him. They had children who are all grown now. This Gypsy girl Tuttus was one of the Locks. The great gentleman she married was from near Welshpool in Wales. The gentleman's people were farmers and were very rich.

Tuttus was my wife's aunt. Nowadays she lives in Heversham. She and her man work all year round in the fields and have been together for a long time. I don't know any Gypsies who are married out of their own people and are happy. It doesn't work out. I know one or two who did it, but are not happy.

I am writing out your songs and will send them when I have done more old songs, please forgive me for not sending them before.

Good night from (the) Sherriff,
Henry

6. POEMS AND SONGS

This chapter has been divided into two sections. These are:

A. *Apparently authentic poems and words from songs from Henry's own folk memory;*

B. *Poems and words from songs apparently composed by Henry himself;*

C. *(Not included) — Such items unquestionably taken verbatim by Henry from printed sources.*

I have identified some songs as originating from previous printed sources but claimed by Henry as traditional and heard by him. These have been omitted, other than to list them in a <u>Section C.</u> They are available as type-written pages from Derbyshire Gypsy Liaison Group – details on request.

I remain firmly of the opinion that several other of these songs were not heard by Henry from other Gypsies but from printed sources. I have never-theless included them and thereby given him the benefit of the doubt.

It has not always proved easy to decide into which category each of this vast array of songs and poems should fall. Only a couple appear in either of the main modern books on Gypsy folk songs (Stanley and Burke; McColl and Seeger) so that most are new. Some are clearly lifted from Leland's book, and therefore belong in the C category (even though Henry claims them as ones he learned off his grandmother) and several are unquestion-ably Henry's original work. But many of the others cannot be placed any-where with total certainty.

It is also noteworthy that some of these songs appear on the tape which Dick made of members of the Hames and Booth families singing at Brails-ford, DBY in 1964.

A. Apparently Authentic, from Henry's Memory

Henry says of a batch of the following:

Miro kamlo prala, Komyer muk mandi jin ifasar tutti komessa o giveliaw, me shan bitcherdas katar tutti jivana a kusi komi ta ti bitcher lendi awaver chairus adray chinamengri katar tute yon si sor tatcho Romani giveliaw a boot purano. Gillava lendi dosta chairusaw adray miro kamora akai. Yek divvus sig ti gilli lendi te tute Koko Bill ti jina poshay sor ofasar len. Komyer putch lesti. A kusi komi Romani lavaw just to fill page up.

My dear brother. Let me know if you like the songs. I have sent to you
where you live a little more and to send it another time in a letter to you, they
are all true Gypsy songs and very old. I have sung them many times in my
cell here. One day soon I will sing them to you. Uncle Bill knows almost all,
of them. Please ask him. A few more Romani words just ...(letter finishes —
ed.)

Komeli Pirini – Bute purane Giveli *(A very old song)*

This poem was reproduced by Dick Wade in an article in the Journal of the
Gypsy Lore Society, 3rd Series, Volume 48, pp 83-91. Dick was satisfied that
it was genuinely from Henry's own memory. I remain extremely suspicious.
The translation is Dick's.

Komeli Pirini

Jinava me o tatcho nav
Kushiko kova adray o gav
Avewr kushtidiro a mengi zi
Si miri komeli pirini.

Beshava sor dovvus adrin o tan
Penava i folki sarishan
Aver beshava ta dikav o mui
O miri komeli pirini.

Komava te vel o bauro rei
Komava ta lel a kushto grei
Aver wuserava i dui avri
Te choomer mi komeli pirini.

My Beloved Sweetheart

I know the loveliest name.
The best in all the town,
The sweetest in all my heart
It is my beloved sweetheart.

I sit all day in the tent
Greeting the folk who pass by,
But I really sit there to watch for the face
Of my beloved sweetheart.

I should love to become a great gentleman
I should love to own a fine horse;
But I would give up both of these
Just to kiss my beloved sweetheart.

Seven Ghosts

Yes my master it's a queer old story
And it's many a year since last I heard it
Since I heard the good father telling
All about the seven night-walking spirits.

Thus he told the story, thus I heard it
If you took an oath upon those spirits
And the oath upon them should be broken
Seven nights will come to you the walkers

Seven nights they'll come each night to wake you
Seven nights you'll always see the seven
But upon the seventh night my master
By the seventh spirit you'll be strangled

Round your neck the ghost will twine his fingers
Then upon your throat you'll feel them pressing
Then they pass away into the midnight
But my master, where could you have heard it?

(*Underneath, Dick Wade has written,* Learned off grandmother Trainette
Boswell.)

There will come a time
This delightful little poem could be one of Henry's own compositions.

What makes you sad papa my darling?
Why are the tears rolling today?
Have I done wrong to thee, pray tell me?
Have I done wrong to thee I pray?

No no my child thou hart *(sic)* an angel
There is no love more pure than thine
But I'm afraid some day you'll leave me
Like your mother did, there will come a time.

There'll come a time some day when you are far away
You'll have no father to find you from day to day
Think of the words I've said, honour the man you'll wed
Always remember my story, there will come a time.

Romany Rye
*(This song is known by almost all Gypsies, with slight variations. In the full
version there are several verses and a chorus, which normally goes something like:*

Kekka chavi, dik akoi,
Father's gone to sell the mush a kushti gry,
And that's why they call him the Romany Rye.

Henry's version is:

I'm a Romany Rye not old didikye
I live in a mansion beneath the blue sky
My home is a tent and I don't pay no rent
That is the reason they call me an old didikye.

I wish mandi *(I)* was jellin *(going)* to puv de grye *(graze the horses)* down by the parni *(river)* side. Still, the time will come hay, Dick. Don't forget please send a biggish notebook for songs and paramish *(stories)*.
Thank you, Henry.

Brishindesko Munthos *(Rainy month, April)*

The Gypsies live beneath the blue sky
Beautiful white clouds passing them by
Sun shining clear till it's lost to view
When a dark brooding cloud covers the blue.

Suddenly the wind grows stronger and cold
Daffodils appear a pale gold
The lambs all cease to race in play
To shelter alongside the rack of hay.

The Gypsies live beneath the blue sky
Pheasants are calling in wood near by
The curlew flies overhead both day and night
It's sad haunting cry a heart-stirring delight

The plough has returned earth to earth
Leaving rich soil as if glowing with mirth
At receiving good seed for waving grain
But depending on God for the sun and the rain.

(Underneath, Dick has written, *Henry's own composition.*)

An oak tree loves a rivulet

An oak tree loves a rivulet but she will never stay
To look at him or hear a word, she runs as fast away
And there beneath the forest boughs the Romanies are free
To take the water from the brook and firewood from the tree.

There's a lord that loves a lady, and she will never stay
To hear him when he speaks of love but lightly trips away.
My Gypsy mother can you tell how all of this was known
The lord and lady came to me and each of them alone.

They came to me so secretly and crossed my hand with gold
They sat inside the Gypsy tent and had their fortune told
From the lover and his lady, from rivulet and tree
From all of them we help ourselves for we are Romanies.

Si o Romani mush

Si o Romani mush se kinlo   *If the Gypsy man is weary,*
Si e grei adray o stanya   *If the horse is in the stable,*
Te o Romano chavo bokaloo   *And the Gypsy is fortunate,*
Si e kani adray o granza   *If the hen is in the barn,*
Shan Romani chalaw trushilo   *You Gypsy boys are thirsty*
Si livinor adray o kitchema   *If there's beer in the pub*
Lela Romani chichi adray lesko vast   *The Gypsy has nothing in his hand*
Shan barveli gorjer adray sar o tem.   *You are wealthier then than all the*
                                       gorjers in the land.

Si Mandi Sar Teero Chavo

Si mandi sar teero chavo   *If I am your boy*
Si tutti sar meeri dei   *If you are my mother*
Komessa del mandi e chooma   *I want you to give me a kiss.*
Keka mi ruzno rei.   *No, my strong gentleman.*
Ava mi shom kek teero chavo   *Come, you are not my child*
Ava tutti shan kek meeri dei   *Come, you are not my mother*
Adova's e waver kova   *That's another thing,*
Ava mi kushto rei.   *Yes my fine gentleman.*

Maybe You've Heard It's the Romany Way

Maybe you've heard it's the Romany way
To say that religion is lies
But I know it's all true what the parson says
For I saw the devil myself one day
With these here blessed eyes.
I was camping out in a field one night
But I couldn't sleep a wink
For I suddenly got a sort of a fright
And I fancied the donkey wasn't all right
Now was prophecy that, I think.

Then I says, I'll take a look around
So out in the air I went
And there in the dim half light I found
That the donkey was standing safe and sound
A grazin' outside the tent.

Come up, I says, says I to the moke
For him and me was friends
An' he always knew me when I spoke
An' he used to canter up and poke
His nose into my hands.

But this here time, and I needn't say
That I thought it rather rum
Though he stood as still as a lump of clay
Yet the further he seemed to get away
The nearer I tried to come.

At last he vanished out of sight
And I knew, when day came round
That the donkey I'd followed all through the night
Was the devil himself for when it was light
I saw my own in the pound.

It's a wrong idea most folks have got
That Romany chaps like me
Haven't any dear God to look after the lot
For the devil he tempts us quite a lot
As anyone else you see.

Tacho Komoben – a Gypsy poem *(True Love)*

I puri dai si jilo	*The grandmother's gone*
Ke dova gav kenaw	*Into that town now*
O puro dadus beshella	*The grandfather sits*
Adrin o kitchema	*In the pub.*
Kek Mush adray sor o tanya	*No man in all the place*
Kek chai te puk a lav	*No girl to chat to*
Mi shom akai akonyo.	*I am here all alone.*
Av, miro kamlo, av	*So come, my love, come*
Dordi sosi mandi kerin	*Oh dear, what am I doing*
Posh o lulo yog,	*Beside the red fire?*
Butti, butti, sor pa tute	*Work, work, all for you*
Tuki kushto bok!	*All for luck to you!*

True love – A Gypsy Poem

Mi dukerdom i rawni	*I told the lady's fortune*
Adray dora bawro ker.	*In that big house nearby,*
Kek kawli chovihani	*No Gypsy could have done it*
Vel ker les kushtider.	*More cleverly than I.*
Man pukkerdom rinkeni kova,	*I promised her she'd marry*
A barvalo rai te sar.	*A Lord with heaps of gold,*
Yoi das amenghi luva	*She filled my hand with silver*
Mi pordo vast ajaw.	*As much as I could hold.*
Oh, mi sosti rocker, duckker	*I can chatter, I can flatter*
Gorgios adrom:	*Gorgios far and near,*
Butti, butti, sor pa tute	*All for you love, all for true love*
Miro kamlo rom.	*All for luck my dear.*
Oh, Romanies shan jonger,	*Oh, Romanies are cunning,*
Mi shom kek dineli chai.	*I know what I'm about.*
Mi gaverdom o vonger	*I hid away the money*
Te kekeno jindas kai.	*Where no one found it out.*
Mi kindom kushto varo	*I bought some flour last evening*
I rati, kunjerni.	*I bought it secretly.*
O moriklo si kero	*Come now, the cake is ready*
Av, diri tatcho, si	*And no one here to see*
Pawno varo, pawno luva,	*Meal so white, money bright*
Drin a moriklo	*Baked together here,*
Butti, butti, sor pa tute,	*All for you love, all for true love*
Kamlo pirino!	*All for luck my dear.*

The Fiddle Maker

This song is in Henry's handwriting but must, surely, be a lift from another source, as otherwise why would he use the phrase Collected ... *and the additional detail. A typically Gypsy song heard by another Gypsy would have some sort of oral history to it, such as how the person was connected to Henry.* Collected Rorrington, Shropshire, 1962. Fiddle maker, upon the field at A2. He made the fiddle and bow in his fine tent.

O bosh kelomengrero beshtas	*The fiddle maker sat*
Oprey o poov arey Ackerlo	*Upon the ground in Ackerley*
Kedas o bosh y balano kosht	*He made the fiddle and the bow*
Adrey i kushti zigaira.	*In the beautiful tent*
Nai man keck diklo	*I have no neckerchief*
Nai man gad,	*I have no shirt*
Nai man keck pushka	*I have no gun*
Nai man staadi	*I have no hat*
Nai man keck rinkeni vongustrin	*I have no pretty rings*
Y nai man bosh y balano kosht.	*But I have my fiddle and bow.*

(The word zigaira *has been starred by Henry to a footnote reading, "Zigaira is now only used by some of the Woods and Ingrams." I have never met the word in Anglo Romani and think it was rare in Welsh Romani.)*

Me Brother's 'Orse

Henry writes: Minty Smith, Stone, A2 Trunk Road, Kent, 1962. Shouted lines after each verse are underlined.
    Did Henry obtain this song directly from Minty Smith? Perhaps, though again I am dubious. If not, where did he get it from? An exact replica of this songs appears in Denise Stanley and Rosy Burke's "Romano Drom Song Book" (post-dating Henry's letters) , where it is stated: "Mrs Minty Smith composed this lament for a specific occasion of sorrow. It shows how Romani song is a living cultural expression of the feelings of the people." *The death of a horse was a major disaster in Gypsy life, since without it travel and some means of earning a living were impossible.)*

I'm a real ol' Gypsy ghel
Borned and reared up in a tent
I spend the best part of me life in the ol' wagon
An the Gypsy life's a hard life to spend –
O dordi dordi – dick at the mullerd gry prey the drom, mush.
(Oh my God, look at the dead horse on the road, mate.)
Me brother's 'orse was killed on the A2

And it wasn't me brother's own fault
'E was a bright one and 'e thought 'e'd be all right
If 'e crossed over the road.
O dordi dordi – dick at the gry mush, dick at the gry.
(Oh my God, look at the horse mate. Look at the horse.)

And that's when the car 'it 'im
And 'e was all mi brother 'ad to make 'is livin' with
'E was a smart 'orse, a real good cart 'orse –
Gord, I wish 'e 'adn't tried to cross the road!
O dordi dordi – dick at the gavver, dick at the gavver.
(Oh my God, look at the policeman, look at the policeman.)

We was charged with causin' an obstruction
And when the old gavvers 'eard me brother's pleas
'E thought 'e was a startin' orf of a big eruption
An' then 'e charged 'im for a breachin' o' the peace.
O dordi dordi – the ol' gavver's nine part dinilo!
(Oh my God, the policeman's nine parts stupid.)

It's a good job we can always change our name like
And scarper orf away to some other verge
Course as me brother's 'orse weren't really to blame like
We aren't goin' to court cos we just don't feel the urge.
O dordi dordi – why don't they leave people like us alone?

Me brother's 'orse was killed on the A2
An''e's all me brother 'ad to make 'is livin' with
An I reckon meself we'll never get another 'orse just like 'im
And then the gavver comed along and breached the peace
O dordi dordi – dick at the gavver.
(Oh my God, look at the policeman"

Come along, chavies, we'll 'ave to shav off a waver drom or we'll be lelled.
(Come on kids, we'll have to set off another way or we'll be arrested.)

On Old Epsom Downs

Jasper Smith, Edenbridge, Kent (Didn't note date). *Similar comments to those appearing with* The Fiddle Maker *should be made. Additionally, why has Henry said, "Didn't note date"?*

On old Epsom Downs we got diddies and liars
They cooked their old food on the smoky wood fires
They had piebalds and skewbalds and flea bitten greys
Like most of the others they'd seen better days.

With a little spavvin' here and a little splint there
They took knacker price for the old 'orses at the fair –
Look round the corner, cos there comes a cop
Old Snobby's been 'it with the old kettle prop.

But Travellers knows nothin' and Travellers don't talk
But the travelling that's done now is halfway to York;
The publics are full, 'ave been open for hours
As old Jasper and Snobby are singin' 'April Showers.'

Mandi Went to Poove the Grys

Frank Cooper, West Kent.
(This is another very well known Gypsy rhyme, though I have never met this version before. Pooving the gry meant to illegally graze a horse. Late at night, the horse was moved from the roadside into a farmer's field and taken out again very early next morning so that it had access to better grass than was found at the roadside.)

Version 1

Mandi went to poov the grys	*I went to graze the horses*
In among the staggers akai	*In among the gates here.*
The gavver's arter mandi	*The policeman's after me*
To lel o' me oprey.	*To arrest me.*
"Ma" says the rakli	*"Don't," says (my) girl*
Dickin at the gavvers	*Looking at the police,*
"Tis like our dear old daddy say	*"It's like our dear old dad said,*
We can't jawl avree."	*We can't go anywhere."*

Version 2

Mandi went to poov the grei	*I went to graze the horse*
In the stigher and over akei.	*Through the gates and over here*
All though mandis rakli kickin up a goodli.	*All through my gel kicking up a noise*
Along jal'd the gairo	*Along came the man*
To lel poor mandi opre	*To arrest poor me*
Mandi lel'd off his tog	*I took off his shirt*
To del the moosh the pur	*To hit him in the gut*
Sos mi dori daddi	*Says my dear daddy*
The moosh koored too well.	*The man fought too well.*

I jal'd up to a bauri kan	*I went up to a mansion*
In the story I laid down.	*With the tale I laid down*
And munged a kani,	*And begged a hen*
And a kushti yag,	*And a good fire*
And the tail o' mi' old nightgown	*And the tail of my old nightgown.*

Henry adds: This is from a tinker in the Red Lion at Thursley Surrey circa 1953. *(Presumably Dick asked Henry where he had learned some of the songs, hence his response.)*

Give me a Kiss

Del mandi a chuma meero rinkeni chei	*Give me a kiss my pretty girl*
Mandi jins mandi'll see bitcherd avri	*I know I will be transported*
Tootis rinkeni mui mand'l kekka dik apopli	*I will not see your pretty face ever again*
Ta mandi jins duva'l poga mandis zee.	*And I know that'll break my heart.*
Chivd mandi peeri adre bauri gav	*I put my feet in the city*
Mandi dikt a gairi jalin tale o drom	*I saw a gorjer man going along the road*
Mandi pukt kova ghero sas a poshora dre lestis putsi	*I asked that man if he had a half penny in his pocket*
Kek o beng te poga lesti zee.	*Not the devil to break his heart.*

Can you Rokker Romani?

This little rhyme, which also exists in song format, is known to almost every Gypsy in Britain. Henry's version is unusual in being in deeper Romani than others, but the message is similar in all its varieties. One version appears in Denise Stanley and Rosy Burke's Romano Drom Song Book, produced by Romanestan Publications. A note in the book states, "(This song) contrasts the insecurity of Gypsy life with the protecting solidarity of friendship. George Borrow wrote down a different version over a hundred years ago.".

<u>Version 1</u>

Mandi rokkers Romanes	*I speak Romani*
Mandi fakes a bosh	*I play the fiddle*
Toot dik o gavmush	*You watch for the policeman,*
Mandi'l chor a kosht	*I'll steal the firewood.*

<u>Version 2</u>

Mandi penchava toot wi jin kova ghiveli *(2 illegible words here – written over the edge of the paper)* folki ghili les. *(think you will know this song ..... people sing it)*

Sastis too rokka Romanes
Sastis too kel de bosh
Wi too dik a gavmash
Mandi wi chor o kosh

Can you talk Romani
Can you play the violin
Will you watch for the police
While I get the firewood.

(One version of this song which I have heard has as its second verse –

Can you rocker Romani
Can you poove the gry
Can you chor a kani
As the muskrer jels by.

The third line means, Can you steal a hen? *On one occasion, some Gypsies of my acquaintance taught a gorjer youth the third line as* Can you suv a kani? *'Suv' means 'to sleep with'. The unsophisticated youth, unaware of the meaning, was then sent to the local hospital where his future mother-in-law lay in bed following a major operation. He recited her the poem to the immense delight of all.)*

I'll Marry a Donkey

Keka mandi koms kek juvel
Mandi'l roma a tarni mailla
If yoi kers wafedo te mandi
Mandi'l biken lati for a balansa

No, I love no woman
I'll marry a young donkey
If it does evil to me
I'll sell it for a pound.

(Translated by Henry as:)
None of women kind I'll wed
Some she-ass I'll love instead
If unkind to me she's found
Then I'll sell her for a pound.

Fortune Telling

Da rashai rokkered penshai dukkerin
Pend duva sas a laj
But keka yov jind mandi dukkered
    yovs chie
Pukkerd yovd roma barvelo rai.
Mandi hatches adray purri Romani
    varda

The priest talked of fortune telling
Said that it was a shame
But he did not know I told his
    daughter's future
Told her she'd marry a wealthy lord.
I live in an old Gypsy wagon

(Henry does
not give
the Romani)

And the roof is all painted in gold
I once thought about getting married
And taking a tent and waggon of my own.

Dik duvva gorjio rokkers mandis a
  Romany chavi
Mandi dia jals a dukkerin for luva
  for mandi
Mandi jals dikkin rinkeni raklies
  peserin
Luva ta jal raklies abrea.

See that Gorjer says I'm a Gypsy gel

*My mother goes fortune telling for
  money for me*
I go looking at beautiful girls paying

Money and the girls go away.

Leaving Home

You're going to leave your old home Jim
You're going far away
Said a poor grey haired mother to her son one summer's day.
You're going to leave your old home Jim,
You're going far away
You're going amongst those city folks to dwell
Said a poor grey haired mother to her son one summer's day
If your mind's made up that way I wish you well.
The old house will be lonely, the fire won't burn so bright
The birds won't sing so sweet while you're away
But if you are in trouble Jim
Just write and let me know
And by these words he gently turned away.
When sickness overtakes you, and all companions hates you
As through this world you wander all alone
When friends you have not any, in your pocket not one penny
There's your mother always waiting for you at home sweet home.

Little Rose

Here, prala, is my favourite song:

Little Rose in a garden of weeds
No-one knows who planted you there
Although you're alone, how sweet you have grown
With no one to tend you or to care
Never mind, little Rose, never mind
Though you're lonely and nobody cares
When the night sheds its dew
There's a tear shed for you
Little Rose in a garden of weeds.

An old fashioned lady

Not very old prala, but a beautiful verse

Just an old fashioned lady
With old fashioned ways
And a smile that means welcome to you
Just an old fashioned bedside
There she kneels and prays
For the return of her wandering boy
Though she wears no fine clothes
No nor yet silken hose
Yet there's something that makes her divine
When the Angels above taught the way how to love
To that old fashioned mother of mine.

I saw the mud cabin

I saw the mud cabin he danced his wild jigs in
A finer mud cabin you never did see
Considering he used to keep poultry and pigs in
It always looked tidy so neat and so clean
But now all around is so dark and so cheery
I'd die if I thought we should ever depart
Now even the sun through the windows shines clearly
Since I lost my darling sweet Tedy O'Niel

I am known as a vagrant

I am known as a vagrant
Well, a vagrant I may be
But before you stop me wandering
Please listen to my plea.

Leave me alone, let me wander
Don't tie my hands, just let me roam
I'm like a bird, crying for space
Give me a brook and some sweet meadow place

Gone is my craving for the city
Give me the moon and I am up high
Leave me to wander the countryside to ponder
A roaming vagabond am I.

(Under this song, Henry writes: A song I heard not so long ago sung by my cousin Billy Boswell was 'Golden Earrings'. I think it is a lovely song and sounds very sweet on a violin. Proper violin music. You are bound to know

it. It starts, 'There's a story that's known to very few. If your love wears golden earrings, she will come to you.' I love to play this song on a mouth organ. Did you see the picture, prala?

A Peg Maker's Wife

Said by Henry to be over 100 years old.

When I was single, I used to skip and play
But now I am married, the cradle's in my way
Oh what a life, a funny, funny life
I'd sooner be a beggar than a peg maker's wife
Now my husband is like me a Gypsy
And believe me he is very strong
Any time that anything wrong happens
He kicks and hits me like a dog.
One day he struck at me his missis
And he also struck at the kids
The kids ran away and the cradle fell over
O what a life, a funny, funny life
I'd sooner be a beggar than a peg man's wife.
If I'd have married a gorjer he would have
Treat me like a queen
But this amongst the Gypsy men
Is a thing you never will see.
Oh what a life, a funny, funny life
I should have had my brains tested
When I became a peg man's wife.

Miro Koko *(My Uncle)*

I'm thinking, you know my Uncle, sir,
And you know his name I'll be bound,
The other day his horse and he
Were travelling the country round.

My uncle went to a public house
And there he got beer enough
But the poor old horse had nothing to eat
But nettles and such like stuff.

Oh beer is the thing to cheer one's heart
So my uncle whistled a song
But the poor old horse had little to eat
So he went but slowly along.

Said the man, when a man has enough o meat
He whistles for joy
And if you'd a mouthful of hay to eat
You'd go faster than this, my boy.

What is that, my horse, oh what is that
On the other sudden of the way
With never a soul a watching it
There's a beautiful stack of hay.

So this my Gypsy loses no time
A jumping over the stile
He didn't guess there was somebody,
A watching him all the while.

A little crooked yellow faced man
Was sitting beneath a tree
My uncle told me he'd never beheld
Such an ugly fellow as he.

My uncle was singing Good luck, Good luck
But he soon let singing alone
For the man jumped up and hollered at him
In Romani like his own.

Wester Lock and Tienni

So early on Christmas morning
No other sound was there
But bells far off a ringing
Through the silent frosty air.

So early on Christmas morning
Between the dark and dawn
When the stars were going like pigeons
As the day like a hawk came on.

I heard a noise in the forest
The voice of a wailing man
And then a rustling cracking
As though a fire began.

I hurried to the burning
And there upon a rock
Beside his blazing wagon
Sat the Gypsy Wester Lock.

Oh have you buried your father
And like a Romani true
Are you burning up his wagon
As the real old Romanies do?
Or is it your dear old mother
Who looked in so many a hand
She will read no more the future
Since she's gone to the future land.

My father is still in London
And my mother is here, said he
This is burnt for a girl who is living
But dead for ever to me.

And whether she walk the South or West
Or live by East or North
That wicked girl is in the grave
To me from this day forth.

Last week we were to marry
With a dinner and a ball
And our Romani Rai, you know him,
Got it ready and paid for all.

The Rai was on the sofa
The parson was in his chair
We waited for Tienni
But Tienni was not there.

So it all broke up in sorrow
And we all went off in shame
Though we stayed till dinner was over
Tienni never came.

And I heard that she said she did it
Because I loved her so
That for twice the trick and trouble
I never would let her go.

We met and she said she was sorry
That I still should be her rom
And the next time to the wedding
She would really be sure to come.

But I said, "While there's dust on the highway
And water is in the sea
There will never be a wedding
In the world between you and me

If every hair of your ringlets
Was a spangle of shining gold
I never would ask to marry
A maiden so bad and bold.

If you had as many fingers
As a hedgehog has pins to show
And all the rings close crowded
Whenever you came I'd go,

And because you have been so cruel
And served me such a turn
I've a wagon I meant to give you
And now that wagon will burn.

He went among the people
Who had stayed to hear him through
I saw a gorjio standing
And the gorjio was weeping too.

And I asked him, Is it the story
Which causes the tears to rise
Or the smoke of the burning wagon
That so affects your eyes?

He answered, I'm not affected
By the smoke nor by what he said
But I sold him that wagon on credit
And I know I shall never be paid.

No more he wasn't and never
While water is in the sea
Will he ever get a copper
From the heart broken Romani.

(Richard Wade has written alongside this poem, in quote marks, "O kotorendi trustal Westo Lock si a tatcheno giveli, kerdo opray li a Romani chal dosta bershaw ghias. A tatcho paramish ta gilli, Romani folki rokker lis, Komeni folki gilli lis, fetterdair to gilli." ("This piece about Wester Lock is a true song done about a Gypsy many years ago. A true story and song. Gypsy people tell it or sing it. Better to sing.")

Mi Duvelesko Tacho Giveli pa Bitti Nell

Titled also as A Hymn for Little Nell. *Little Nell was Ellie, Dick Wade's daughter.*

Into a tent where a Gypsy boy lay
Dying alone at the close of the day
News of Salvation we carried, said he
Nobody ever has told it to me.

Did he so love me, a poor Gypsy boy
Send unto me the good tidings of joy
Need I not perish, my hands will behold
Nobody ever the story has told.

Bending, we caught the last word of his breath
Just as he entered the Valley of Death
God sent his son – Whosoever, said he,
Then I am sure that e sent him for me.

Smiling he said as his last sigh was spent
I am so glad that for me, he was sent
Whispered, while low, seeing the sun in the west
Lord I believe, tell it now to the rest.

The Gypsy Boy

The Gypsy boy, the poet and the tramp
Discuss philosophies they have of life
Words forming mists above the dewy damp
Their laughter cuts the morning like a knife
Echoing and drifting to the dreaming Gypsy camp.
Two eyes like needles watch from high above
And thread their way across the fields of morning
Gliding warmly on the winds of love
Shouting to the clouds that another day is dawning.
Gipsy David lives in dreams a solitary mind
His brains pursuing abstract shapes of thought
Half of it he knows, the other yet to find
A cobweb in his senses holds a butterfly he caught.
In his ignorance he freed it, to its value being blind
A butterfly named Tina recalls the touch of love
She built her faith upon a worthless dream.
Still caught in the web because it's fitted like a glove
Holding memories, reversing down their stream
Picturing in thought form, the kisses of the wind
Her body being ravished by the sun
Searching for the mind place hope and dreams were pinned
The thought reflecting echoes minus one.

(Underneath this extract, Dick Wade has written: Note Asked, a few days
later, when did he write this poem, Henry replied, 'I went straight and

wrote it after you left me the other day.' I remarked that he was very clever is using words in any language and I could not just write a poem straight out like that.'They just come easily to me,' he said. 'I often lie on my bed for hours thinking of the fields and the trees.' But are these genuinely his own?)

Lel Trad

Lel rak prala atch opray	*Watch out if you stay here brother,*
Jal i greiaw praster	*Make the horses run*
Plaster pa tiro meriben	*Run for your life*
I rei avella tachipen	*Truly the lord is coming.*
Tu loordas a greiaw kaliko	*For you stole a horse yesterday.*
Te vel yov diksa tutti	*He is coming seeking you*
Yov shellela avri talla yakengro	*He whistles from behind his gun*
Te bitcheraw tutti te stariben	*To send you to jail.*
Lel-drum lel-trad	*Take the road, be on your guard.*

Bold Robin Hood

Henry has added a note, Mostly sung when half-drunk.

Bold Robin Hood in the forest he stood
He wished all his men good-bye,
For a journey he took, it lay over a brook
Where a stranger he happened to spy.

Now they happened to meet on a long narrow bridge
And neither of them would give way.
And bold Robin Hood he quite gallantly stood
While the stranger he boldly did say

"They call me John Little because I am large.
"My bounty is seven foot three.
"Seven foot and a half, it would knock down a calf
"And surely it will knock down thee."

Now Robin, he run, to the thick of the wood
Where he choosed a staff of brown oak.
When this he had done, to the stranger he run,
But he tippled him into the brook.

"Oh! Where are you now, my jolly fellow,
"Oh! Where do you laugh or you cry?"
"No matter of thine", said bold Robin Hood,
"I'll be floating along with the tide"

He dived, he dived, he dived low;
He pulled himself out by a thorn.
When this he had done, to the stranger he run
And he pulled out a fine bugle horn

Now he blew on this horn so loud and so shrill,
 He caused all the valleys to ring.
Men clothed in green, they were plain to be seen
And surrounded their master as well.

Now up spoke the first. It was Bill Studderley.
"Why, Master, you're wet to the skin!"
"For the boy that you see; he is standing by me.
"We've been fighting; he tippled me in".

"Now none shall harm him" cried bold Robin Hood.
"Oh! No one shall harm him" cried he.
"I've got three score – and – nine, and if he will be mine,
"He shall my dear livery wear"

"They call me John Little because I am large.
"My bounty is seven foot three.
"Seven foot and a half, it would knock down a calf
"And surely it will knock down thee"

A Young Married Man

Henry has added: Ghiveli sor Romani *(song all in Romani)*

Kanna mandi sas e tarno chavo	*When I was a young boy*
Meero dei siklo te ghili kater mandi	*My mother taught me how to sing.*
Yek ofasar laki ghiveliaw sas kova.	*One of her songs was this*
O ghiveli meero poori dei siklo te ghili	*The song my old mother taught me to sing:*

I am a young married man who is tired of life
Ten years I've been wed to a sick dying wife
She does nothing all day only sit down and cry
And wishing to God that she would die.

A friend of mine came to see me one day
And he said that my wife, she was pining away.
He afterwards told me that she would get strong
If I bought her a bottle from dear Doctor John.

I bought her a bottle just for to try
And the way that she drank it you would swear she was dry
I bought her another, it fanished *(sic)* the same
Well you'd swear she had cod liver oil on the brain.

Now my house resembles a dear doctor's shop
It's covered with bottles from bottom to top
And early in the morning when the kettle it boils
You'd swear its singing out Cod Liver Oil.

O doctor, o doctor, o dear Doctor John
Your cod liver oil is so pure and so strong
I'm afraid for my life, I'll go down in the soil
If my wife don't stop drinking your cod liver oil.

Now my house resembles a dear doctor's shop
It's covered with bottles from bottom to top
And early in the morning when the kettle would boil
You'd swear it was singing out cod liver oil.

Henry appends a note: There is one more verse but I am sorry I just can't remember it. It is years ago at Appleby Fair that I last sang it, maybe you know it. You can dance to the tune of it. I have played it many a time with two dessert spoons and on the bosh, also the mouth organ. A lot of the mushaw here have mouth organs. I sometimes borrow one and play it to little Hopey. He chitta chatters when he hears music. I wish you could hear him. *Little Opey was the bird which Dick Wade loaned him the money to buy).*

I'm a young travelling Gypsy boy

I'm a young travelling Gypsy boy
Who has travelled the country through
In search of occupation and other lands to view
With me shingla under mi shoulder and a wee black dutch in mi hand
I strolled into America to view that handsome land.

It was the Queen's Old Tavern boys, that's where we spent the night
The landlady's daughter, to me she takes delight.
Oh daughter, o daughter, what's this you're going to do
To fall in love with a Gypsy boy, a boy you never knew
Who sailed across the ocean and thought of a jolly good plan
Well, you'll sail out of America with a roving Gypsy man.

Henry asks Dick, "Do you jin any gillio adray Romanes?" *(Do you know any songs in Romani?)*

The Beauty of Ireland

Oh, there's a beauty in old Ireland
That will live in memory
From the lofty Cherry Mountains
To the shores of Loch Swilly

But in dear old county Wexford
It's a paradise, God knows
In the lovely Lyland valley
Where the Rime Slang flows

Many months in I've wandered
From that little isle of green
But in all my fruitless wanderings
No contentment have I seen
A fair maiden said I will.

My Mother Said I Never Should

Version one:

My mother said I never should
Play with the Gypsies in the wood
Pulling my hair and breaking my comb,
Or I'd get beaten when I got home

Version two:

My mother said I never should
Play with the Gypsies in the wood
For, she said, if ever I did
They'd break my head with their tin pot lid.

For if I did she would say
'Naughty girl to run away!
'your hair wont curl, your boots wont shine;
'Naughty girl, you shan't be mine

On the banks of the sweet Dundee

Now Mary she was walking
All in her uncle's grove
She met now with the Squire
All in her uncle's grove.

He flung his arms around her
And tried to sling her down.
Two pistols and a sword she spied
Beneath his morning gown

Now she took those pistols from his side
And the sword she used so free
Then she fired and shot the Squire
On the banks of the sweet Dundee

"My bride I will make you,
"Before this is long,
"For taking of your own part
"And a firing of your gun"

Now the Doctor he was sent for,
A man of great skill.
Likewise the lawyer
For him to sign his will.

He willed his gold to Mary
Who fought so manfully
Then he closed his (eyes) no more to rise
On the banks of the sweet Dundee

Bold Robert Eammon

Bold Robert Eammon, the darling of Ireland
Bold Robert Eammon will die with a smile
I don't blame my comrades for doing their duty.
A hero I lived and a hero I'll die.

Hark now Sir William; you hear your death sentence
Tried like a traitor, no rebel was I.
I don't blame my comrades for doing their duty,
A hero I lived and a hero I'll die.

Now hark the bells' tolling; we all know its meaning
"Ah!" said bold Robert "I'm waiting my doom;
My chest is exposed to the point of the rifle
A hero I lived and a hero I'll die."

The Old Bog Road

My feet are here on Broadway this blessed harvest morn
But oh the ache that's in them for the place that I was born
My weary hands are blistered through the toil and cold and heat
But oh to swing a scythe today through field of Irish wheat
But here am I on Broadway building bricks by loads
I would rather see the hawthorn tree down the old bog road.

My mother died last springtime when Ireland's fields were green
The neighbours said her waking was the finest ever seen
There was snowdrops and primroses strewn all around the grave
And the village church was crowded when the funeral march was played
But here was I on Broadway building bricks by loads
When they carried out her coffin down the old bog road.

Henry, taken a few months before his death.

Newbold War memorial, Thomas Sherriff

Newbold War Memorial, Chesterfield

Henry with Lily Walker

LAWN MOWER SPECIALISTS

CALLING TODAY

CRAFTSMEN GRINDERS AND CUTLERS

Dear Sir or Madam,

We are in your district today with our Mobile Grinding Machine. We sharpen and reset on the spot:

ELECTRIC MOWERS MOTOR MOWERS
HAND MOWERS ROTARY MOWER BLADES
GARDEN SHEARS BORDER SHEARS
GARDEN TOOLS ETC.
SCISSORS TAILORS SHEARS
CUTTING OUT SHEARS PINKING SHEARS
KNIVES STAINLESS STEEL PRESTIGE KNIVES
CARVING KNIVES SAW KNIVES ETC.

This leaflet will be called for within 2 hours. Anticipating your kind patronage,

Yours faithfully,

G.H. SHERRIFF

Henry's Hawking Bill

D5

H M Prison Dartmoor
4 - 7 - 65.

~~Roi~~ Roi

~~spoon.~~ spoon.

these are the two words most chals use   Posomengro
                                          Fork.
~~but they are Kek latchge Sherrff~~

these is a "tatchi" Romani Paramish Prala.
Latcho divvus nogo prala, ser sham me prala.
Jis a shilino divvus. Outli yusyela, kei see
tooti koko ghilo tadivrus, tov ghias troliko divrus
ta lalo peero wagyaura. Kei see tooti sinkeni
penya, Meiri penyas adray adoova gav
a dukkerin, ~~shoon~~ Prala Boshela jukkeal
Dik sava see a goryis, De ~~gestronmengro~~
Maw poga aduwa bor dinelo keka prala
tis a bauri kei, Yovs a Latcho Kestamengra
Ous. and yovs kohto rooda, Dik Aduwa
see lesti ~~filishun~~ Ranya tooti stardi
Mook's jal adray akova kitchema fo choomoni
ta pee. Besh tooki la prala. Akova see wavedo
livena, Latcho fa dichi. Mook's pee a wova
trooshni livena. Latcho bok ta tooti prala
Aduwa thindi-lemengra's posh mūto. Kova
mush is a gorje-engro Wel apre prala
Mook's jal avri purpli. Ous meiri tamos a
Latcho door fon akei. Savo see da tatchi
drom Jale aduwa dibeli drom Dik akei's
de patrin apre da bongo vas.

Jis a Latcho door ta o forus. Outli kini shom.
Besh tooki la Dei an mook, mendi jal ta mong
a bitti Hoben. Keka ma prala Jis doosh ta
jal adis. O bauri rye, as jivs adoi is a

Part of a letter to Dick Wade written from Dartmoor Prison

Henry and a woman thought to be called Elizabeth Mary, a Traveller from Leicester

Henry and one of his partners, probably Sarah Lock or Jane Swales

Example of a whoopy cart, this on a Hartman postcard dating from 1907

An ornate knife grinding barrow once owned by John Smith.
Photo copyright Hereford and Worcester County Museum and reproduced by
kind permission.

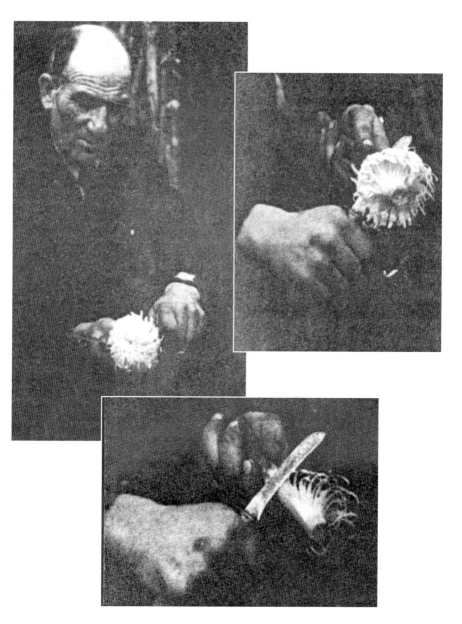

Copies of photos, copyright Dick Wade, showing Henry making wooden flowers in 1967

1964.—(D).—No. 43

In the High Court of Justice,

PROBATE, DIVORCE & ADMIRALTY DIVISION

(DIVORCE).

LEICESTER DISTRICT REGISTRY.]

BETWEEN

GEORGE WILLIAM SHERRIFF

AND

LILY SHERRIFF

AND

GEORGE WILLIAM DEAKIN

Notice of Petition

(Respondent Spouse)

Henry's notice of petition for his divorce from Lily. Note Henry's incorrect second name of William.

Henry's son George and daughter in law Susan Sherriff

George's cousin Arthur Sherriff

Owen Durkin (left), Basil Smith and Bev Durkin.

Dick Wade with Siobhan Spencer

Miro Nogo Chei Tu Mandi *(My own Gypsy girl and I)*

1. On my wall hangs a beautiful picture
Of a girl who is only small
She is a beautiful Gipsy girl
And to me the best one of all.

2. Her hair it hangs over her shoulders
I think of the Queen of the land
Her apron is full of penny winkles
She 'as a black velvet band in her hand

3. Every time I look at this picture
My mind it travels away
It goes to some old fashioned village
Or lane where this girl may stay

4. Someday in the near future
With this girl I'm hoping to be
You see Sir, this girl is my daughter
And she means all the world to me

5. I always pray to God to protect her
And this I know he will do
You see Sir, he has no race or colour
Whether you be Gipsy or Jew

6. So I know my daughter is safe Sir
As she is left in good hands
Our Lord Almighty will protect her
Until I can rejoin my own band

7. Please Sir always remember
There is good in the worst of us
You cannot judge a book by its cover
Whether it is bad or good

8. It is a crime to be a Gipsy in this world Sir
This is a thing, that I feel sure you know
If you are a Gipsy nobody wants you
And they don't care where you go

9. There is one thing that I am sure of
My Lord will forgive me for this
That is more than I can say about people
Who are supposed to be good and all this

10. So here ends my little sad story
Please Sir, don't look down on me
I am like thousands of others
There for the grace of God goes me.

Mandi kairdo akova bitti kova opre mi-kokero. Estist tootii kom les. Mandi kefin tooto kel. *I wrote this little thing by myself. I hope you like it. I will play you it.*

Sar Les Jinsa Tutti *(How do you know (it))*

Oh jinsa tutti, mi chavi sar rinkeni tut shan
Savo avali miri dai
Awer si kek dikamengro adray moro bitti tan
Sar jinsa tutti les, miri chi
Me foki apray o drom
O gorgio te o Rom
Shan sig ta pukker mandi sor rinkeni mi shom
Adray savo jib, mi chavi pukkerin i folki les
Maw len mengi hokkerben mi chi
Rokker, yon nasti rokker chichi, miro dai
Yon sasti pen kek lav
Awer dik ajaw te sav
Te jinava shom, i komlidiri juvel adray o gav.

Oh you know my child how pretty you are
How came you to my mother
Yes, (and) there is no mirror in my little tent
How do you know, my girl?
My people on the road,
The gorjer and the Gypsy
Are quick to tell me how beautiful I am.

In all my life, my child, saying it to the people
Do not lie to them, my girl
Talk, they cannot say anything my mother
They can say nothing
Yes, now I can laugh
To know I am the most dearly desired woman in town.

B. Poems and Song Words Composed by Henry Himself
Gypsy Boy to a Gorjer

Yek Romani chal te a gorgio
Ye poori daieski dai
Pawnch chavaw te a gairo
A chukeno didikai
Awer o rom sas ruzno
Si bawro opray o chib
Te shordas sas lesti kokero
Si deep-dirus adray Romani jib

A Gypsy and a gorjer
You old grandma
Five sons and a man
A poor half breed
Come, the man was strong
He is a loud mouth
He made himself heard
His Romani is pure

The Death of A Child

It is unclear whether the first bit about the pregnant Gypsy girl is connected with the second. At first, I thought the second part related to the child Henry had by a gorjer girl before his partnership with Anna Howard, but after the first bit this seems more likely to be unrelated to Henry's life.

Pendas e Romani chei ke laki di
Said the Gypsy girl to her mother
Miri diri di miri chomb kambri
My dear mother, I am pregnant
Koined kerdi tutti kambri
Who made you pregnant?
Oh miri di e gorgio grei e bavalo.
Oh my mother, the rich gorjer stallion.
A tikno rai avakli yekorus amandi lel'd yek
A little gentleman once came to me, delivered
A bitti chavi sar rinkeni sar tule komessa ta dik
A little child, so beautiful, full of love to see
Kana yoi vias ararti adray moro puro tan
Her coming that night in my old tent
Sos pensi o dud o de saula a pukkerin Sarshan.
Was like the moon of the morning saying Hello
Miro juvel sos bute mishto te sa lakis tikno te yoi
My wife was very good to her little one and she
Sos beshin tuller i rukkor te masker i ruzhior odoi
Was sitting under the trees and amidst the flowers there.
Mi latcherdom yek muiengri man dikt adray a budika
I registered (the baby's birth) at the Registrar's office
I fokli pendas sos Miduvel a beshin posh leski dai.
The people said it was God sitting beside her mother.
I mila i juvel te mandi jasedo kettenas opray o drom
The donkey, the wife and I went together travelling
Sar i chavi adray yek trushero oh shomas a baktalo Rom
With the child in one pannier, oh I was a lucky Gypsy
Te kana i rarti sos vellin sar dur fon i gavior
And when the night began to fall far from the towns
Amandi atchd moro tan posh o tatto rik o de bor.
I pitched our tent in the sheltered side of the hedge

Posh o yog rikkorus o tan mendui beshdom alay
Around the fireside by the tent we sat down
Ta rokkerd ajar kon i chavi sos sutto pukeno adray
And talked thus of the child who was silently asleep within

Sor men sosti sikker laki ta kil adray i welgoros
How we would show her off when we did the fairs
Te lel bute adosta vongor a dukkerin Gorjios.
In order to get a great deal of money from the gorjers.

Aver adray o rinkeno cheirus te pauli o bauro ven
There came the beautiful time (=Spring) after the long winter.
Moro diri komeli chavi leld o wafedo naflopen
My beloved child caught a fever.
Lakin Tarni pirror sos shilo sar shileri sims (?) I yiv
Her young feet were icy as if they were snow
Aver lakis chomyor loldi pensi rushior masker o giv.
Her lips were red like flowers in the corn
Miri juval pukkerdas mandi "Rom atch apray te ja
My wife asked me, Husband, get up and go
Keti gav te mong o drabengro awer kon amendi veld ketteni
to the town to beg the doctor to come, therefore we came together
Mi diktom yov nasti keir chichi i chavi sos suttied avri
I saw he could not do anything, as the child was slipping away.
Mi juvel rovella butti awer mandi pendom kek lav
My wife wept much but I said not a word
Til apray o waver posh divvus a mush avel fon o gav
Till upon the other afternoon a man came from the town
Lesti roodapen sikkeras mandi yov sos o bauro rashai
His gentle coaxing showed me he was a great priest.
Yov komd te rokker bute kovas ke mengi te miro ch... (*remainder of word missing – chavi?*)
He wanted to talk of many things about us and my ...child(?)

Meer Dei

Following the introduction, the words are apparently intended as a song, though there is no clue as to the music. It was clearly Henry's own invention.
   Henry uses the noun dooma *below in entirely the wrong way. Dooma means the back of a person or animal. There is no sound Anglo Romani word for the adverb back, but* apopli *would be the nearest.*
   Meero dai, yos sas tachi, katar laki chavaw ta laki kairr'e, yoi sas komelo ta tachi ta komoben mendi sor. Sas laki vast duva chalavaw meero kor. Mandi sastis penchava troostal les kenaw. Toot kek-komi nisser tooti Dei tallugno yoi sar jalaw. Dadus yov sas latcho ta komelo pukkarus mendi – sor Men keker kek-komi latch awaver yek Katar shan moro nasfelo ta dooka. Mandi monya Juvel fon laki guidlo nav fon yoiaw sorkomn-cheerus sig o sanuvo toot kek-komi nisser tooti Dei talluyaw yoi sar jalaw. Me shom jaw door avri fon kairi. Me shan jaldaw kek latcho. Meero Dei Sorkon-cheerus monya fon man at kairi. Kelobens yoi sorkon-cheerus tallopen ta jiv A

jivoben jaw tatcho ta dik meero kamelo pooro dei adre yoiaw hev.

Kanna mandi sas yekino meero putsi sas Sorkon-cheerus pordo pa luva. Kenaw mandi shom romedi meero putsi see kek pordo jaw mendi monya katar wel kek romedi apopli. Men Romanies righer o peiastas jivoben. Moro opre o drom see kek-komi kerdo Sorkon cheerus mendi atch-meero-tan. O muskra pens jal opre jal opre. O gairo pendas mantchi-too Bongo toot. Mandi pendas boot latcho kenaw toot sastis pessa pa meero livenor Sor rarti. Mandi'll pessa toot dooma kanna mandi lel o luva. Ajaw mandi besh adray akova stariben kamora me penchava pa toot meero komelo O kongnusti akei shan pensa bengesko tan but mandi'll avel pauli, kel kek trash. O Gavengro aduva lino mandi adrom Si keker komoben pa mandi aduva divvus YoYon lie mandi adray stariben, adoi katar atch. Parikarova Duvel mandi'll vel avri yek divvus

My mother, she was true to her children, to her offspring, she was loving and true and loved us all. It was her hand that soothed my brow. I can think about it now. You never forget your mother throughout all her actions. My father was good and kindly speaking to us all. I never found another to help us through our illnesses and pains. I pray for the woman for her sweet name they always .... you never forget your mother throughout all her actions. I have gone far from home. It has not gone well for me. My mother always begged for me at houses, for the things we needed to live. A life goes truly and sees my dear old mother in her grave.

When I was single, my pocket was always full of money. Now I am married my pocket is never full, so I beg never to marry again.

We Gypsies keep to a life of fun
Our being on the road is never done.

We forever make our camp (And) the police say, get away, get away. The (Gypsy) man said, 'Cheer up you will get some crooked money. I said, 'Very good, now you can pay for my beer all night. I'll pay you back when I get the money. Now I sit here in my prison cell, I think of you my sweetheart. The cleric here has spoken of hell but I'll come back, never you fear. The policeman that took me away is not liked by me to this day. They put me in prison, there to stay. Thank God I'll come away one day.

When My Travelling Days are Over

When my travelling days are over
And my life is nearly done
I shall put my tent and waggon
Right beside a country pub

Every Sunday I'll go coursing
After rabbits with my dog
Maybe he will catch a Kanengro *(hare)*
And I will roast it on the yog *(fire)*

Every night I'll sit and Rokka *(chat)*
About the good times on the drom *(road)*
And the tales about the devil
Also paramishes *(stories)* of fun

Once I chor'd a bauri Kanni *(stole a pheasant)*
And the Ghivengro *(farmer)* had me lel'd *(arrested)*
They sent me to Stafford prison
And there they put me in a cell.

I have lots of things to remember
How some people have treat me
They have been so good and kind Sir
Like you, and your family.

When you sit beside your fire
Please Sir, always remember this
Our Lord Almighty will protect you
I shall always pray for this

When our days are finished and over
We shall meet in an happy land
Not like this one, full of trouble
But one where we all walk hand in hand.

I have often sat and wondered
And thought how nice it would be
If all the people in this world
Could live in harmony

No more wars, no more ling,
No more killing just for fun.
But instead live happily together
Until our life on earth is done

Have you ever thought of people
And how silly they really are
They just go and kill each other
And it never gets them very far.

Some rich man with plenty of money
He is greedy like us all
But not satisfied with a little
He goes and starts a bloody war.

We are expected for to fight it
But thank God I can say
I have more sense than lots of others
So at home I will always stay

I would not have it on my mind Sir
That I had ever killed a man
So when my travelling days are over
I can look forward to the happy land.

Avri miro Koko shero *(from my own head)*

You Call to me

Henry sent the following to Fred Huth, who sent it on to Dick Wade with the following comment:
   Really two poems, I suppose. Just as he sent it to me. I have only re-arranged the punctuation (which was chaotic) and inserted the question marks (which were absent). So unlikely that he has copied it out of a book. But he may have heard it, or part of it, perhaps even as a child, and therefore be plagiarising consciously or unconsciously. F Huth

You Call to Me

You call to me, who have no will to wander
Content am I to know in a traveller's tale
The paradises I shall visit never
Beyond the ocean I shall never sail.
And yet, past reason, in this one small country
I sigh for the woods, the streams, unvisited
So many valleys happy under heaven.
So many fields that I shall never tread.

Who would prefer a smooth-clipped lawn.
Though birds hop there at silver dawn,
To uncouth grass, drugged meadowsweet
And boggy earth as black as peat
Who a trim garden would prefer
Though bees hum in its lavender
To the green smells and lights and stains
Of hot, high-banked sun filtering lanes.

Romanano ghiveli adre Anitrakero *(English Gypsy Song)*

I am a travelling Gypsy man and a scissor grinder too.
I travel around the country side my trade for to do
 Some people are glad to see me and some they are not
This does not make any difference because to me they are soon forgot
Sometimes I meet young women and their fortunes I do tell.
This gets me my living and a glass of beer as well.
I lost my dear old mother, when I was but a boy
I can truthfully tell you Sir, that this was not a joy.
My father treat us kindly and did the best he could
But kind Sir I'm sorry to say, not as my mother would.
One day I finally got married and took a Gypsy wife
Now I know I shall be happy, for the rest of my life.
Kind Sir take a warning and listen to my plea
Never treat a travelling Gypsy man as a lot treat me.
I have been hounded around the country and knocked from pillar to post
I can truthfully tell you Sir this is no boast
I kindly thank my father, who taught me all he knew
For getting through my hardships and getting my living too
Some days you may have friends aplenty.
Other days but a few
So please kind Sir, think of the Gypsy man
Who could be the best friend you ever knew.
I finally end my story and wish you all the best
If ever you see a Gypsy camp, please God let them rest
You never know yourself Sir what you may go through
So please Sir do unto the Gypsy, that which you would like done to you

Mandi shan Ghiledi akova ghiveli adre Kitchema as sor paudel Anghiterra.
Ses see e pooro Romano ghiveli. Me hopesar tooti Kom les. *(I have sung this song in pubs all over England. It is an old Gypsy song. I hope you like it.)*

About Dick

This piece is marked by Dick, Henry's own composition. *It is introduced by Henry with the words,* Kek bute kushto, to kel fettedair awaver chairus – *'Not very good, to improve another time.' After the poem, Henry has written,* 'The piece about tiro kokero *(yourself),* I have a nice tune to it. You will like it when you hear me gilli *(sing)* it.

Notice Henry's variation in the spelling of chavies/chavvies in Verse 1, line 3 and Verse 2, line 2.

Nell is Dick's daughter, Ellie, who spent some time with Henry and who was shown various traditional crafts by him. Whilst in prison he made a wagon of matchsticks for her, but this cannot now be located.

In a village in Lincolnshire there stands a dwelling
It is owned by a Romani Rai *(Gypsy gentleman)*.
He has a Romni and trin chavies *((wife and three children)*
He goes to most Gypsy meetings
And also rokkers their jib *(talks their language)*
One of his bitti chavies is a rinkeni chie *(little children is a pretty girl)*
Her name is little Nell
She plays with Gypsy chavvies *(children)*
Who she knows very well.
In time she'll learn to rokker *(talk Romani)*
And learn to dukker too *(tell fortunes)*
Also to make kushti hobben *(good food)*
As all tatcho Romanies do. *(True Gypsies)*
One day she will travel like her father, to the fairs
And become a Romani rawni, *(Gypsy lady)*
Who for the Gypsies cares.
She may marry a pukkersamengro *(lawyer)*
Or yet a gorgio bauro rai *(great gorjer lord)*
But there is one thing certain
Her love for Gypsies will never die.
This family will always prosper
And have the best of luck
You see, they are not like most people
Who always get stuck up.
They have no class distinction
And are really tatcho friends *(true)*
This I can truly tell you
They are the Gypsies friends.

C. Poems and Songs From Other Sources

Henry plagiarised many items from LELAND, Charles G. English Gipsy Songs in Rommany. London, Trubner and Co. Though Leland was the main person behind this book, he was assisted in the translation into Romani of traditional or popular items – but not necessarily of Gypsy origin – by E.H. Palmer and Janet Tuckey. This is an extremely rare and valuable book – my own copy, purchased many years ago, cost me £65 then. It is interesting to speculate how Henry managed to get sight of this book as it is difficult to believe that it was in the prison library. Perhaps it was through Fred Huth, but there is no evidence for this.

John Brune's Analysis

In correspondence in August 1969 and April 1970, between Dick Wade and the folk song specialist John Brune, Brune correctly identifies the following borrowings claimed by Henry as ones he has heard in his family, as originating from Leland's book:

Meriben Pa Komoben	Tuckey, p 42
Yoraws ta Balovas	Charles G. Leyland, and several Gypsies, p 87.
Tatcho Rom	Leyland, p 33
Komoben Tattopen	Tucky, p 196
Muledo Kuramengro	E.H. Palmer, (after Tennyson) p, 5
Frank and Alice Cooper	Tuckey, p 158
O Romani Patrin	Tuckey p, 205

Brune gives Henry the considerable benefit of doubt as to how Henry learned these songs, and presumes that, because of minor differences in text, Henry must have learned these from his family and that therefore, on the balance of probability, they were original songs.

Henry gives most of the songs in both English and Romani, the latter being very archaic and mostly gorjer translations which would have never stood up to authentic Gypsy eyes.

These letters almost certainly date to after the break-up of the friendship between Henry and Dick.
Brune writes:

Perry Vale
LONDON
17. 8. 1969

Dear Mr. Wade

Thank you very much for your last letter and the free copy of July/Oct. issue of the JGLS. I am very sorry I did not reply earlier but I have been landed with a whole rash of deadline articles on a variety of subjects that required a certain amount of original research. Incidentally, I did not try to rush you into sending me your vocabularies – I merely thanked you for your promise to let me have them in due course.

Now to the Romany songs of Henry Sherriff:- judging by the specimens so far, his entire repertoire would appear to have originated with the Lelend, Palmer and Tuckey book I mentioned to you in a previous letter. Only ' HUNNALO PARNI' is an original Romani verse by Matthew Cooper – translated into English by Charles G. Leland – p 129; 'ROCKERIN ROMANI' by Leland, p 219; 'TALKING ROMANI', Leland, p 221; MIRI KOMELI PIRINI', Leland, p 149, no English words; 'O PATRIN', Leland, p. 203; THE TRAIL SIGN', Tuckey, p. 205; 'AS DRUNK AS A GENTLE-MAN NEEDS BE', in Romany on p 101; by E.H.Palmer, English, also by Palmer, p 103; I will send you the original versions by the end of September when I am a bit less harassed.

I am under the distinct impression that Henry Sherriff learned all these verses traditionally, probably at third hand rather than at second-hand. There are enough minor differences in his versions to justify such an opinion. I would further say that the fact that they have been passed on for a Century in at least one Romany family is proof enough that they are in the true Romany tradition and that they should be regarded by now as Romany and not Rye songs; after all what constitutes a tradition? Is it not the process and the memory that keeps it going rather than the details of its origin? Do you remember Henrich Heine, the German Jewish poet who wrote many popular 'folk songs' in the last Century? Well, when the Nazis came to power, Heine was banned, but his songs were still issued as anonymous folk songs. They had become so much part of the German tradition that not even the Nazis could erase them from the folk – memory. I would say that people like Henry Sherriff greatly help us in sorting out which of the 'ENG-LISH – GYPSY SONGS IN ROMANY' have any significance within the context of present day Romany Society, and which are plain chaff. It would be good to know the full extent of his repertoire.

All the best.
J. A. Brune

P.S. I am only collecting currently spoken Traveller's cant – so if you have any of this, and if you can remember whether you got it from English, Scottish or Irish 'tinkers', I would be very grateful for any snatches you may send me. But with Romany I am not particular as to whether the terms are obsolete, just as long as they were still remembered as late as 1850. I will incorporate the more important lists (Sampson, Smart, Crofton, Leland and much of *Romano Lavo Lil*) as well these works have been sadly under-printed. Incidently the sections will include tape transcripts of more general interest on the life. My material on dog breeding and training and on the Romany horse doctoring is rather deplete as yet. If you have anything on these subjects I would be grateful if I could use it too.

Yours sincerely
JAB

9.4.1970

Dear Mr Wade,
Christmas is long over and so is Easter – and you have probably written me off as a bad egg. I was rather overloaded with work of one description and another and I also hoped to trace the rest of the original sources of your collection before writing to you, – but without success. These may well be original material, but more probably half or more originated with Janet Tuckey and appeared scattered here and there. If I trace any more of the items I will certainly know right away. It may be well worth issuing the lot as you have it as there are enough changes in the words as Henry Sherriff remembers them for them to serve as a interesting example of the "folk process ". Sorry for the odd wording and typing errors I am a bit tired just now.
All good wishes
John Brune

Underneath one song Meriben pa komoben *(Living for Love), Henry has written:* Another six giveli prala *(songs brother).* Another six or seven next chairus *(time)* and so on until me jinova kekkomi *(I know no more).* Please let me know if these are then kind of giveli you like and want. Teero prala Henry *(Your brother Henry.*

Of the remainder, the only one I have personally heard a version of is the very fine, As Drunk as a Gentleman Needs to Be, *which I here reproduce in Henry's 'borrowed' version, which differs from those I have heard:*

As Drunk As A Gentleman Needs to Be

A Gypsy lad in his tent did lie
"How do you do my boy?" said I
He laughs outright and he says, says he,
"Things is a going all right with me
"I'm drunk as a gentleman needs to be."

His girl she gave the fire a poke
And into the tent came clouds of smoke.
"Now dammit," he says, "I can hardly see,
That smoke has got in my eyes," says he,
As drunk as a gentleman needs to be.

Out of the tent he bundles quick
And takes his fiddle and fiddle-stick,
Down on the grass outside he sits
Singing away in Romani,
As drunk as a gentleman needs to be.

The Gorjers when they heard the sound
Came running up and crowded round
To hear him singing in Romani
Crying, "Oh look at Mister Lee,
"Drunk as a gentleman needs to be."

The Gypsy's daughter was standing by
And hearing him sing began to cry:
"Oh stop his singing," she says, says she,
"A teaching of Gorjers Romani,
"As drunk as ever a man could be."

"I loves to see a Gypsy lad
"A-singing and playing away like mad
"But this is what seems a sin to me,
"To talk before Gorjers in Romani,
"If a man is as drunk as a man can be."

Thorneymoor Fields

This song is written in syllables to fit the music, and is in Dick Wade's writing. It appears on Dick's tape of the Hames and Booth singers. I think it should be assumed that it is not in fact one of Henry's, though it is certainly an authentic Gypsy song.

In Thorn-ey-moor Field in Nott-ing-ham-shire;
Fol-de-dol-da-ra-ri-ful-a-ri-day,
In Thor-ney-moor Fields in Nott-ing-ham-shire,
Three keepers' houses stood in a square
Their ord-ers was to look af-ter the deer,
Ri-fol-de-dol-da-ra-li-day

Epping Forest (Talking Romani)

*The following song is unquestionably a straight lift by Henry from Leland,
but I have heard fairly similar ones which suggests that Leland's version
may have been an adaption of something which was originally authentically
Gypsy. A similar version appears on Bob Lovell's tape of New Zealand Gypsy
songs. It is for this reason that Henry's is here reproduced:*

Talay o shelni patrinya
Aposh o de kitchema
Mandi rokkerdom puri Rosa
Te yoi rokkerdas sig aglal.

Kana sig yoi pukkerdas shukaro
Maw rokessa Romanes
Adoi avella o muskero
Te vel bengus shunnel-les.

Tew vel shunella amengi
Si chickji o lesti pen
Maw jinessa tute mi rai
Sis chinger ye sig avel o tem.

Mandi shundom mi dadus pen les
Tute man pennis si chin
Te bute folki shan nashedi
Ajafera rokkerin.

Sin chindo adray o lilyaw
Te si kekana lins avri
Len panderenna tute
Pa rokkeraw Romani.

*Translated by Dick Wade as follows. In his original, here and there, Dick
has pencilled in translations of obscure words, or alternative Romani
orthography.*

Epping Forest (Talking Romani)

One morning in Epping Forest
Beside the kitchema door
I talked with the Gypsy Rosa
As I often had done before.

When she whispered quick and softly
Don't speak in Romani
For there is a policeman
Who can hear as well as see.

But if he hears us talking
He will not understand
Why, don't you know, my master,
It's against the law of the land.

I have heard it from my father
It may not be spoken or writ
And many have swung on the gallows
For nothing but talking it.

And it's still down in the law books
And was never struck out, you see
They may swing you off the crossbeam
For a talking much more for a writing
A book in the Romani.

And though you're a gentleman truly
Don't go in the way to be hung
For I say it's a hanging matter
This talking the Romani tongue.

The music for Thorneymoor Fields

7. DICK'S QUESTIONS TO HENRY

At some stage in their relationship, Dick sent a series of four batches of questions to Henry, leaving spaces on the right had part of the page for Henry to append responses. It is clear from the content of the Romani in these, that they originated early in their relationship, therefore they provide probably totally accurate samples of Henry's Romani before he 'discovered' Smart and Crofton. It is clear from these that Henry already had a good knowledge of some fine Romani, and this certainly helps to explain why Henry was able to pick up Puri Chib so quickly.

One page, consisting of three questions from Dick, has at the top of the page, in Richard Wade's handwriting, appears: "R.A.R. Wade to 92 Sherriff. Extra paper for folk tales and folk songs with Governor's permission."

It is not possible to surmise the exact order of these four documents, but the following is as likely as any:

Document 1

<u>*Question from RAR Wade*</u>   <u>Answer from Henry Sherriff</u>

A. The following words of yours I don't know at all. What do they mean?

1. Jigger	1. Door. Wuder
2. Bochadok	2. Sheep
3. Glade	3. Window

B. The following I think I understand but tell me if I am right or wrong.

1. Pernell (or is it pennell?) – leg or arm	1. Pero, perros
2. Covell usually means thing or a licence, but do you use it for year?	2. Licence is slang. Besh – year. Kushti covvel
3. Yorals – eggs?	3. Yora, yoralls
4. Jog – shilling	4. Jog. Trin mushni collos
5. Budrus – same as wudrus (bed)	5. Wudrus
6. Pawno chiriklo – ?	6. Swan, goose, dove
7. Matchago – cat?	7. Cat. Fish is matchis.

C. What are your words for:

1. Grinding barrow?	1. Chinamestros
2. Lawyer?	2. Bitcherin mush
3. Duck?	3. Tickno pappni

4. Goose?   4. Pauno rani
5. Harness?   5. Solivanis (*could read Solivaris*)
6. Fork?   6. Rooys
7. Who?   7. ?
8. What?   8. ?
9. When?   9. ?
10. Wheel?   10. Putti
11. Shafts (of a cart)?   11. Trullos
12. Candle?   12. Momeli dood

D. How do you count?

One	Yeck
Two	Dui
Three	Trin
Four	Shtar
Five	Pange
Six	Shove
Seven	Lono
Eight	Pate
Nine	Wanner
Ten	Desh
Twenty	(*Left blank*)

Document 2

1. Why is Macclesfield called Mong-dikla-kova-gav?

It is because they make silk there and Travellers can beg or buy some silk off of the people who work in the mills to make silk diklas.

2. What is your word for:

(*There then follows a list of 7 English words with Romanes besides, and 70 Romanes words and phrases, most of which also have an English translation beside them. The exceptions are: otcherimengri, panamengri, panigurni, drabni, choovikan, lesti, berkeris, kekavi, and the sentence* Dordi dordi, duvva mush delled mandi (*Oh dear, that man hit me.*) *All the words are incorporated into the fuller Anglo Romanes vocabulary and so are not additionally shown here.*)

Dick writes: Yes I have heard chittybank before from Kit Hames, but always assumed it was not tatchi Romani, but when you think about it, it could be. Chitti in Romanes means "Nothing". Do you think it is Romanes or cant?

Henry's reply: I am not sure Dick, we have used this word for years. I think nearly all the Romany chals use it. You will know better than I if it is tatcho, myself don't think it is.

Dick: You say "Bivan tan" for "Green tent". This is an old word not often heard these days, but always used to mean "raw" e.g." Bivan mas" means "Raw meat although they used to say "bivan kosht" for green (i.e. raw) wood. You seem to have several words for "green"; which would you say is the best and the most used in your family.

Henry: Bivan means raw but we sometimes use it for green proper word is the true word that we have been taught is greeno but we use three or four other words for Green. I have sent you a couple of them. I think Greeno is the proper word.

Document 3

Question from RAR Wade   *Answer from Henry Sherriff*

How would you say?:

1. How are you?
2. What's your name and prala, what line are you? Where are you from?
3. Look out! The keeper's coming!
4. Tell the man to go away
5. Under the hedge
6. Down the road
7. We'll stop in the next village
8. He is a bad man
9. She is a bad woman
10. Bring your dad a bucket of water

1. Sarishan
2. Pukker your nav my Prala
3. Divki, vasher havin shoon aki, Waster jellin.
4. Jell, on dinlo.
5. Adjuta the bor
6. Vangus the drom
7. Latch in the neser lewe
8. Waffety gerri
9. Flocktin lubnee
10. Ker your dadus pani, nixie aki.

From RAR Wade: Please write down some more rare words you think I may not know. Don't say what they mean. Let's see how many I can make out.

Reply from Henry:

Gruvni	Fawney	Chovey	Piimangros
Pirrabin	Grome	Lollo	Beshin
Nockengro	Wastos	Nasher	Kawm
Wongushees	Kanengro	Cangry Puv	Trushnees
Givescro	Chuchnee	Solivengro	Muttermengri
HorasChorri	Buttika	Shekori	Weshni

Sigaben	Bory	Lastered	Sovaken
Chickli	Gavingroes	Pockamyes	Gudlo
Juckals	Mushis	Danlymengro	Kam
Krallis	Dumo	Chuvveny-	Shummy
Pash	Wuder	choomerin	Sarserin
Puvengro	Ballos	Chinamangril	Chinned
Wen	Shubo	Ker chungs	Ballovas
Ruvvin	Hocabin	Sunaben	Chingaree
Hovalas	Chongurs	Ranyas	Delemscro
Miraben	Cottar	Toves	Horra
Shuvalo	Pen	Pale	Cullos

Richard – hope you have some joy with these. Nash.

I am sorry prala I send you a wrong word, we use pallani – choka for petticoat. The word pallani as I used it and my folki use means under. Pallani poodj – means under bridge.

I was not thinking what I was doing when I wrote petty, please excuse me I would not like to give you a wrong word if I can help it, so pallani means – under. I am very sorry for the mistake. I have to think back many a time to bring back some of the lavs back to me. As I have said before prala, there is no one here to talk to in Romanes, and sometimes I have to think twice. It is the best thing that ever happened having you write to me in Romanes jib. It keeps my mind on it, not as I shall ever forget as I love my breedopen to much. I could never be Gorgerfied if I lived amongst them all my life. I don't like their life or ways.

Tooti sastis kek kair e tatchi Romani chal adrey e gorger, Yon shan kairdo lenti kushtiest te kair mandi adray yek. Lenti sastis – kek parik duvel ta kek – komi willasar. Sastra Vala hero Vardo. Do you jin this?

Pallani – underneath, underneath
Pallani – choka – underneath coat, petticoat
Palla – after.......Some chals say Tallani – choka....Talla – after, under
We say palla – after – under pauli – back or palla
You can use palla for after. Under or back. It all depends on the breed you are talking to, as I said we use Pauli- back Palla – under Pallani underneath.

Document 4

Questions from RAR Wade   *Answers from Henry Sherriff*

1. Out of your last list, the following words I do not know. What do they mean?

Sigaben	Chance
Shubo	Gown
Shummy	Tent, canvas bag
Sarserin	Broken trail
Cullos	Shilling
Collos	Coconuts
Chovey	Shop
Buttika	Shop
Ballos	Hair
Chuvveny ker	Workhouse
Krallismush	Judge = king's man

2. When you give putti for wheel, what does this mean literally?

Putti — The word for wheel is usually hero, same as for leg.

Changed her name again, another woman's

Purabend lakis nav ajaw. Geeris

3. The words you didn't jin are:

Who – kon, eg Kon see adoi – who is there?
What – savo, eg Savo gra te biken? – which horse to buy?
When – kanna, eg kanna sas mandi tikno – when I was a child.

4. Do you know any other of these small words which help to put a sentence together?

Chichi – any, none
Kairs – makes, does, do
Bongo – sad

	Eg
Here	Acai
There	Adoi
Away	Going away – puroben, yuzhered
Down	Avree
	Longo duras adre the tem
Again	?
Before	?
Behind	Pauli
After On	?
In	Apre, pre, dree – in, on
Under	

Tale the koshters – under the wood
Shooned – heard

5. Have you any word for goat? *(Left blank)*

6. What do you call:-

Pheasant	Weshni canni
Partridge	Weshni canni
Fly	?
Bee	Gudlo, Sugar.
Beehive	Gudlo ker
	Pishom
Foxes	Gudlo jukali

At the bottom of this page, in Henry's writing, appear the tantalising words
– That's to say, Dovos to pen, chivved adre the puv, and was buried.

This may be a carry-over from a list of phrases on another page, but appears to be referring to wayside burials. Henry's own mother Eliza Sherriff/Boswell, was interred with the stillborn baby in a wayside grave at an identified location near Bakewell, DBY.

8. ROMANI

The quality of Henry's Romani varies massively. It is not simply marked by his acquisition of Puri Chib Romani, as the quality of the Romani which can be attributed with certainty to his pre-Smart and Crofton discovery is good. After Smart and Crofton is where the real variation occurs, and this is because he is mixing his own compositions (which are often presented in good Romani) with the plagiarised. The quality of the latter, especially those produced by gorjers such as in the Leland book, is very mixed.

Some of the Romani is so archaic that it cannot be translated. Whilst it is perfectly true that Gypsies take Romani words and amend them, and their meaning, for a particular context, some of the words in the Leland songs have been composed in ways that no Gypsy would have done and therefore the intended meaning sometimes remains obscure.

The Romani in this section is therefore very mixed. Passages taken almost verbatim by Henry from either Smart and Crofton or Leland have been omitted. Passages which are partly from those sources but which have been substantially changed or added to are reproduced. Several original passages provide splendid examples of the way Henry has absorbed and can now use his language.

The first section is Henry's claim to be the last surviving speaker of old Romani, a claim which, as had already been shown, is bogus.

The English word 'deep' is used customarily by all English and Welsh Gypsies to indicate purer forms of Romani.

Sor tatcho Romano-chalaw wi pulska toot kova. Kanna sas mandi e tikno sor o pooro folki, rokerdi tatcho pooro Romani lavaw. Kek nanei see jaw siklo. Konaw see sas beshaw dosta palal. Konaw o tarno folki kek yon rokerenna tatcho konaw Boot gorki-kani folki see-le konaw. Kek ne junenna lenghi kokeri so see tatcho ta wafedo. Kanna too putches lendi tatcho lavaw. Kek yon sastis, pukka toot o tatcho drom o lendi. Meero kokero riherova o tatvcho pooro lavaw. Mandi penova meero kokero. Kek

Romani chalaw jivenna konaw pensa mi kokero adray tatcho pooro Romani-chal rokerimus, ta latcho pooro tatcho lavaw. Sor gorjjio see o folki konaw. Mandi see e tatcho pooro Romano-chal pardel sor mokadi posh-kedo Romani-chalaw. Komovas te rokka troostal jafri poori rokeriben. Sorbon breedopen adre kova temeskri, jinnena kova koosi rokerbon.

All true Gypsy boys will tell you this. When I was a child, all the old people spoke true deep Romani. It's not used at all. Now they are getting far behind. Now the young people do not talk correctly they are more like gorjer people now. They don't themselves know what is right or wrong when you say proper words to them. They can't speak the right way themselves. I alone keep to the true deep words. I talk it to myself. No Gypsy boy alive knows how to speak in true deep old Gypsy-boy Romani talk and good old deep words. It's all Gorjer people (talk) now. I am a true old Gypsy boy, superior to all stinking half-breed Gypsy boys. I want to talk about such deep language. All breeds in this country know a little Romani.

I have never met a real old Romani moosh who could not tell you this little story. It is true as well as you know. I am making a good long piece up and putting nearly every travelling breed in it. I think you will like it when I send it next time.

Kushti rarti bor. *(Good night my friend)*
    Duvel parav toot ta teero Romni ta chavies. *(God bless you and your wife and children.)* By the way Dick, Romni is the tatcho lav *(correct word)* for wife. Rom – husband.

Dick's Romani Lesson

The following document is in Henry's handwriting, and is apparently intended as a lesson in Romani, for under each Romanes line is Dick Wade's translation. Some of the Romani is quite clumsy and it may well be one of Henry's early attempts at writing the original language (puri chib) as he learned it. That said, I have a gut feeling that I have come across part of this passage elsewhere, so it may not all be original.

Gaujo see o mush pardal odoi, ta i monoshi akai see Romani chai.Romadi see yov te les. Yoi see kushti tarni gairi te wafedo gairo see yov. Kek see yon bokale ketane. Kek nanai tatcho kova see for a Riomani rakli te rommer a hindo Gaujo moosh pensa lesti.
    Gorgio is the man over there, and the woman here is Gypsy lass. Married is he to her. She is good young woman but bad man is he. Not are they happy together. No not right thing is for a Gypsy girl to marry a dirty Gorgio man like him.
    Dova bauro grai odoi see lesti's grai, ta kova jookli see lesko tai. Kek nanai komova mandi o jookels; hinde see yon, keker penaa graiaw. Graiaw see sor tatcho, kooshto dikin kovaw. I grasni akai see sor kauli, sar yek porno kotor akonyo.
    That big horse there is his horse and this bitch is his too. Not not love I the dogs; dirty are they, not like horses. Horses are all right, good looking things. The mare here is all black with one white piece only.
    O kam see opre, ta dikova les adre i paani. "Kam" see mooshlenjo lav, ta "paani" see joovioko lav. "Joovrel" see a waver lav for "monoshi" or "gairi". Penova mendi "o kam", "o grai", ta "o mooi" ta penova "i paani",

"i graasni", "i monoshi". Maw penessa toot "o paani". Wafedo drom te rokker Romanes see dova! Pensa dinilo Gaujo choorodo! A "choorodo" see a mumper. "Chooro" see o lav for "poor."Kek komi tatche Romanichale jalenna sar hinde choorode. Joovle see yon. Lel trad! "Joova" see o lav for "louse", "joovel" see a waver lav for "monoshi." Joovlo mush see choorado sorkon-cheerus.

The sun is up and I see it in the water. "Kam" is masculine word, and "paani" is feminine word. "Juvel" is another word for "Monoshi" or "gairi". Say we "o kam," "o grai", and "o mooi" but we say "i paani", "i grasni", "i monishi". Don't you "o paani". Bad way to speak Romani is that! Like foolish Gorgio tramp. A "choorodo" is a tramp. "Chooro" is the word for "poor". Never, true Romanies go they with dirty tramps. Lousy are they. Take care! "Joova" is the word for "louse", "joovel" is another word for "monishi" (woman). Lousy man is tramp all time (always).

Meero pooro dad see moosh. Meero poori dai see monoshi. Teero pal see a chavo. Meeri rinkeni pen see rakli. Waver lav for a rakli see "chai". Meero chavo ta chai see chave. Tatcho bauro chavo see yov, ta rinkeni tikni chai see yoi. Lesko nav see 'Nilus; laki nav see Sinfi. Pen teero nav te mandi. Kon see teero dad? Kon see teeri dai? Konaw jinova me teero nav, ta jinessa too savo nav see mandi. O divvus see o cheerus for booti; i raati see o cheerus te jal te sooter. O kam see opre adre o divvus. O choom see opre 'dre i raati. Dosta dosta divvusaw see 'dre a besh Bish beshaw see bauro cheerus. Dossta dromaw jalova me dre yek bersh.

My old father is man. My old mother is woman. Your brother is a boy. My pretty sister is a girl. Other word for a girl is "chai". My son and daughter are children. Right big boy is he, and pretty little lass is she. His name is 'Nilus, Her name is Sinfi. Tell your name to me. Who is your father? Who is your mother? Now I know your name and know you what name is (to) me. The day is the time for work; the night is the time to go to sleep. The sun is up in the day. The moon is up in the night. Many many days are in a year. Twenty years is great time. Many roads go I in one year.

Sorkon mooshaw see dooi yokaw, dooi vastaw ta dooi kanyaw, ta kek yon see dooi nokaw or trin peere. O yok o nok o kan see opre o shero. O vastaw see desh vongushte. Pansh vongushte see yek vast. Yek moosh, yeklo shero. Dooi shere see dooi mooshaw. Dova chooro moosh see yek peero akonyo. See stor bokre dre dova poov. Keker yek bokro adre kolli poovyaw. See dosta bokre pardal odoi? Dik for mandi.Penessa mandi. Yek, dooi, trin, stor, pansh, shov, dooi trinyaw ta yek, dooi storaw, dooi storaw ta yek, desh, desh ta yek, desh ta dooi, desh ta trin, desh ta stor, desh ta pansh, desh ta shov, desh ta dooi trinyaw ta yek, desh ta dooi storaw. Dordi! Dordi! Kino shom mandi; dikessa ti-kokero. Bauro balo see odoi ta poori bauli, ta shov tikne baule. Kooshto mas see baulo mas. Chorova yek o dulla baule for meero hoben te raati.

All men have 2 eyes, 2 hands and 2 ears, but not they have two noses or three feet. The eye, the nose, the ear are on the head. The hands have 10 fingers. Five fingers has one hand. One man, one head. Two heads have two men. That poor man has one foot only. (There) are four sheep in that field. Not sheep in these fields.

(There) are many sheep over there? Look for me. Tell me. 1, 2, 3, 4, 5, 6, 7, 8, 9, 10, 11, 12, 13, 14, 15, 16, 17, 18. Dear oh dear! Tired am I; look after yourself. Big pig is there and old sow and 6 little pigs. Good meat is pork. I shall steal one of these pigs for my food tonight.

Another Romani lesson

The following piece follows the Romani account titled Romano chei adray stariben.

I have wrote these as near to the English way of speaking as I can. You know prala that we say a lot of our sentences different, such as 'Tooti dias o bauri churi katar mush'?, which means, 'Did you given the big knife to the man?' Instead of saying, 'I don't know,' we say, 'Kek jinova me. – not know I.' When we speak Romanes properly a lot of it sounds back to front in English. 'Kelassa toot' – do you see, this is right. 'Kel tooti dik,' this is bad Romanes. So the proper way to say 'Do you see my waggon?' is, 'Kelessa tott mi-vardo?', instead of 'Kel tooti dik meero vardo.' Anyway prala, I know that you know more about this than I do. I will send you more paramish next time. Did you get the addresses of the swag shops all right? You never told me. I once told you that the word 'shan' is used in cant. Some Travellers say Shanengro meaning a man who tells hokobens, they use the word 'shan' for bad and lies. We use the word 'shan' meaning 'have'. 'Shan toot?', 'have you?'. We also say 'shanengro' for 'lawyer' but mostly say 'pukersamengro'.

After an extract taken directly from Smart and Crofton, Henry writes:

Lel-kushtoben pukka mandi if toot jin meero Romanes lavs. Mendi jin sor teero Romanes, sor teero lavs shan tatcho Romanes.

Please tell me if you understand my Romani words. I know all your Romani, all your words are correct Romani.

You once asked me what Curlew was. I have heard some chals say 'kurlew', they meant 'hide it'.

Henry on Dialects

I once told you prala a long whole back that I could 'rokker komi Romanes dan vaniso-waver Romani mush jivo tedivvus.' Would you say I was wrong in making this statement to you? I do believe in my own mind that I jib every dialect in this Temeskri. There is scores of different dialects as you know, same as cherki, star, and chakano, star. Both are tacho lavaw, just different dialects. There is five different words for lawyer and all of them are right. It all depends on which part of the country you are in I suppose it is the same with English, different counties use different words. I would never use the word "shanengro" connected with you. "Shanengro" means the lawyer on the Police's side. prosecuting lawyer, informer. Did you know this prala? Pukeromengero is the lawyer on the prisoner's side. Chibalengero is a barrister often used for lawyer. Komi awaver chairus, Henry.

Three Romani extracts

Three extracts from Smart and Crofton deserve mention in being the only ones to be dated – 4.7.65. They were sent from HM prison Dartmoor. Until the discovery of this letter, it was always assumed that Henry spent all his prison service at Leicester before Dick got him transferred to the Open prison at Ashwell. This proves that Henry spent time at Dartmoor, presumably before transfer to Leicester.

Henry introduces the extracts thus:

Roi – spoon. Posomengro – fork. These are the two words most Chals *(Gypsies)* use but they are not lacho *(good)*.
   Here is a tatchi Romani Paramish prala *(good Gypsy story, Brother.) In fact they are not stories at all, which shows that Henry simply copied them from his source without seeking a translation. In the first piece, there are minor changes made by Henry from the original Smart and Crofton. In the second, the changes are much more significant and, interestingly, Henry changes the standard* puri chib *ending* -o, *into* -a, *which is the normal modern day pronunciation in the Midlands. He also changes one or two words into preferred Romani, for instance substituting* gavamengra *for the more obscure* nashermengro *and* staraben *for* steripen, *and* ratli *for Smart and Crofton's original English* she'll. *For that reason, the second piece (for which cp Smart and Crofton , pp 256-7) follows.*

Second piece
   Tis a latcho door to o forus. Ourli, kini shom. Besh tooki le dei an mook mandi jal ta mong a bitti hoben. Keka ma prala. Tis doosh ta jal adio*. O

bauri rye, as jivs adoi is a pokenyus. He'll bitcha o gavamengra to lel tooti ta stareben. Mooks jal a wova drom. Me beebi's a steromeskri kenaw at a bauri gav fa chorin at a moilesto gav. Ratli be bitchadi paudel. Dik o gavamengra is lelin a mongamengra ta staraben.

It's along way to the city. Yes, I'm tired. Sit yourself down, mother, and let me go to beg a little food. No my brother. It's no good going there. The gentleman who lives there is a magistrate. He'll send the police to put you in prison. Let's go another way. My aunt's in prison now at a large town for stealing at Doncaster. The girl will be transported (to Australia). Look, the policeman is taking a beggar to prison.

The word adio *above is a mis-writing by Henry for* adoi.

Henry ends the letter,

There is a few more verses of this, will send them when I get your paper or notebook. Nearly every tatchi chal jins this paramish *(proper Gypsy knows this story)*. My folki *(people)*, Boswells, have handed a lot of tatchi Romanes paramish *(proper Gypsy stories)* down through the years.

Henry on Romanes

Anyway, prala *(brother)* we can have a good talk about these things when I come to either Ashwell or Lincoln for visits to see you. You will not find any 'cant' words in my Rokaben *(Romani talk)* as I was not brought up to use cant words. My folki *(people)* would never use cant, sometimes today you have to use a lot of 'cant' words otherwise a lot of chals *(the boys)* would not know what you were talking about. I feel sure you know this by mixing and talking to different chals.

A few years back they were proud of their tatchi Rokoben *(proper Romani)*, today they are aladj *(ashamed)* of it. You very rarely see the chals with the trailers with a stick fire and having their food outside, they like to be like Rawnies *(ladies)* and Reis *(lords)* and have their food inside their trailers. My old Dei *(mother)* would turn in his *(sic)* grave if she saw some of the ways of the chals today

Different breeds use different words such as we say vast , some say wast *(hand)*; vardo and wardo *(wagon)*; voodres – woodres *(bed)*; talla – palla *(after)*. You see Dick one breed may use a 'w' and another like us would use 'v' . My people and myself always use the 'v', same as for vudres or voodres – bed. Vudar or vooda – door; others say wooda or wudar. That is the reason it is hard to write Romanes without you know the breed you are writing to . If I was talking to a Penfold or Loveridge or Lovell, I would use the 'w' instead of the 'v'. Wongar – Vongar, they both mean the same – coal. Some chals say wonga for luva – money.

I have given you all different words of different breeds. Biggest part of them are pure Romanes jib *(Gypsy language)*. It is handy for you to know all the breed Rokerben then you can talk to any of them in their own Rokerben. As you know, three parts of my folki cannot read or write and we say the words as we know them. To a jinomeskro *(scholar)* like yourself our way of putting words are all wrong. You see prala that is the best of being a good Delomus – opre *(writer)*. I would never be able to write Romanes like you. I have never had the teaching of writing Romanes, as you can see prala my English spelling is not so good. I only learned in Stariben *(jail)*.

I never went to school. My schooling was going out with my pooro Dadus *(grandfather)* fetching rushes and willows for reseating rush chairs and willows for pegs and 'tushnies' – baskets. Also at the age of seven I used to go out grinding with my pooro Dei *(grandmother)*. You will see when I come on visits to see you, that I can speak Romanes far better than I can write it. I am sure there are not many words I do not know, and that includes all different breeds' Rokerben. If I make mistakes in spelling please forgive me. It is different talking to anyone as you know. You can pick up straight away what kind of Rokerben they use. We have so many different words meaning the same thing as you know:

Apre – opre paudel – pardelo are see;
Shan have shan- si;
Pepper – Tattamengri;
Danomeskri – mustard;

These two are the tatchi lavs but you will hear a lot more tatti – kova . Dandameskri these also mean pepper.

Here is another: Xotchermongri; Tattermengro; Masali. These three words are all used for frying pan. *(Note that the letter X in Xotchermengri, above, is meant to represent the Romani sound 'ch', pronounced as in the 'ch' of Scots loch.)*

Some say talengala – pepper
Shoon – Listen
Some say shunta
Have – Shan
Nai
Kele me nai chichi te pen ke yon — I have nothing to say to them

There is another difference:

Moro Dadus jivs pray doy kon tirous nav. – moro Dadus jivs adre miduveleski – tem kom teero nav *(Our father who lives in heaven, hallowed be thy name.)*

These both mean the same. Me ghiom avree. Me jaldas avree garadas de doods – you garad o duds

You can see prala there is so many different words and sayings . I could give you scores of different words. A lot put pen at the end of words, we put ben.

Rivoben – linen

Stariben keliben meriben etc.

Jivoben is the word for life, we always say jivomus

We say Ruknies for trousers; some say bulengreis. Kal – ?????. a lot say Calum

Stikka or stika. I think it is one k. A few say Stekas or stigher. These three words all mean gate.

Stikla – jug swigler – pipe. A few say sweglar our word swigler.

Ruzliben – power

Shuzlo – strong

Delom – opre write

Delomus – opre writing

Del opre – read

Do you use these words, prala.

Spiniars – carrots

We say – pukerin kosht, same thing but said different.

Welsh Romani

The list below is of interest in being clearly authentic, since it contains words which are non-Romani or amended words. I believe it to be 100% authentic. That said, the Welsh Romani purist might not always equate it to Sampson's Dialect of the Gypsies of Wales: It is Welsh Romani as Henry heard it, probably from the Prices. Cp the main Welsh Romani list below.

The pooro tatcho Romanes jib *(The proper old Gypsy language)* is more or less the same amongst all Romani-chalaw *(Gypsies)*. It is just a few different families who put some of their own jibberish in it.

Even pure Welsh Romanies use the same only for a few different words such as,

Vissa, come	Keraw, boil
Ker-abba, make haste	Lulla, blush
Bishava, rain	Okaw, eyes
Dino, given	Poordas, stairs
Chinda, shilling	Kurri-tin
Holon, landlord	togram, peg
Ghias, sing	Moth, drunk

Jom, went

Ne, he

Les, has

Jolta, go

Chalava, bother

Wi, with

Ko, to

Munthos, month

Sikermengro, signpost

Misali, table

Mulla, devil

Karlo, throat

Trineskni, three shillings

Duikolor, two shillings

Bulengries, trousers

All their other words are more or less like ours. They always say 'keker' and never use the word 'Dordi'

Dordi   a lot

Dordi-Hoki

I am rather puzzled as to the significance of these last few words.

I would love to know where you learned your Romanes. Surely there is never a book with all the Romani lavaw *(words)* in that you know. Who could have ever written one *(sic)*, as Romanies years ago could neither read or write.

It has me puzzled wondering if you are a tatcho Romani-chal, as I could never imagine a Gorgio knowing so much – are you sure Dick that none of your folki were Romani folki? I cannot believe that some were in your family *(and that)* there is no Romani-ratveli *(Gypsy blood)*.

(I don't think this requires any comment from me!)

A short lesson in Romani

I have write these as near to the English way of speaking as I can. You know prala *(brother)* that we say a lot of our sentences different:

Such as, Tooti dias o bauri churi batar mush? Which means, Did you give the big knife to the man?

Instead of saying, I don't know, We say, Kek jinova me – Not know I.

When we speak Romanes properly a lot of it sounds back to front in English.

Kelassa toot – do you see? This is right. Kel tooti dik? This is bad Romanes.

So the proper way to say, Do you see my wagon – is – Kelassa toot mivardo. Instead of Kel tooti dik meero vardo.

Anyway prala, I know that you know more about this than I do. I will send you more paramish *(stories)* next time. Did you get the addresses of the swag shops alright? You never told me. I once told you that the word Shan is used in cant. Some travellers say Shanengro, meaning a man who tells hokobens. They use the word shan for bad and lies. We use the word shan meaning "have". Shan-toot, have you. We also say Shanengro for lawyer but mostly say Pukerisamengro.

Regional Romani Variations

You will be able to see prala *(brother)* with all the notes I have sent you, the different words you can use for certain words. All the words I send you are tatcho Romanes *(proper Romani)*, no cant words included. I can assure you on that.

I should think prala that Romanes is a very hard language for anyone who was not brought up to speak it from a child to learn. There are so many different dialects, and to be able to talk to any Romani-foki *(Gypsy people)* a person would have to know them all. There is still a few Romani-foki like myself who knows them all. You see prala a Sussex Romani calls hair hamel instead of bal. We use the word hamel for attack, but we also know it means hair to the South of England chies and chals.

Some Romani foki never use the word muttermongri but piameski *(both meaning tea)*. We never use piameski, only if we are talking to a south country Traveller. They call a water well a hanikus, we say parnieskri hev. Different breeds have different names for colours. Bad, wafedo, vasavo. These two words are pure Romanies but are used in different breeds. We say wafedo, a South Country chal would say vasavo. Saster ravnos chirklo, iron sky bird, aeroplane. Brishindesko ravnos, rainy sky. Such words as these are used by all Romani folki.

Now you can see prala how many different words there are meaning the same thing, and all tatcho Romanes. There are hundreds more, as you know. I am making a big list out with all the Romani words meaning one thing. This is what I mean. Lel kushtoben *(and)* komyer both mean please; hupasin *(and)* kor both mean shout, puri dai *(and)* daieski Dai both mean grandmother; misali *(and)* salamanka both mean table.

You see prala the word saster, iron, is universal, so are hundreds more Romani words.

You will know Dick that nearly every different Romany breeds as different words for some things that is the reason I have mixed my Romanes a bit. It will give you an idea of the different words used in parts of the country such as South of England Chals call tea Ramenski although the Coopers and other south of England Chals use different words than the Midland and and North Chals.

I feel sure it would be a very hard thing to do write a Romanes dictionary as there are so many different words used for the same meaning.

Here is a word – Police; here are the Romanes words for it, they are all
tatchi: Gavengro – Gavamengro – Gava mush- Prastamingri Muskra.
These are all tatchi Romani lavs and are understood by all tatchi Romani
chals – choose which one you used. Here is another: Gamekeeper – Vesh-
engro – yogmush – Vesheskro mush. The Taylors call trousers Bulengries
where we call them Rukenies. Pepper – we call it Tallamengri, south of
England Dander; North Chals they understand our words and we understand theirs. This is where a Gorgio who has travelled with one breed
would be beat with the language. I feel sure you know this.

A lot of the words I have sent you are used by other Romani Chals. But
biggest part of them are used by my folki; eski – some call it tattilon. (*do
not understand this phrase. Eski may be a mis-write for esti, meaning for,
and tattilon is presumably tattiben, meaning heating.*)

Stariben is our lav for prison – south of England, Steripen. I could give
you a hundred and one different words meaning the same things if you are
interested. Please let me know. You see Prala, the trouble is that a lot of
Romani chals never travel out of their own county for that is the main
reason that they stick to their own Rokabon.

Another thing is they use a lot of cant today. Instead of saying Vong-
nishni *(ring)* they say grauni which you must have heard at different
Romani fairs. Biggest part of the Northern travellers call tuvels *(tobacco)*
– foggus. I doubt very much if there is fifty Romani chals who would
understand your mized of English and Cant with it.*(The word mized here
may be an error for mixed, or Shelta, meaning 'confusion'.)* I know I have
spoken to different breeds and a lot of my Romanes has been like double
Dutch to them. I thank God that my children and folki understand Tatchi
Romanes *(good Romani)*, also my juvvels folki ta Rokka Latcho Romanes
(also my wife's people and speak good Romani).

Please let me know if you want different words for things, they may
come in very useful at times when tooti opre o drom *(you go on the road)*.
I am writing a lot of paramish for you, a bit of it is about my folki and
myself and juvvel. Will send it when finished.

Have you ever heard the Romani Word Chitibok – it is a three legged
kettle iron with a chain hanging from the top it folds in when you have
finished with it. *(Note that Chitibok is not actually Romani but Cant.)*

Some Little Notes from Henry

Please excuse me if I have put them down twice. I just put them down as they come into my head.

I suppose you know all these lavaw prala but there may be an odd one new to you.

Enough for you to be going on with for now. Any English words that you do not know in Romanes please let me know and I will send them.

From the back page of the prison notebook: Kamlo pal, This should just about make your Romani lavaw list complete. Please let me know if there are any words I have not write *(sic)* down in any of the lists I have sent you. Please forgive me if I have sent you the same word more than once. I have sent you so many I forget which ones I have sent, and the ones I have not sent I have written them down as they come into my mind. Please excuse my spelling prala. Teero prala sorkon chairus, *(Your brother for all time),*Henry.

From part way through the same notebook: Kamlo prala. These lists of words should just about make your collection up. If there is any words I have not written in any of the lists I have sent you, please let me know. I will be more than pleased to send them. I have just put down words that came into my head. So please excuse me if I have wrote a word down more than once. You see prala I have not kept a list myself, so cannot remember all the words I have sent, so it is quite possible I have sent you a few words more than once. I have put a few different dialects prala as you will notice but all tatcho Romani lavaw.

If you want the names of any other birds please put names on a piece of paper and send it. That includes fish-towns-counties – anything that grows or crawls such as sapengri – snake, kermo – worm. Also any word in English that you dio not know in Romanes. I am certain I can give you the tatcho lavaw adre Romanes. Mandi kefi te kair-posh tooti wi lavaw tooti keker jin. Mandi penehava tooti jin len so ordoi estist yek o dui tooti kek jin. *(I am certain I can give you the correct word in Romani. I wish to present you with words you don't know. Maybe I will tell you some you don't know, one or two you don't know.)*

From a mixed page containing songs and Romanes:
You will know Dick that nearly all different Romany breeds have different have different words for some things, that is the reason I have mixed my Romanes a bit. It will give you an idea of the different words used in parts of the country such as South of England chals call tea Rameskri, although the Coopers and other South of England chals use different words than the Midland and North chals. They understand our

words and we understand theirs. This is where a gorgio who has travelled with one breed would be beat with the language. I feel sure you know this. A lot of the words I have sent you are used by other Romani chals but biggest part of them are used by my folki and Midland and North chals.

9. VOCABULARY

Henry's Anglo Romani Word List

This consists of 12 foolscap pages with the listed Romani in random order, some written on prison paper, sundry lists in letters, and a prison service notebook consisting of 12 pages of Romani . The note book is also random, but Henry has obviously attempted to place them in some kind of logical order, for instance by listing together nouns and adjectives ending in -alo, -eskero/i, and -ben. Here and there are notes from Henry. In the following, Henry's notes are given first, and these are followed by an alphabetical list of the Romani. His listings do not follow Smart and Crofton, and there are some significant differences, but of course he may well have learned many from Smart and Crofton's book. Some words may be from Derek Tipler, who was himself a great 'borrower' of other peoples' recordings.

Though Henry claims that all, his words here are Romani, a few are Cant or Dialect, obvious examples being docket, driz, fergio, fiz, fricha, joig and sanus. Three other words need special comment.

Marime is the Continental equivalent of Anglo and Welsh Romani Mokhadi. I am unaware of its ever having been used in Britain, though it is not impossible that it was brought here by one or other of the influxes of foreign Gypsies. I am more inclined to take the less charitable view that Henry came across the word in the Journal of the Gypsy Lore Society *and had not realised that it was not, in fact, British Romani.*

Another very interesting word is nila. This is a borrowing from Arabic, and means blue. Henry presumably picked this up whilst on the run with the Bedouin in North Africa. Again, I know of no evidence that it has entered British Romani but it is the kind of word which could easily do so, being first used by one family, then spreading to others. However, in this case, nila (Romanified as nilo) is still a one-man word.

Another fascinating word is puzshakero, for marksman. It is a very good Romani word, but to the best of my knowledge the root word, puzsha, is only found in Scoto Romani with the meaning gun. It is probable that Henry has found this written in JGLS or elsewhere, but without direct evidence, he should be given the benefit of the doubt.

Finally, note the use of the rare prefix bi – meaning without or not.

Abrea – going
achilo – stagnant
acoi – here
adlimos – idle
adray – in
adray pesko chairus – in his lifetime
adrin – inside
adrom – away
adusta chairuses – many a time; much
aglal – before anything, in front of
ajar – again
ajaw – so, as
akersesko – squire
akonya – alone
akyasavo – such as this
alav – kindle
alay – down
alriz – lace
ana – bring
and – to bring, have
andadas – they brought
andadom – I brought
andadom opre – I brought up
andas – he brought
andedom – I brought
andessa – you bring
andia – brought
andlo– fetch
ando – brought
andova – I bring
anduro – farther
anerjal – against
anglanani rig – front
ani – whether; caused
Anitrakero – Englishman
anjer – strip
ankair – to begin
anlo – brought
anlo opre – brought up
annerela – it brings
anvias – come on
apopli – again
aposh – against
apre – in
asar – also
aser –lift
asivasin – to join
astilo – wait

asti si – it can be, it is to be
ataviben – forgiveness, mercy
atchava – I stop
atchdo – stay
atchiben – stopping place
atchimasko parni – stagnant water
atchimaskro/maskero – station
atchin opray apopli – Resurrection
atch pawli kanni – guinea fowl
ativabin – forgiveness
atrasht – frightened
atut – cross
avakei – come here
avali – yes
avas – to come
avava – I come
avel – he comes
avenna – they come
avessa – you come
av kater – should
av kom – could
avo – you
avos – come
avree – out
avri – out
avrial – outside
avri-avri – abroad
avri pesko tan – out of place
awaver divvus – tomorrow
awel – be
azer – to lift
azerdas – he lifted

bahtali – happy
bai – bough
bai – sleeve
bairo – boat
bakterimaski – magic
bal – hair
Balaws – Hernes
Balengro – Gray (family)
baleno – hairy
baleno bokro – hairy sheep
baleno matcho – herring
banyer – to bend
banyerava – I bend
baresko ker – stone house
baresk(e)ro – grindstone

barshani – mule
barvalipen – wealth, wealthy
barvalo – rich; diamond
Barvelo Tem – Yorkshire
Barvelo Tem Matchesko Gav – Hull
bauri – big
Bauri Beresta Gav – Liverpool
Bauri Driz Gav – Nottingham
bauri holomengra – glutton
Bauri lon gav – Northwich
Bauri machengro (munthos) –
   November
bauri pukenyuski-beshopen-
   pukersomengro – barrister
Bauri Veshaw Tem – Essex
bauro – deep
bauro boshno chirklo – pheasant
bauro rasher – bishop
bauro rokkerin chiriklo – parrot
bavalesko vardo – car
Bavalyakero (munthos) – March
bavalyako – stormy
bavalyer – to winnow
baviakero – windmill
baw – edge
bawlesko bal – bristle
bawri boshimengri – harp
bawri gavesti dromaw – streets
bawro – chief
bawro bavalesti vardo – lorry
bawro staribenengro – prison chief
bebee – aunt
beeno – born
beeno mullo – stillborn
bengesko gairo – enemy
bereneskro dud – lighthouse
beresto tilomengro – anchor
berk – breast
bershor – years
besh – sit
beshimaskeri maneri – sofa
beshiben – beside
beshipen – sessions
biano mullo – still born
bi-baktalo – unlucky
bichardo pardel – transported
bichaviben – sentence
bi-doshako – harmless

bignas – begin
bignipen – beginning
Bignomus chairus – Spring
bikonyo – alone
bilav – melt
bi-masesko – vegetarian
bish – 20
bi-shilalo – sheltered
bisser – forget
bisserdom – I forgot
bitchadas – he sent
bitchama – sentence
bitcharava – I sent
bitchas – sent
bitcherenna – they sent, they send
bitcherava – I sent
bitcherdas – he sent
bitcherenna – they sent
bi-trashedo – fearless
bitta kawlo (munthos) – February
bitteder – fainter
bitti – small
bitti barengro keliben – marbles
bittiben – smallness; small quantity
bittider – fainter
bitti gavesti dromaw – lanes
bitti lalo pobi – cherries, small red
   apple
Bitti Peeresto Koppa Gav –
   Kidderminster
bitti rinkeno rokkerin chirklo –
   budgerigar
bitti skamin – chair mender
Bitti Tem – Rutland
bitti trad – hint
bivan – green, raw
bivan kosht – green wood
bivan mas – raw meat
bivan tan – green tent
blajvano – bold
blav – suspended
bodyer – feel
boinelopus – swaggering
boiri parni – sea
boker – to starve
bolaviben – baptism
bolesko – pig sty
bonek – to hold

bongno – left side, etc
bongo – wrong; lame; crooked
Bongo Kongri Gav – Chesterfield
boobni boshno (chiriklo) – peacock
booino – proud
boot boot – very much
bootodair – most
bor – friend
bora – great
borali – greatest
borengri – hedge stake
boriakero ta gutrenengro – hedger and
   ditcher
Bori Gav – London
borodir – greater
Boronashemescrutan – Epsom Race
   Course
borshana – weak
bosharus – cough
boshav – music
boshaviben – music
boshimangri – fiddle
boshimengriako kosht – fiddle bow
boshtardus chiriklo – cuckoo
boshtik – saddle
bov – oven
Bozlemengro – Boswell
brishameskris – umbrella
Brishindesko munthos – April
brishindesko ravnos – rainy sky
brishindeskri/kero – rainbow
brishindo – rained
brishno – hail
brunos – brown
budika divvus – shopping day
budikamengero – shopkeeper
bulengries – trousers
bulomengro – backside
bulsta – green
bunnerin – building
bunyela – cider
burla – bee
bute – much
bute bute – very much
butti – work
buzno – goat

Cambria gav – Cambridge

chairas – time
chairuses – sometimes; time while
chakanengro – astrologer
chakano – star
chakano dudus – starlight
chalava – bother
chalav – to touch
cham – tin
chamyer – to chew
chamyor – cheeks
changyer – to kneel
charava – I touch
chavali –mate
chavalo – grassy
chaveskro – little boy
chavori – chicken, chicken hearted
chaw – grass
chawyer – to graze
chein – moon
cheldo – yellow
cheldo shol chirklo – canary
chepalo – sharp
cherki – star
cherki dudus – starlight
chibalengero –lawyer, barrister
chibalengri – scold
chibando – sermon
chibengro – linguist
chibyer – to lick
chichi – nothing
chik – dust
chikalo – dirty
chikeno kolli – brick
chiket – to soil
chin cut
chin bal moi – shaving
chinengro – postman
chinimangeri – letter
chingaraw – sparks
chingoras – sparks
chinger – bother
chingerimasko – quarrelsome
chingeripen – to have a row
chinoben – wound
chin odotar – straight on
chinomengro – hatchet
chin-opray – straight up
chin-talay – straight down

chiriklesto nok – bird's beak
chitti – nothing
chitti-bok – three legged kettle prop, tripod
chiv avri – put away
chivdom – I put
chivestri te voodrus – confined
chiv les adray tutti shero – remember
chivs – puts
chivvin tulipen prey da chokkars – greasing the shoes
chivlo gorjio – justice of the peace
choir – steal
chol – whole
cho(l)lo – whole, entire
chome(-a)ni – something
chomono – something
chong – knee, hill
choom – kiss
chooro bitto dandomengro chiriklo – bat
Choovena Tem – Worcestershire
chooventas – cunning, sly
choovikan – witch, wizard
chorda – cover (verb and noun)
chordas – covered
chordom – I stole
chorien – poverty
chorn – lock of hair
chornalo – curly
choro – plate
chorodi – outcast
chororo – outcast
chorvano ker – workhouse
choryer – to graze
choveo ker – workhouse
chuibengri – caterpillar
Chumba Gav — Derby
Chumba kalesko Tem – Derbyshire
Chumba Tem – Derbyshire
chumoni – somebody, something
chungalo – loathsome
chungar – to spit
chunger – spittle
churelo – bearded
churi – knife
churiengro morlo – knife grinding, knife grinder

Churiesta Gav – Sheffield
churimengri vardas – grinding barrow
churoknay – mumper
churomengro – tramp
chuveno – humble
chuvno gorjio – Justice of the Peace

da – and, the
dadesko – fatherly
dadesko dadrus – grandfather
dadlo – bastard
daieski dai –grandmother
dandimengri chor – nettles
danomeskri – pepper
dariav – sea
deenos – knock
deep deeras — deeper
del – give; I give
deldom – I gave
delenako dudengri kosh – match
del kan – listen
del lav katar – answer
del opray – write, read
del opray vastesti rokkerben – writing, to write
derav – to frighten
des – gave
desch – ten
deshniben – slavery
deshni rarti chiriklo – owl
desto horri – one and sixpence
dias – I gave
dick tan ta duva – did you see that?
dikasimengeri – mirror
dikasimengro – photograph
dikas mendi – let us look
dikesti hev – window
dikimengri – picture
dikimengro – mirror
dikkin hev – window
dikio – look here
dikno – I saw; seen
dikomengro – watchman
dikomus – eyesight
dikova – I see
dik palla – watch
dik pawlay – look back, remember
dili – hearty

dilleri – clever
dinvariben – stupidity
diora – watch,
dir – dear
diviengro ker – assylum
divio – wild
doieng(e)ri – net
dooi lendi – they two
dooi mendi – we two
dooker – ache
dooket – pedlar's certificate
doomeskno grei – broken winded horse
door avree – a long way off
doordair – further
doordair avri – further away
door dooriel – far far away
Door doriev temesti – East Anglia
door dosta – far away
doodum – womb
doori – navel
dooriben – distance
door paulay – far back
door ta poshay – from far and near
dordi dordi – oh dear
dori – ribboned
doriengeri – net
dorier –to lace
dorya poringero – watch chain
doshvalo – harmful, mischevious
dosta – enough, plenty
Dova-Gav-kei-o-shorokni-rais- jiv –
　　Cambridge
dovalay – down there
dov-e-lo – what is that?
Dovrus – distance
doyai – river
drabengri – druggist
drabengro – doctor
drak – grape
drakengro ker – vinery
dralano drom – by road
dree – into
driz –lace
drochin – dew
dromos – roadway
drom sikkerinengri – sign post
drovenelas – forcibly
druveno – tiresome

dui – two
dui desch – 20
dui muiengri – gas mask
dui pansch ta yek – 11
dui – efta – 14
dui efta yek – 15
dui-engo – 18
dui-engo-ta-yek – 19
dui lendi – they too
dui mendi – we two
dui-ochta – 16
dui-ochta-yek – 17
dui pansch ta yek – 11
dui schok – 12
dui schok ta yek – 13
dui tengs ta yek – nineteeen
dui vasteno – two handed
dui vasteno koro – two handed cup
dukav – to hurt
dukkerela i vastesa – fortunes by hand
dulla – those
dulla kolla – those things
dumbo – mountain
dumeskero –hunchback
dur – far
durer – remove
duril – berries
durmi – among
durodirus – longer, further
dush – wrong
dushalo – unlucky
dusherari – difficult
duva sas a laj – that was a shame
Duveleskero – religious
Duvelesto chairus – eternity
Duvelkanesto – holly
Duvel nasherdo – God forsaken
Duvels ken gairo – preacher

efta – seven
engo – nine
esti – for
estis(t) – maybe
exunyes varda – shafts

faino – grand
fergio– fig
ferri – entice

ferridiro – better
fettadair – better
finishin – hall
fino – fine
finyer – to enlighten, tell a secret
fiz – charm
foki – people
fordel – forgive
foros – city
foshadi – quarrel
fosheno – false
fosheno vongushni – imitation gold ring
foshiben – falseness
fricha – fridge

gad (kosht) kova – clothes pegs
gampana – bell
gani – embrace
garav – hide
garaviben – hiding
garonas, garovas – secretly
gavamush – police
gavengro – policeman
gavotemengro – this-country- man
ghiom – I went
ghiom adre – I entered
ghiom palla – I followed
ghiveskeri – harrow
Ghiveskro munthos – August
ghivesti chairus – harvest
gias – ago; went
gilaviben – singing
giliava – we sing
gilienna – they sing
gilivenna – they sang
giliola – he sang
gilo – gone
gilyaw – bills for ragging etc
ginya – reckon
giom – I went
gister – trunk, chest
givamengro – farmer
giveski henli – scythe
givesko chairus – harvest time
givesko ker – farmhouse
Giveskro – August
glaver – solder
glinja – count (money etc)

glistas – to shine
godiakeri – bell
godiako – noisy
godli-kelomengrio chirklo – pea-wit
goodli – summons
goorono chirklo – sparrow
gostago – thick
Gozivero (or Gozwero) tem – Yorkshire
gozvero – sly, cunning
gozwero – cunning
granza – barn
granza chiriklo – sparrow
grasniben – cantankerous
greeno – green
greiesta chok – horse shoe
greiesta grasni – mare
geriesta menegro – horse collar
greiesta peleno – stallion
greiesto koppa – horse rug
groveneska mas – beef
grovneski bul – beef steak
gruveno roozho – cowslip
gudlimengro – bailiff
gudnengriaw – parsnips
gurni – cucumber
gurniava – cucumber
gurunin – thunder
guzer – tremble

hagiben – worrying
hai – understand
hai aduva – understand that
haiaw – understand
hairas – harness
hairi – leg
hamav – yawn
hamel – attack
hamel – hair
hameviben – yawning
hamil– attack
hanav –to scratch
handadas – they brought
handadom – I brought
handava – I dig
handessa – you bring
handilo – dug
handiom – I dug
hanikus/haniko – water well

hanj – itch
Hanjvalo tem – Scotland
hanlo – brought
hashas – to join
hashiben –splice
hatav – tickle
haurongo – copper
Haveliakeri – Cinderella
hawra – penny
heb – sky
heka – haste
hekor kair – *(not trans.)*
heni – spring (water)
herengro matcho – crab
hevakeri – water well
hevengri – shutters
hgas – worry
hindi ker – lavatory
Hindi Temengra – Irishman
Hindi Temengri Kongri – Catholic
    Church
Hindo Tem – Ireland
hoieriben – rage
hoiniben – angry
hoinomus – vexed, angry
hokano dai – step mother
hokaw – deceive
hokiben – lie
hokki – haste
hokter – jump
hol – eat
holdom – I ate
holomeskro chirikla– cuckoo
holov – stocking
hongralo – horrible
honj – itch
honjedom – I itched
honji – mange
hotcherimongri – frying pan
hud – squeeze
hudilo – grasp
hufa – cap
hufengri gairo – captain
hukki – already
hulani – landlady
hulano –landlord
hulyer – to part
hulyeriben – separation

hunalo – roar, roaring
hupasin – shout, shouting
huredo – miniature
hutlo – shallow
hutto – hung up

iv – snow
Iveskro Munthos – January
Iveskro – January
izengri – clothes line
izengro – clothier

jadilo – tear
jafra – as such, such
jafri – such
jafri kovaw – such things
jal – go
jalamengri – train
jalava – I go
jaldas – I went
jal shukker – go slowly
jas(a) mengi – let us go
java – I go
jav tavesto – cotton
jib adray savo – in what language?
Jibengro – *(meaning unsure – appears
    to be* bailiff *but normally means*
    barrister.)
Jido – alive
jin – to know
jinaw – I know
jindas – he knew
jinuoennaa – they knew
jinusava – we know
jinussela – he knew
jinusenna – they know
jinusoava – I knew
jiv(a)mus – year
jivo – alive
joig – shilling
jookli – bitch
jukel – dog
juker – to track
justa konaw – just now
Jutano – Jew
juvalo –lively
juviaki stardi – bonnet

kabni – mare in foal
kai – where
kai na koi – neither here nor there
kaird kin – sharpened
kairdom – I made
Kairi Kamora – Home Office
kairikeni – housekeeper
kairova – I make
kairs – do
kaisheno – silken
kaisheno dikla – silk handkerchief
kakavengri – tramp, tinker
kalengri – buttermilk
kali – treacle
kaliko sawlo – tomorrow morning
kal kelimus – cheese making
kam – sun
kamakonyo – a mouse
kambri – pregnant
kam(i)eskero – sun dial
kamlo – sunny
kamoro – room
kandava – stink
kander – to stink
kandeskri – earwig
kandesko rokkeriben – telephone
kandilo – attentive
kanela – it stinks
kanjones – unknown
kanna – what time is it, when
kanna sig – by and by, soon, presently
kanomengri – earring
kanomengro tatcho sonakei – solid gold
    earings
kanro – thorn
kar – shout, call
karin – gleam
karo – thorn
kas – hay
kasaukay – deaf
Kaseskro (munthos) – July
kashti – leg
kasoni – billhook
kat – build
katar – to
katcher – blaze
katsaki verani – nail file
katsies – scissors

kaula – black
Kaula Bals – Lee (family)
Kaula Gav – Birmingham
Kaula Tem – Staffordshire
kauli boreskro – blackthorn
kaulikano – blackish
kaulikano chei – brunette
Kaula Parni Gav – Blackpool
kauli rauni – turkey
kaulo – black
Kaulobals – Lees
kaulo chiriklo – black bird
kaun – ear
kaun vongishti – earrings
kauro – thorn
Kauromengra Gav – Aldershot
Kauromengra ta Veshengra Gav –
    Hampshire
kavakai – this here
kavi – kettle
kavi kosht – kettle prop
kavi sastern– kettle iron
kavadoi – that there
kawlikani – brunette
kawli kareskro – blackthorn
kawliko – yesterday
kawlo dirus – blacker
kawlo rarteskro – dark night
ke – to
kefi – wish
kefidus – wished
kefipen – wishing
kek – no
kek adusta nevvi – nothing much new
kek adray lin – empty
kekauvia – kettle
kekavi saster – kettle iron
kekavisko saster – kettle iron
kek av kater – should not
kek av kom – could not
kekavvi mokto – kettle box under back
    of wagon
Kek Chumni Tem – Lincolnshire
kekkano mush's poov – a common
kekkeno – none, nothing
kek-kom – to hate
kek-komeni – nobody
kek-komi – no more, never. Did not

kek-mi-kom – would not
kek nanay – is not
kekovengra – tramp
kek sig – no right
kel – to play, put
kela – he dances
kelava – I dance
kelassa – we dance
keldas – done
kelenna – they dance
kelepen – spree
kelessa – you dance
keliben wardensa – card party
kelimas – hornpipe
kelimaski tanas – dancing booth
kelimeskri – woman dancer
kelimus – making
keloben – quarrel
kelobens – trouble
kelomengro – performer
kelsta – blue
kelyeriben – merry making
kenaw – already
ken sigaw – immediately
kerado – boiled
keras mengi – let us make
kerav – cook
keraviben – cooking place
keravimaskeri – saucepan
keravit – to do; do it
ker bongo – to bend
keriben – business, behaviour
kerikeni – house keeper
kerimus – behaviour
ker kek – do not
kerlengro – feneed (?)
Kermo – worm
kermo chiriklo – thrush
kerova me – I will do
keseriben – matter
kesser – care
kesserova – care
Kestermengri Gav – Newmarket
Ketri – towards
kettenus – together
kiler – bloom
kileskero – churn
kileskri – butterfly

kil koro – buttercup
kimba – book
kindo – sweaty, wet
kinger – to tease
kinlo – tired
kino ta bokalo – tired and hungry
kino ta hoyano – tired and cross
kinyermengro – a bore to people
kirivo – cashier, clerk
kishano diklo – silk neckerchief
kishli – thin
kister – ride
kistermengro – rider
kistero – rider
kitchemeskro – innkeeper
klaimas – to climb
klastengro – pliers
kleembra – table
klisin – key
klispas – to lisp
klininas – to lock
Klizinaw – Lock (family)
klisomengra – bridewell
klisomengro – rabbit trap
klura – colour
kluras – to colour
kluriben – colouring
kodav – to hurt
kokalengro – skeleton
kokalo – bone
kokalus – bone
kokolo – rib
kokoolas – thigh
kokoriben – solitude
kola – those
koli – these
kolla – these
kolyaw – bones
kom – like
komaben chiriklo – love bird, dove
kom bawri – pregnant
kombri – pregnant
komdilo – popular
komeli – darling
Komeloeskro – Lovell (family)
komelo gairo – friend
komesa – you wish
komeskro – lover

komi – more
komiben – love
komimasko giliben – love song
komipen lil – love letter
komodair – more
komomusti – however
konleder – kindest
komles – pleasantly
komlo – loving
komlo baval – fair wind
komomusti – however
komyer – please
komyerdo – pleased
konglier – comb
kongnusti – comforts
kongri puv – church yard
kon sigaw – just now
konta – fork
konya – quiet
konyiben – peace
koonshi – corner
Koppa Gav Tem – Wiltshire
Koppari Gav – Witney
kor – shout; brow
korauna – crown
koraviben – place of call
kordi – blind
Kordum Gav – Kidderminster
korimangero – hawker
korni – ill tempered
korodiben – blindness
korodomus – blindness
koroesko vasteskero – cup handle
korro sastarn – pot hook
koru – cup
korubikna – hawker; pot hawker
kosh chinamengri – saw
koshchirikla – aeroplane
kosh pukka drom – sign post
koshtani purdimangeri – flute
kosht chinamengri – saw
kosht pukker drom – signpost
kosser – to wipe
kotorendi – pieces, fragment
kotorendi poktan – pieces of cloth
kottorengeris – bits and pieces
kovantsa – anvil
kovli – fine

kovvas – things
kovvus – something
kovyer – smooth
krafnier – nail
kraila – toad
kraliska rook kitchema – Royal Oak
    Public House
kralisko – castle
kralis matcho chirklo – kingfisher
krarfonengriaw – turnips
krili – funny
Krukingros – Sunday; sun
Krukingros Divvus – Sunday
kuch bar – diamond
kuchikano – careful
kuini – quiet
kuknidkay – nettle
kumi – quiet
kumini – fellow
kumoni – somebody
kunji – narrow, close
kunjikano – secret
kunsas – corner
kur – to beat
kuri – tin
kurido – beaten
Kurko krukingrus divvus – Sunday
kurlo – throat
kuro – thorn
kuroko – week
Kusakos – Saturday
kush – to blame
kusher-opray – to flatter anyone
Kushti Chokka Gav – Luton
Kushti Koro Gavesti – Black Country,
    Staffordshire
kushtodar, kushtodirus – better
kushtomus – goodness
kusi – little
kusi rarti dudesti – moon
kuv – to plait
kuvdo – plaited
kuvimangero – weaver

lachas mengi – let us find
lacho – good
ladiben – a burden, load
ladipen – fine, penalty

ladipen chirklo – swallow
lalo –red
lalo halomengri – radish
lalo pabo – tomato
lalo Gav – Reading
Lalo Peeri Gav – Redford, Retford
lanani peeri – forefeet
lanano – foremost
latch(d)as meng(h)i – let us find
latchipen – goodness
Latcho butti gav – Coventry
lati – her
latimangro – detective
latimeskro lil – guide book
lats – kick
latsiben –kicking
lav – word; to read or write
lavado – dumb
lavengro lil – dictionary, almanack
Lavines Tem – Wales
le – they
leeno – taken
lel – get, put
lel kushtoben – please
lel opray – apprehend
lelova – I do
lel veeno – take notice
lenay – lake
lenghi – theirs
lengris – their, of them
lensa – with them
lenti – their
lesti – him, his
lestist – maybe
lestis kukero – himself
lias – he took
lil – letter
likalo – nitty
lilay – summer
Lilaiesko munthos – June
Lilayesko – June
lilayesko lil – almanack
Lilengreski Gav – Cambridge
lilengro ker – library
lilesko kolli – paper
lilesti – book
limalengro zumin – snail broth
limala– snotty

limaloo nok – snotty nose
lindalo – drousy
lino – taken, caught
liom – took, I took, got
liri – law
lishedo – horrified
lishiben – nervousness
Livenomengri gav – Burton on Trent
Liveno(r) Tem – Kent
livenormengris – hops
livinako koro – beer mug
lo – he
lodiben – lodging
lodimaskro ker – lodging house
lokeder – lighter
lokker – to lighten
loko – heavy
loli – rose
lolyeriben – blushing
londeskeri – salt cellar
longay – fame
longo duro – farther
loor – rob
looriben – taking
looripen chiriklo – jackdaw
luber – unchaste
luli– farthing
luller – vanish
Lundrameskro jib – London talk,
     Cockney

mach – fish
mairas – blaggard, trouble maker
maklo – painter
mal – die
malawar – dead
maleli – smutty
malyaw – companions
mamuchi – midwife
manch – to take comfort
mancha –perhaps
manchi tu – clear up
mangkay – before (of time)
mankay – before (of time)
mankay posh divvus – morning
man(n)ay – forbid
mansi – with me
mantchi-tu – cheer up

marikiengro – confectioner
marime – unclean*
masali – frying pan
masengro mawin ker – slaughter house
maseski churi – carving knife
maskal – amidst
maskal o rukka – in the middle of the
    forest
maskari – middle
Matchesko Gav Ten – Norfolk
maw – don't
maw dusher – don't harm
mazalo – frosty
mel – die
melali – smutty
Melali Gav – Sheffield
melano – amber, yellow
menakeri – necklace
menakero – collar
merenna – they do
merikli – bead
meriklo – gem
meriklongeri/meriklengeri – rosary
mia bor – milestone
mi-Duvelesk(e)ro munthos – December
mi dir Duvelesko koro – chalice
mi-Duvel's chirklo – wren
mi-Duvelesko bitti folki – fairies
mi-Duvelesko chairus – world
mi-Duvelesko mauromengri – Jews
mi-kom – would
minas – mean
mingrer – policeman
mino – mine
misali – table
misaliakero potan – table cloth
misha-dosta – quite well
mishto – well
mishtoga – sure
misto – well
mizak – harmful
Mo – May
mokado – dirty
moker – dirtily
mol – wine
mol – worth
moleno – lead
moleno tatchi – new *(sic)*

molivesko koro – pewter mug
mollasar – never mind
molus/-os – lead
molyerdo – groomed
Mong-Dikla-kova-gav – Macclesfield
mongish – desire
mongramengro – beggar
mongyay – prayers
mont – without
mookli – lent
mooklo – left (behind)
mooktas – left
moosheno hev – armpit
mootsi – skin
moraviben – shearing
morda – ground (eg a knife)
morimengero – hangman
morlo – grind
mornis – our own
moro – our
morov – share
moser – taste
moseriben – tasting
muiben – drilling
Muieski Boshimengri – mouth organ
muieski shukerimaskri – face towel
muiesko mokto a kamorer – face box
muk – let
mukerdi avri – flown away, let out
mukiben – leavings
muk les bikonga – let him go
muklis – drop it
muklo – forsaken; left a place
mukova – I do
mul – wine
mulano – dismal
muli dab – knock-out blow
mulla de puv – graveyard
mulleno ruk – yew tree
mullerdi puv – graveyard
mullo mokto – coffin
mulomengro/-a – halter
mumbli – candle
mumbliyakero dudus – search light
mumliakeri – candlesticks
munjadom – squeezed
munya – pincers
murako – mountain

muran – lazy
muri – mountain
musengro – cart shaft
musheskra sastra – bike
mushkeno bawlo – boar
mushkeno matcho – cod fish
mushkeno papinengri – gander
muskra – policeman
mutchimengero – tanner
muterimengreriako mokto – tea caddy
mutterdo koro – chamber pot
muttermongri – tea
muttomengri – tea
muza – porridge

na – than
nak – to pass
nakav – to swallow
nakela – passes
nakeskri – snuff
nak o ye divvus – end of the day
naksati – to reach
nanai – not
nashavdo – hung
nasheda gairi – hangman
nasherd(o) – lost
nashkado – lost
nashki gallows
nastissa – unable, cannot
naveskro – namesake
nershavdo – ruined
netra – nature
nevibemn – new
nevimaskero – newcomer
nevus – rascal
nila – blue*
nillo –blue*
nisser – miss, avoid
nisser kova – strange thing
nitchi – peevish
nokengro – glandered
nolta – hold
nogo – own
nongiben – nakkedness
nongo – bald
notherenghi chiriklo – grouse

o – the

ochta – eight
odotar – parts
olish – hungry
oparl miro shero – over my head
opray akei – up here
opray door – highup
opray talay – deep down
opray ta talay –up and down
ora – clock
orengero – watchmaker
oriben – rising
otcherimengri – frying pan
ovavo – the next

paburna – rush
paburnengri skamin – rush chair
pakker – to defend
pakni – cradle
pako – ripe
pala dova – thereafter
palal – after
pala pesko chairus – late, behind time
palani rig – back
paleno grei – stallion
palay posh divvus – afternoon
pale – round
palla – behind
Palla Chairus – Autumn
paller shero – overhead
pallini – under, after
pallini chokka – petticoat
palyer – to follow
palyeriben – following
Panamengro – Penfold
pand – shut
pandili vastensay – bound hands
pandilo – slung
pandimangeri – snare
pandimangero – safe
pandlo – closed
pando bavalesti vardo – van
pand opray – close
panlo – fast, closed
panomengro – compound
pansch – 5
panser – to approve
pansh dorieni boshimengeri – banjo
panshengro – £5 note

papalay – again
paparis – paper
papinengri – goose
papinyaw – geese
papiresko tulaben – cigarette
para – change
paracrow tute/toot – thank you
parakai – this way
paramikri – snare
paramish – tale, story
paramishus – tales
parano – ancient
parasko – Friday
parav – bless
paraviben – change
paravimangero – money changer
paravit – split
pardel – across
pardel o parni – across the water
pardel vaverkendi – crosswise
pardo – hidden
parikeriben – thanking
parikerimasko – thankful
parl o shero – over head
parnieskeri – water pipe
parniesk(e)ro – pump
parniesko hev – water well
parnieskri hev – water well
parnigurni – frog
Parni Karesko Munthos – May
parnimengri – bucket
parni pori chiriklo – water wagtail
parni shok – watercress
parnugo hev – well
parnyerdo – watery
pas – to mock
pasado – mock
paserimangria – nurse
pash – by; with; near; next to
pashal lesti – with him
pashavo – side rib
patreni – trails
patrinyengero – herbalist
patsiben – faith
patsilo – trust
patsimangero – believer
patvalo – honourable
paunch – five

paunch dorieni boshimengri– banjo
paunch kolengri yek – a five shilling
 one
PaunoTem – Norfolk
paver – to rear, nourish
paverdi dai – foster mother
paverdo – protect
paverelo – protected
paverimangeri – nurse
paverimaskeri – foster mother
pawdel – over
pawlay – back
pawnago hev – water well
pawnch – 5
pawnch koruner – crown
pawnel kolengri yek – a five shilling
 one
Pawno Kareskro – May
pawno sastarn – tin
pawnshengro – £5 note
pawnugo hev – well for water
pawrvaliben – poverty
peaser stekas – turnpike
pedom – I fell
peerdos – Travellers
Peeri delin Tem – Lancashire
peeromengro – stile
peerdo – vagrant
peeresko kokolos – uncle
Peeresto Koppa Gav – Axminster
Peeri Delin Tem – Lancashire
peeeri kekavi – cauldron
peevli gairi – widow
peevlo gairo – widower
peevlo – widowed
peevlo gairo – widower
peias – fun, play
peiastas – funny
pel – to fall
pel alay – broken off
pel – fall
peleno – strong
pello – fallen
pelonas – testicles
pel alay – fallen off
penava – I say
pench – to think
pencher – think

pencherdas – thought
peneher – think
penella – he says
penenna– they say
penesko rom – brother in law
penessa – you say
pensa – like
per – belly
peraviben – felling
peresko – belly
pervimus – dazzled
pesado – paid
perastas – funny
peserimeskero – paymaster
pesko – its
Petulengro – Smith (family)
pevrasin – blinking
pi – drink
piameski – tea
Piaseskro mush – actor
pikalo – shoulder
pincher – to comprehend
pincheriben – understanding
pindro – hoof
pins – fun
pirand – bottom of anything
pirand misali – foot of table
piranglo – bare footed
pirav – to woo
piraviben – love affair
pirdo – half breed
piriengri – ladder
pirini – sweetheart
piriv – woo; to open
pirivdo – opened
pi tiro komoben – drink your health
plashtengri – mantle maker
Pobeski Piemeskri Tan – Devonshire
Pobeski Rook Tem – Kent
Pobomeski Gav – Norwich
pobomus – orange
pogerdo – broken
poggado jib – broken language
pointimus – appointment
pokonyesko kair – magistrate's house
pokonyos – justice of the peace
poktan kelomengro – weaver
poller – nourish

pondishlo – handkerchief
pongdishla – pocket handkerchief
poodado – blown
poodar – shoot
poodas – to shoot
poodamengri – bellows
poodj – bridge
poodj peias chiriklo – skylark
poordas – star
poorikano – ancient
poorokono – old fashioned
Poorumi Gav – Leek
poosham – wool
pooshumengro – spurs
porano – feather
porder – to fill
pordo – full
porengro – made of feathers
poringero – watch
porni doriov chiriklo – seagull
pornikano – whitish pale
porni rauni – swan
porno – white
porno bukesko – consumption
porno buko –lungs, white liver
Pornomestris – Price (family)
poryakeri koshteno bavaleski vardo –
       aeroplane
posadas – dug
posado – buried
posh aglal – opposite
posh ajal – neighbouring
poshano – near, adjoining
poshav – to prick
poshavo – side rib
poshawra – halfpenny
poshay – close, by, near
poshayder – nearer
poshay o peeray – at one's feet
posh bar – ten shillings
posh buklo – half gallon
posh divvus– noon; afternoon
posh dromesko kitchema – half way
       house. *After this is written what
       appears to be the word* puplie. *This
       is possibly meant to read purply, ie
       a purple colour, but much more
       likely, it is a mis-spelling for public.*

posher – divide, share
posherra – halfpenny
posh korauna – half a crown
posh koruner – half crown
posh posherra – farthing
posh rig – besides
Poshumesko Tem – Westmoreland
poshteno – cover
poshti – animal hide
poshumesko – woollen
posinajos – handkerchief
posomengri – fork
praio – upper
prakos trin praki – three legged kettle
    prop
prala – brother
pralacha – will brother
prarstomengro – policeman
prasteri kista – railway station
prasterin kolli – train
Prasterin Koli Gav – Crewe
prasser – to abuse
pre – in; up
prech – to rise
prechdo opray – arise
pre-engro folki – upper class
pudi(?) Gudlo kolli – sugar beet
pukasamengrai – lawyer
pukavimangero – speaker
pukavimaskero – informer
pukeno – quiet
Pukersomengro – lawyer on the
    prisoner's side
pukersomengro-shanengro-
    rokermengro – lawyer
pukkerin kosh(t) – signpost
pukni – udder, bladder
pumyer – to fester (In a list of Henry's
    words, in his own writing, Dick
    Wade has translated pumyer as
    jester. This is a misreading.)
puraben – exchange
purano – ancient
purdimangero – bellows
purdimengro – whistle
purdimengro bauro boshimengeri –
    harp
purerd – changed

purj – bridge
puro dadrus – grandfather
puri dai – grandmother
purikano –old fashioned
purri dadus – grandfather
purri dia – grandmother
purro – grey
pus – straw
pusav – to bury
pusesekri – pitchfork
pushkakero – marksman
pusomengri – fork
putchas – I ask
putchava – I ask(ed)
putchdom – I ask
putchem – we ask
putchena – we ask
putchtas – he asks((asked)
putchte – they ask(ed)
putchtem – we asked
puterdo – to undo
putsi lil – pocket book
puttan – tinder
puttar – unfasten
puvengriaw – potatoes
puvesti chirkla
puvesto churi – plough
puvyerdas – turned out in field (horses
    etc)
puzhkakero – marksman

radiben – departure
rak – protect
rakdo – keep
rakelo – keep
rak toot – take care
ran – rod
ranglas – angling
rangliben – fishing
ranjer (?) – take care
rankni – gaily coloured
ranya, ranyay – remove
ranyedo – tainted, putrid
ranyengero – fishing rod dealer
rartenghi chirikla – owl
ranyengri – cane
ranyengri skamin – cane chair
rartenghi-chei-chiriklo – nightingale

rashai/rasher – parson
rashni – parson's wife
rateskeri – artery
ratsilo – to bleed
ratvalo – blood stained
ravalo – noble
ravnesko – heaven
razumay – gum
Reltum Gav – Wrexham
repper toot – remember
ressi tut – make haste
resta – duck
rhiger – lead
ridjil – partridge
rigger – bring, lead
riggerdas – kept
Riggermeskro munthos – September
rikkerorus – the side of anything
rikker – carry
rikkers – to keep, retain
ril – break wind
rinkeni – pretty, handsome
rinkeni bar matcho – trout
rinkeni kelimaskeri – pretty dancer
Rinkeni Rakli Gav – Nottingham
Rinkeni Tem – Cumberland
rino fine
risher – to bribe
risser – tremble, shake
ritchera – elephant
riv – wear
roi – spoon
rokava – I talk
rokeras – you talk, speak
rokerdas – he talks
rokerde – they talk
rokkadas – he talked
rokkade – they talked
rokka shookas – speak low
rokkerde – they talked
Romaneskras – Gypsy fashion
Romani chirklo – magpie
Romani velgooras – Gypsy Fair
roodipen – search
roopni roi – silver spoon
roozho puv – garden
roshengri – stag
ruchano – tall

rucho – high
ruderipen –
rukenies – trousers
rukni – tree
rumman – spoon
rupavi purdimengeri – a whistle
rushni – flower
Rushni Tem – Lincolnshire
rus o de saulo – dawn
rutni – nostril
ruz – strength
ruzlipen – power
ruzlo – coarse, strong
ruzlipen – power
ruzlo – strong
ruzlopen – strength
ruzno– strong, harsh, stiff
ruzvalo – powerful

safran – yellow
sakos, sakas – sake
sakumi – as ever
salamanka – table
salav – to peel
salava – I laugh
salvas – tray
sani – soft, silken
sanus – same
sapesko matcho mutsi – eel skin
sar – with; as
sarishan – how are you?
sar komessa – if you please
sar see – how is
sar talay – in ruins
sar the wen – all the winter
sas – was
sastani mushesko vardo – motor bike
sastarni graieski – engine
satarni misali – iron table
sastarni herro – iron wheel
saster ravnos chirklo – aeroplane
sasti – maybe, should
sastis – can, if possible, possible
sastra grei – train
sastra grei kolli – train
sastus – should
saveri – cruel
savimasko chirklo – wood pecker

savo – which, that, what
savo chairus – what time, when
see le – are they
shalav – to peel
Shelengros – Hames
shinlo – ill tempered
schok – 6
schov – 6
schtor – 4
screeve – car
selano – green
sensus, sensas – since
setlimen – settled
shamado – ragged
shan – have
shanengro – lawyer on the police side, informer, prosecuting lawyer
shaniben – delicacy
shar – to praise
shel – 100
Shelengro – Booth (family), Hames (family)
shelengro – whistler
shelyer – to whistle
shenakeri – water well
sherengro – leader
shereskano-looromengro's- rokeringairo – lawyer
shereski venderay – brains
shereskro – chief, head man
sheromengro – lawyer
sherokno – chief
sherno – best
shian – perhaps
shilalo – cool, cold
shilalo naflopen – a cold
shil(l)eri – chilly
shilyeriben – shudder
shinalo – horn
shing – horn
shingaw – horns
shinlo – ill tempered
shir avri – to pour out
shirro – sour
shishlo – hardy
shooka – dry
shookar atchlo – still
shokengriaw – cabbages

Shookamauro – Sherriff (family)
    (*Henry explains:* The name Shookamauro, drybread, was given us years ago. They used to call us dry bread without any butter on.)
Shooka Mauro Gav – Worcester
shootlo – sour, bitter
shorokno – chief
shumas – I was
si – have
simensa –cousin
solverkon – curse
shom – am
shomas – I was, were
shoobli – pregnant
shoonamengri – newspaper
shookiben – drought
shootlo – bitter
shootlo pobi – sour apple, bitter apple
shoovlo – *(not trans.)*
shorokno – clever; chief
shor opray – to praise
shov – 6
shovawri – sixpence
shublo – swollen
shukerdo – dried
shukiben – drought
shuknid – empty
shukyer – to make dry
shulavka – shovel
shunadom – dreamed
shun lendi – remember
shuns – sounds
shushengri hevyaw – rabbit holes
shushlo – damp
shuveni –beautiful
shuvla pordi – shovel full
shuvlo – swollen
si – is, are
siddi – naughty
sideli – naughty
sig – quick(ly)
sigaben – a chance
sigan – straight on
sig o miro zi – anxious
sigo-tooti – be quick
sik – to taste
sikaviben – showing

sikeromengro – signpost
sikker – taught
sikkerin – sign
siklo – used
sikomengro – circus
si komlo – it is likely
sik o tem – the law
simensa(y) – relation
simer – to pawn, pledge
simeromeskro – pawnbroker
sini – tray
si posh sig – perhaps
siran – faster
siro – reaped
siro puv – reaped field
siva – stitch
sivomengro – tailor; Taylor (family)
skamin – chair
skamin(y)engro – chair mender or
    bottomer
skopelo – lazy
skucher – empty
skudalin – plate
skudela – dish
skudilyaw – dishes
Skutenengro – Scotsman
slatchery – slate
smentini – cream
solabon – swear
sonakei petulengro – goldsmith
soonakei chiriklo – goldfinch
sorasor – forever
soridui – both
sor kettenay – altogether
sorkon – every
sorkon kolensa – for everything
sorkon kolli – everything
sorkon yekesti – for everyone
sor opray – all over
sor ruzlo – almighty
so si – what is?
so si les – what is it?
Soski – what is, why
soski kedas les talla – why did you do
    it?
sosti – has to, must, ought
sov –coire. (Richard Wade has added,
    'Never to sleep.')

soridui – both
sovahalled – swear
sovel– oath
sovel khaliom – I have sworn
sovloholaben – oath
spilav – to push
spiniars – carrots
spinibgriaw – carrots
staka – tread
stanimamengro – groom
stanya – stable
stardi – hat
stariben – prison
staribenengero – prison officer
stariben gav – county town
stariben raiesko – prison governor
stari chirklo, – starling
stastis – if I can
stekas – gate
stiffi chai – daughter in law
stiffi chavo – son in law
stiffi dai – mother in law
stiffi pen(or penya) – sister in law
stiffo prala – brother in law
stiglo – lonely
stikla – jug
stor – 4
stugi – stack
suji dova – what is that?
sulverkon lavaw – swear words
suneli – handsome
suner – to dream
sur – deep
surelo – hard
sus – was
sutilo – sleeping
sutti – sleep
sutti mishto – sleep well
sutti penchayray – dream
sutto mishto – sleep well
suvali – infirm
swigla – pipe
swishi – ugly

tabno – to run water
tachani ziengri – true hearted
tachiben – truth
tacho – true

takeno – to paint; paint
takimengro – painter
talal o kam – on the hearth, under the sun
talal o puv – underground, buried
talay – under, down
talay koi – down there
talay o drom – along
tale – under
talengalo – pepper
talkiben – dented
talkipen – dented
talla – except, but, beneath
tallani – under
tallapen – endure
tallay – off
talleni – flannel
tallen(o) – wool
tallopen – to endure
tallugno – until
tambuskos – drum
tamliben – youth
tamlo – black
tamlo rarti – dark night
tangri – tight
tangiben – bell
tard – to
tarda – longer
tarder – to pull
tardimengri – drawers, knickers
tardimos – drawing
tarno – young; little
tarnodar – younger
tarnomus – youth
tasav – to choke
tasaviben – strangulation
tasho peeri – right foot
tasser – draw
tatchiben – truth
tateriben – heating
tattermengri – pepper
tatto – sting
tatto andi – expert
Tattoben chairus – Summer
tav – cotton
Tavesta Gav – Manchester
tavyer – to thread, shake
teakli – strong

tei – too
tem – country
teray – entice
tikno – child
tikno matchka – kitten
til – to hold
tiliben – grasp
tilimang(e)ro – poacher
tilameskeri – trap, snare
till – I hold; to hold
tilomengri – snare
til opray – raise
timas – to pour
tippoti – spiteful
Tippoti Tem – Herefordshire
tivdas – knitted
tootchi – nipples
torro – high
torropen – height
tovdo – washed
tovelas – washing
tover – axe
tovimang(e)ri – washerwoman
tovin divvus – Monday
tradiben – warned
tradis – to warn
tranglumi – tools
trin – 3
trin desch – 30
trin desh – 13
tringushni – shilling
trin koshtengri purdimengri – bag pipes
trinushni – three shillings
trito – third
trom – to dare
tromaviben – challenge
tromiben – risk, peril
tromin – gold coin
trooshal – about
trooshal – a cross; about
trooshal-akei– hereabouts
trooshalo – thirsty
trooshal o tan – in the neighbourhood
trooshni – quart
troostal – about *(? in error for trooshal)*
trothipen – betrothed
trupas – body

trupesko – bodily
trupesk(e)ro undertaker
trushel – about; around
trushlar – to twist
tuchi – nipples
tudeskro – milkman
tugano – sorrow
tugno – grief, sad
tukal – friend
tukali – friendly
tukalipen/ben – kindness
tukalo – kind
tuki – to (or for) you
tuknus – sorrow
tul – drive a car, horse, cart
tulak – behind, back of
tuley, tulei – below
tulipen – grease
tulipenasko/eski koro – dripping pot
tulkar – bitter
tullay – below
tulld – held
tullin – drawing a cart
Tulo Mas Tem – Lincolnshire
tulyer – fatten
tumay – you also
tuneri – fierce
turel – barrel
turrali – cask
tu sastis dikavit – you should
tushni – basket
tussa – you
tussar – to comfort
tuveski –smokey
tuvimasko koro – chimney pot

ucherdo – cast off
uklisto – I rode
ulav – to share
Urcheng(r)o munthos – October
useder – worse
ushlo – sour
utar – west
uzlo – guilty

val – hair
val(l)a – wheel
valinas – to bottle

valinesko – bottle
Valinesko Men Gav – Grimsby
valin o duk – vessel of wrath
valoboshamengra – harp player
vaniso – any
vaniso kai – anywhere
vaniso ka(-o)meni – anybody
varaso – whatever
vardameskra – waggon dweller
Vardengro – Miller (family)
vardesko kola (or kolli) – harness
vardesko musengero – waggon shaft
vardesko prastermengri – wheel
vardo pano – 'the spindled pens on the
　　side of ledge sided waggons,
　　sometimes on bow topped wagon
　　sides'
varekai – whatever
vareki –wherever
varekon – whoever
varesavo – whichever
vareso – whatever
vartiben – watched
vartinini – watching
vartni mush – watchman
vasavo – bad (fruit, person etc)
vasesko rokkerimos – writing
vastengri rokkerben – writing
vastengri tattomus – ironing
vastermengris – handcuffs
vasteseko rokkerimos – writing
vastus – hand
vastustengri – thimble, gloves
vasteskero – handle
vastusteskero – thimble
vava – will
vava me tussa – am I going with you?
vaverken – another; each other
veena – excuse
veenlo – excused
veeno – notice
velas – you come
veld te duk – come to grief
velgorako – of the fair
vendri – bowels
Venesto – Winter
Venesto chairus – Winter
venlo – wintry

venlo chirklo – linnet
verani – file
verigay – chain
vesh – woods
veshengra – gamekeeper
veshengreski chorin – poaching
veshni mullo – owl
vigina(y) – bog, marsh
vina – excuse
vitcher – to hate
Vonga Hev Tem – Durham
Vongali Gairi Tem – Durham
Vongar Divvus – Friday
vongushni – ring
vongushtengro – of the fingers
vongushter – to finger
vongushti chiriklo – pidgeon
vongushto – finger
vonka – when
vudda – door
vuddres – bed
Vudres Gav Tem – Bedfordshire

wafedi keriben – bad behaviour
wafedi kolli – evil thing(s)
wafedo(i) – bad (man etc), wicked
wafedodair – worse
wardi – cards
wataviben – wantonness
wava temengra – foreigner
waver – other
waver temeni – another country
waveskro – otherwise
welled – came
weshni rarti chiriklo – owl
wisht –lip
woklen – duck
Wolshengro – Welshman
wooser opray – to vomit
woozerdom – threw

yadlipen – addled
yek – one
yekati waver – one to another
yekeno – only
yeke(s)ti waver – one to another
yekino – only
yekli – only

yekno –single (one)
yekorus – once
yek palal e waver – one after another
yek(o)rus – once
yekto – first
yelma – elm
yiv – snow
yivyela – it snows
yogakeri – poker
yogako muzerimaskero – fire engine
yogako sastarn – poker
yogengeri – clock
yohenghi naflopen – fever
yogesti bavalesti vardo – fire engine
yogesto vastaw – tongs
yogni – fiery
yogomeskro – *no meaning given*
yogongo tan – fireplace
yokesto vastaw – tongs for fire
yooser opray – to clean up
yoozhoben – cleanliness
yuv – he

zee – heart
zelano – green
zeravo – left
zido – alive
zil – vein
zilvas – to envy
zilver – to make jealous
zilviben – jealousy
zimin – soup
zi-ush – shrewd
zumav – to interrogate
zumaviben – interrogation
zumavimaskro – coroner
zumin – broth, soup

Sentences and phrases

Though a high proportion of the following are borrowings from Smart and Crofton, about 60% are original and many others amended. Large Smart and Crofton borrowings, however, have been omitted.

Bauro opray o chib – *great on the tongue.*

Len lullan avri – *they vanish away.*

Jinava kai jivessa – *I know where you live.*

Tala velas pawlay talay kai – *Then he came back down here.*

Beeno sas lo – *He was born.*

Poshay desh bbershaw pawalay – *About ten years ago.*

Shov divvusaw tute bootiessa – *six days you shall work.*

Chomoni sas adray loko – *something inside was heavy.*

O ora si paulay – *the clock is slow.*

Basavi monushni si mursengro si-li – *She is always a bad woman..*

Kair les praykas – *do it in company.*

Jib adray savo jib – *in what language?*

O hev sas hanilo – *the hole was dug..*

Radias peski – *she hoped it.*

Meero feterdair plokta – *my best robe.*

Teero gadesto bei see keker pandad – *your shirt sleeve is not fastened.*

Yek shushi adray o korro see mol dui adray o vesh – *a rabbit in the pot is worth two in the wood.*

Wantsenna o churio te ven morday – *the knives need sharpening.*

Tei o katsies – *also the scissors.*

Maskal o rukka – *in the middle of the forest.*

Moro Dadus jivo praye doy varta tooti, varta tootis juvel si tikni chavvies, latch tooti, tooti's folki bashtali opray da drom. Mandi pens monya ta Duveltis rarti. – *May Our Father above watch your wife and tiny children find you (and) your people staying on the road. I earnestly pray God this night.*

Dik tan ta duva – *did you see that?*

Duva sas a laj – *that was a shame.*

Kek latcho ke jel to starebon. – *It is not good to go to jail.*

Kom si a legbareda barali – *love is the greatest wealth.*

Kek me nai chichi te pen ke yov– *I have nothing to say to them.*

Akova koliko dui kurrokiaw – *this last two weeks.*

Komani rokerela troostal mandi – *someone is talking about me.*

Estist tooti jin sor jafri nevaw si koli – *you know all such new things.*

Kek na komova jafri tanaw si koli – *I don't like such places as that.*

Yooshadom o vardo boot yooser koliko rarti – *I swept the wagon very clean last night.*

Voodrus-dandimengri – *biting bed (ie lousy).*

Duva rakli see o mairas – *that girl is a trouble maker.*

Dosta dosta Romani chalaw – *very many Gypsy lads.*

Soski kedas les talla – *why did you do it?*

Soski tooti nanei rokka te mandi – *why don't you speak to me?*

Prasterdas peski opensa grei – *he ran like a horse.*

Beeno shumas adray Chumba Kalesko Tem – *I was born in Derbyshire.*

Adray o Gavesto pa o Bongo Kongri – *in the town of the crooked church (Chesterfield).*

Kamli see le – *they are putrid.*

Besh tooti le kon – *sit down then.*

Akei see navaw of chirklos akuva mandi jin – *here are names of birds which I know.*

Mandi sham akei tedivvus ta ghilo ovavo-divvus opre o drom te vaniso kei, akova see mendi Romani chel. – *I am here today and gone tomorrow on the road to anywhere, that's why we are Gypsies.*

Can you set a shushi paramikri prala – *(rabbit snare, brother)?* sometimes we say Tilomengri instead of paramikri – *snare.*

Dias miro kokeri wafedo kerimus – *he made me act badly.*

Parikerava mi-Doovel me sastis bonek meero sherro opre torro sorkon-chairus adray vanisso tatcho Romani tan. – *Thank God I can hold my head up high in any true Gypsy place.*

Kek nay komova jafri tanaw si kolli – *I do not like such places as these.*

Purikani chikeski bawri hobenaski kamora – *large old fashioned clay floor kitchen.*

Veom akai mangkay meero chairus – *I came here early.*

Veas pawlay talay kai – *he came back down here.*

Kon se duva dadus? – *Who is that father?*

Yon ghias – *they went.*

Bisserdas tu – *have you forgotten?*

Hokki lel les tutti – *here, take it.*

Kalengri sar kisi – *how much is buttermilk?*

Kalmarikli savo kisi – *how much is cheesecake?*

Kek chalaw choredo kovas – *Don't touch stolen things.*

Nakela sigs sigo o bersh – *the year passes very quickly.*

Kanela akova balavas– *this bacon stinks.*

Tasho poshaglal o gavomengro kair – *right opposite the police house.*

Mandi droven opre o vooda – *I knocked hard on the door.*

Kerova mi kushtodair les – *I will do my best.*

Kek komeni sastis gili pensa tooti – *nobody can sing like you.*

Beeno shomas dray Chambay Kalesko Tem, awer andias opray sor parl o temeskri – *I was born in Derbyshire but brought up all over the country.*

Jinava kai jivessa – *I know where you live.*

Jinessa kai atchava – *you know where I stop.*

Savo see de tatchi drom. Dik. Akais de patrin apre de bongo vas – *Which is the right way? Look. Here's a trail sign on the left.*

Riserela gairo – *Poxy man (lit. Trembling), Parkinson's Disease sufferer.*

Mantchi too prala – *Cheer up, brother.*

Til opre tiro zee. Maw be a ladj. – *Lift your heart. Don't be ashamed.*

Lesti nok is sor rat – *his nose is bleeding.*

Yovs a kushti kooromengro – *he's a good fighter.*

Pukka a tatchipen. Maw rokka hokrapens – *Tell the truth! Don't lie!*

Sig in the sala – *early in the morning.*

Tools their jivaben – *keep alive.*

Hatch mullo adre the wen – *remain dead in the winter.*

Chivved a wudrus pre the puvvis – *born in an open field.*

Henry's Welsh Romani Word Lists

These consist of several pages, some numbered in Romani, of words from Welsh Romani. They appear to have been sent to Richard Wade in three batches. For ease of reference, the vocabulary has here been listed in alphabetical order, with sentences following.

It is possible that Henry obtained this from Sampson, but if so there are significant differences. On the other hand, Derek Tipler printed a list of Welsh Romani words in JGLS which Henry might have seen. However, Henry may have heard this Romani first-hand, as he certainly travelled with several Welsh Romani Lees and Prices. Even today, these families are renowned for the quality of their Romani.

Here and there, Henry adds a note about the significance of some structure in Romani, thus:

The words ending in iben are the same as "ing" in English

On one page he writes:

As you can see prala, Walsheni Kale Romanes is not a lot of difference than English jib. The words are said a little different in some cases. I think Walsheni Romanes is more deep than a lot of English Rokerben. The trouble is there is not many can rokka it. Old Fred Huth is one on his own, as you may know. He surprised me and I take a lot of surprising. But without a doubt you are a master and on your own as regards of English Rokerben. As I have said before, you must be the best in the country without a doubt. I have heard some good ones Romani chalaw but none as good as teero kokero *(yourself)*, you stand on your own.

I hope you like the bit of Walsheno Rokerben I have sent. I once prided myself as knowing Romanes as good as anyone, but I take my stardi *(hat – ed)* off to you. You are the Dadi of us all.

aka – this
Akala tema – British Isles
akana – now
andre – within
Anitrakero – English
anlan – in front
anle – before
asavasin – join
asavibenimos – laughter
astis mangi – I can
atav – forgive
avela – comes
avri – outside
avrial – outside

backnas – backwards
baghtimen – fortunate
baleski tulimaskri – hair oil
baleskro – acorn
balovesko marikli – bacon fritter
bareskero – grindstone
baribeneski – gardening
baro noiyelus – harp
barvali folki – rich people
basvaimasko mokto – musical box
Bauri machengero munthos –
    November
Baviakero – March
Bavalyakero munthos – March
beshdo – sit

beshimaski maneri – sofa
beshto ta salivengro – saddle and bridle
biando – born
bianiben – birth
bi-baiengoro – sleeveless
bichado – send
bi-Dadeskero – illegitimate
bi-doshhako – harmless
bikado – send
bikindo – sell
Bikinimaski budika – swag shop
bi-parniesko – without water
bisserdo – forget
bis ta yek – 21
Bita kaulo munthos – February
bitti barameno keliben – marbles
bi-tuvyerimangero – non smoker
blavdo – hang
blavimeskro – hangman
blui jardoka – blue apron
booteder – more
boshela – barks
Brishindeskeri – rainbow
brishindeski purj – rainbow
Brishindesko munthos – April
brishinela – rains
buklimen – bottle
buklo bi rukeno tan – bleak treeless
   place
Buzneski kitchema – Goat Inn

chalaviben – interference
cheperimangero (?) – knife grinder
cheriklo – bird
chibalengro – lawyer
chibengro – linguist
chikali krafni – rusty nail
chido – put
chinimageriakero – postman
chinimos – sharpness
chivela – puts
chiviben – order
chorvanoben – poverty
chumaben – nastiness
chumerimaskeri – mistletoe

daki bauri dei – great grandmother
dandava – bite
dandesko duk – toothache
desarla – morning

dikesa – seest
dita – look
dino – give
divesendi – for days
dralano drom – by-way, by road
dudimaskeri kosht – lamp post
dui des bi yek – 19
dumano – lonely
dureder – further
duveri star des – 80

eglos – eagle

fededer – better
filishimakero – lord of a castle or
   mansion
fokendi – people
foshano bal ta foshane danda – wig and
   false teeth

gadeski bai – shirt sleeve
Ghivesk(r)o munthos – August
gladimen – glad
grasniaki – mare
grasniben – cantankerous
griga – heather
gudla tud – buttermilk
gudleskeri – sugar tongs
guruvaskero ta puruma – steak and
   onions
guruvesko – bullock

haiaviben – understanding
haiaw – understand

iveskeri – frosty
Ivesko munthos – January

jala – goes
jalimengri – train
jasa – goest
jido – live
jinesa – knowest
jivesa – livest
jukelengero – huntsman
julvino – guilty
junelo – know
junesa – you know
Jutani juvel – Jewess
Jutano – Jew

kairesa – do
kaishano diklo – silk neckerchief
k'akerdo – lime
k'akerdom – scalded
Kale – Gypsy
Kalesko nav – Gypsy name
kaliako mui si dolata – Gypsy- like
    female
kalikani chei – brunette
kalo maresko – barley
kamdo – love
kamimasko gilioben – love song
kana sig – presently
kandeskero – earwig
kandeskrios – earrings
kanro – thorn
kamimen – beside
kamyerdo – pleased
kan de trad – beware
kanela – stinks
kardo – call
Kaseskro munthos – July
katilo – knotted
kedilo – gather
kedimaskro – collector
kediom – collected
kedipen – collection
kekaviaki yakani – kettle prop
kekavi keriola – the kettle is boiling
keker manki – never before
kekomi – never again
keldo – play
keliben – dancing
kerado – boiled
keraviben – cooking
keravimaskri – saucepan
keresko gilimangero – canary bird
kerirela (?) Makes
keseriben – matter
kessa – care
kestiar – window
Kialeski marikli – cheese cake
Kialmaresko tem – Montgomeryshire
kiki – nothing
kindo – cut
kindilo – cut
kiniben – bought
kishliben – slender
kishlo – thin
kistilo – ride

kitchimaris – innkeeper
kivarteris – quarter
klizinimaskeri danda – lock-jaw
klizinimen – locked
kluriben – colouring
kolensa – everything
kom – love
komesa – lovest
komiben – loving
kon – who
konyo – quiet
koppi – blankets
koro – pot
kosdo – wipe
koshtano koro – wooden bowl
koshtenengro chik – sawdust
kosht purdimangero – flute
kovlo – soft
kralisos – king
krudasas – curdled
Kuparis – cooper (also Cooper family)
kusdo – blame
kusi – little
lajilo – ashamed
latsilo – kick
lava – take
lekero – theirs

lija – village
Lilaiesko Munthos – June
limalo nok – snotty nose
lino – take
lurdo – robluriben – robbing
lutrakeri – scullery maid

manke – before
marimaskero – murderer
maseneri – meat safe
masesko kosht – butcher's block
maskal – middle
maskel me duiendi – between us two
mazin – freeze
melano – ripe corn
melesko – oatmeal
Mi-Dubleskero munthos – December
mokadi gaveneri – dirty town people
mokado – unclean
molivo – pewter
molyerdo – groomed
mongiben – begging

moravimaskro – barber
moskerero – policeman
muleskri – coffin
munjerdo – narrow
munthos – month

nasherela – loses
nevi avrimaskero – new comer

odoleski – because
oja sar – such as like
opre – upwards
orinmasko cherikli gili – skylark's song

paburnaki – rush
paiano – peacock
pal – brother
palal – behind
panj des – 50
papali – again
parasko – Friday
parikedo – thank
parniesko – pump
Parni karesko munthos – May
Paro – heavy
paro deimangero – heavy hitter
pasavo – rib
pas durika des – 60
pas durikei – half crown
pas mia – half mile
pas poshera – farthing
patuv – honour
patvalo – prosperous
paverdo – nurse
pavuna – porridge
pendo – say
perdo – fall
pesko – his
pielo – drink
piko – shoulder
pinjeriben – knowledge
piravibenkro (?) nasvaliben – love
    sickness
piraviomaski oram – opening time
piravimaski vongustri – engagement
    ring
pirdilo – walk
planeta – planet
pointimus – appointment
poori rivimengro – old clothes dealer

porno maresko – wheat
poshteno – carpet
prastilo – run
purdilo – blow
purdo – blow
puiako – old woman
pukeras – tellest
puklo – ask
puroikano – ancient

raikaneder – prettier
ridilo – dress
rigako wuva – side door
Rigerimaskero munthos – September
rodilo – seek
Roiengro – spoon maker
rokeras – speakest
rokerdo – talk
rokerela – talks
rokerela misto – she talks well
Rupavi oraki – silver chain
rusdo – angry

saniben – slim
sardilo – praise
savimasko cherikla – wood pecker bird
shelo – whole
sherengri – umbrella
shoonesa – hearest
shun – hear
shundilo – hear
shuniben – hearing
sigisher – sooner
sikav – show
sivdo – sew
skaminyakero – chairman
slutaki – rag
so – what
sovekeriben – curse
star des – 40
star ta panj des – 90
stithius – tinker's anvil
sunakei – gold
sunakeski oraki – silver chain
sutilo – sleep
sutlo – sour
suvelyenero – besom maker
swedla – flute

taktino – paint

tala dandeskro – false person, sly
talal – underneath
talani choka – petticoat
tangimeskro – bell ringer
tap pesko koshtenengro grei – on his wooden horse
tatader ta tateder – hotter and hotter
tov – wash
toviben – washing
tovilo – wash
tovimaskri – washerwoman
trashela – fears
trin des – 30
trin des bi yek – 29
trin prashki – tripod, kettle iron
trin ta star des – 70
trusal – around
trusal akei – hereabouts
trusuleski akimagere (?) – stations of the cross
tukaliben – kindness
uladom – shared
tuleder – fattest

Urchengro munthos – October
urkos – hedgehog
uzin rook – elder tree

valgora – fair

varekai – wherever
varekana – whenever
varesar – howsoever
varesava – whichever
varesavo – whichever
vartimis – watching
vaver – other
vaverben – each other
venderi – insides
vias – came
vodreski – dressing gown
vongli – earring
Walsenengro – Welshman
wantsava – I want
wantsessa – you want
waverkendi – others
welefantos – elephant

yakenkeri – clock
yekar bersesti – once a year
yivela – snows

zelano – green
Zelano Musheski kitchima – Green Man Inn
zozvalo – strong
zuluna (?) – plums
zumavimaskero – coroner
Zuminako-gav-tem – Cardiganshire

Sentences and phrases

Shan pias mi Duvels divvus dosta ov livna adray o kitchema tei dosta ov ghiveliaw te gili. Wi tutti kel o bosh. Me wi vel penchavani troostal tutti opre mi Duvels divvus tei nevo divvus bershaw. Me kefi tutti sor o bahtalipen adre o mi Duvels Temeskri. – *I have often drunk beer in the pub on Christmas Day and sung lots of songs. Will you play the fiddle? I will think about you on Christmas day and New Year's Day. I wish you all the luck in heaven.*

Kushti bok sokon chairus tutti se o tatchiest mush me jinaw fetedair na posh a Romani chalaw tedivvus. – *Good luck to you for ever, You are the truest man I know. Better than half the Gypsies today.*

Please let me know if you want all the Lavines tem Romanes jib *(Welsh Gypsy language)*.

Kushti bok pa mi Duvels beeno divvus ta nevo bershaw. Teero prala sorkon-chairus, Henriasar Shooka Moira – *Best wishes for Christmas and the New Year, Your brother for ever, Henry Sherriff.*

Temeskri ov Ghiveli – *(the name of a country, but unclear which. It translates literally as the Land of Wheat – USA?.)*

Lavines Temeskri – *Welsh.*

Dordi pal, latchiom me komoni kana latchiom drom – *Well, brother, I found someone when I took to the road.*

Staven tumeni sar – *Off with you all.*

Kardas les o rei ta pukadas leski te andel komi kaliko. – *He made the gentleman tell him to bring more the next day.*

Silalo vela kaliko divvus – *It will be cold tomorrow*

Leski danda dili vaverkendi trashavimasta – *His teeth chattered with fright.*

Zaleno si dova rook sa o bersh – *That tree is an evergreen.*

Dosta foshniben kelova lensa ta basavava lengi oke sar. – *Many falsehoods will cause evil to them.*

Akei see o navan ov o munthos adre Walshana Kale Rokerben. *(There then follows a list of the months in Welsh Romani with English translations.)*

Sis kamyerava les me – *I cannot please him.*

Kushto divvus kedivvus yumengri – *Good day today* (yumengri). *(I cannot translate the word* yumengri).

Dew hoben i mulengri – *Give food to the dead.*

Bersha kedivvus – *(lit. Years today.)*

Na haiavava maia kologro rokeriben sar– *I do not understand the words on the mile post.*

Kushto baghtibben kala divesa tuki – *The compliments of the season to you.*

Sor Walsengero Romanesm jib – *All Welsh Romani language.*

Baktalo mui si lesti – *she has a lucky face.*

Kide pen tale – *they lay down.*

Jakai ta dosi buzno – *go and milk the goat, girl.*

Wantsenas lubo livinaki junes – *they want money for beer.*

Na mukela men mari dei te vas – *our mother will not let us come.*

Java to bisava kaia tarni juvel keri dadi –
I am going to see this young man of father (sic).

Kidas o pus tale dudyerdas les – *he layed down in the straw.*

Nai man ki te kenaw tusa kekkomi – *I will have nothing to do with him.*

O kekavi keriolas – *the kettle's boiling.*

Trashases te javo (?) pasi lendi boot boot juveli sas le –
We were so frightened to go near them, they were very lousy.

Rokerana o gaje kitanes kon so kava. I musugeskero – *The gorjers talk together about this and that. The* musugeskero. *(Note that -eskero is the masculine genitive but musug is a new word to me. It may be connected with mootsi, skin, or with musos, mouse – but this is an extremely tentative thought.)*

Ake tiro sastiben ta boot bersha te jives ta dosta te rigerel tutti –
There is your health and may you live many years.

Puilo si-li ta yek tiknoro lesti – *She is a widow with one child.*

Tala pukesa mandi kai si kekaviaki yakani –
Then you asked me where is the kettle prop.

Rokerela misto – *She talks well.*

Raikani sas li – *She was beautiful.*

Bokale si-le – *They are hungry.*

Baro pekiben gavaski – *Biggest roast in town*

Pekiben sis berava les tukki kanna – *I will cook the roast for you now.*

(Berava is a mis-write for kerava.)

Sis hola kek pagerdandengri si – *She cannot eat, she has broken teeth.*

Nasis azava les me kek – *I cannot lift it.*

Velas te juvel romnimus rokeras romnimus –
If she had known Romani, I would have spoken in Romani.

Si dui droma ki vlija dotar to katar –
There are two roads to the village, one that way and one this.

Druba guruva dosta guruva ta greia ta bakeri –
A herd of cattle, a good stock of cows, horses and sheep.

Yoi si pirani manki bersendi dola divusendi – *Problems with translation –*
something like, She is a sweetheart, let us stay those days.)

Keradom kotorendi sas-lo – *It was boiled to shreds.*

Ma ker kek dosvali kola – *Don't do anything wrong.*

Akekon lena o drom – *Now they take the road.*

Pandela ta piravela ma dumo wi nafelas –
My back opens and shuts with pain.

O basno giavelas kedisarla manki sutiom –
The cock crew this morning before I fell asleep.

O koraki kena bari godli – *The rooks are crowing loudly.*

O kamleder kirchimaris ar o temeskri –
The friendliest landlord in the country.

Jivenas bita keresti maskal murendi –
They lived in a cottage in among the hills.

Na jesara me boot kola nevi dromeni –
I do not care for these new fangled ways.

Ratver i grei bita, nai-lo misto kek –
Bleed the horse a little, something is wrong.

Vias i rauniako bokt palal – *The lady's good fortune came at last.*

So rigeresa ta sar o rokeriben kunyibikanes kokoreski –
Why keep all the talk to yourself.

Kardom me livinaki – *I called for beer.*

Piravava les me – *I will open it.*

Beshtokm tale – *I sat down.*

Dikas lati komdias lati romerdas lati –
He saw her, fell in love with her and married her.

Jundas te na bikindom les – *She knew I had not sold it.*

Gias o pooro petalengro opre ki mo dir duvel odoi sas-lo te basavelas bari basimengri ta dikasa les sar me te ne jasa ko beng. Pendas lenti te basvaen opre e basadi gili – *The old smith went up to God, there he was, and played the cello and saw how he did not want to go to the devil. He said he would be there to play the harp.*

Note: This alleged Welsh Romani is a straight lift from Smart and Crofton's English Romani.

Kel tutti jin duvaw, yaun se sor Lavines-temeskri Romanes – *Did you know those, they are all Welsh Romani?*

Comparison between Romani and Cant

Henry states, Dick, you will ten to one have a lot of these cant words used today, mostly in the Midlands and the North. The Winters, Elliotts, Millers, Howards, Crosbys always use them.

Romani	Cant	English
eezaw	tuggies	clothes
wafedi	gamy	bad
duket	slang	license
livenor	peeve	alcoholic drink
Gavengro kair	Bogey hatch	police house
Pogado	pagged*	broken
kil	spread	butter
yog	glim	fire
drabengro	crocus	doctor
churi	chiv	knife
katsies	snips	scissors
mullo	mard	dead
stekas	bur	gate
juvel	buer	woman
motto	gatted	drunk
gili	chant	song
sonakei	mulek	gold
kitchema	peever*	pub
sasta	mulecky	iron
loodopen	nethers ken	lodging
cholo mauro	panam chat	loaf of bread
gudo	sweetner	sugar
keromengro	faker	maker
vonga	blacky	coal
sherengro	mushti	leader

kanni	kackler	hen
stariben	stir	prison
pukersamengro	brief	lawyer
booti kair	spike	work house
kin	keen*	buy
shunta	hark	listen
poringera	slang and kettle	a watch
bikenin	grafting	hawking
brishinameskris mush	mush faker	umbrella mender
chorrin	nickin	stealing
woodres	kip	bed
prikler	china	faker
Hindi temengri	Yurikan	Irishman
Diora	kettle	watch
luva	thoniks	money
tarderamengro	shan poke mush	drawers
mumbli	waxa	candle
tattamengri	mas chat	pepper
dadus	die	father
tattermengro	scran cover	pepper
dei	my	mother
moleivo	bluey	lead
churimengro vardo	chiv chat	knife grinding barrow
pukkerin kosht	tober chat	signpost
kek kushti	snide	no good
kordum	spread	See note
hobben	scran	food
kleembra	misali*	table
mutterimengri	slopy	tea
wafedi rei	shan mush	bad man

kan	lugs	ears
pukka les	mang* it	ask him
puvengries	growers	potatoes
atch	stall	stop
vongishni	grauni	ring
dikla	wipe	neckerchief
nok	snitch	nose
jal avre	jawl* on	go away
ridgil	kanni*	partridge
muskero	horney	policeman
muledi	crawked	died
marime	emparnid	unclean
brishindo	parni*	rain
mamlei	smut	smutty
nogo	newzy	new
nafelo	gamy	ill
nasfelo	gamy	ill
kanvongushni	luggrauny	earring
pushimosko	pushan*	wool
Boronashemescrutan	Epsom gry cover	Epsom races
sikermengro	gav gaji	signpost

Note: the word kordum *is the adjective,* blind, *whilst* spread *is slang for* butter. *I cannot see a connection.*

Second List

Romani	Cant	English
tushni	*kipsi	basket
dud	glima	light
mush	*gaji	man
balovas	sauni	bacon
budika	shova	shop
koor	*pager	fight
tuvlo	foggus	tobacco
nav	monika	name
putch	*mang	ask
maura	panam	read
baula	grunta	pig
stardi	cadey	hat
wooda	jiger	door
dikin hev	glazer	window
gorjio	flaty	non-Gypsy
luva	poke	money
barlansei	nicker	pound
posh rat	*didikai	person of mixed blood
kair	kenna	house
gav	monkrey	town
shovori	sparzi	sixpence
tringushni	jog	shilling
ora	win	penny
posh koorona	half slat	half crown
pansh koorona	caiser	five shillings
peerdomengro	needi pek	tramp
tilomengro	snickel	?poacher

vastus	fams	hands
posh ora	nage	halfpenny
dinelo	*dingla, rajd	stupid
gava mush	*mingra	policeman
drom	tober	road

*These words are actually Romani, not Cant

10. OTHERS OF DICK WADE'S ROMANY PAPERS

The following papers were also housed with those relating to Henry Sherriff but have no apparent connection with Henry. However, they have been included as valuable notes made by Dick Wade during his encounters with Gypsies.

The first batch of these is a list of mainly Shelta words. No source is given. The words are all close to the list produced by MacAlister (see Bibliography). It seems likely that Dick read words from the MacAlister source and these were then confirmed or rejected by his source, and the confirmed ones were those which Dick then noted. The quality of the Shelta is outstanding.

Although the source is not named, it was probably Adam Miller, brother of Henry Miller who was in turn my first Romani brother. Adam was that rare person of the 1960s, a fine Shelta speaker – see the Appleby section below – and there is no-one else of Dick's known Gypsy friends who would fit the bill as well as he. I met Adam in Skipton in about 1963 but as a youth I was below the social and intellectual sphere of such an eminent Gypsy. Other than passing the time of day, he did not involve himself in chats with me.

Shelta itself is the language which was spoken by previous generations of Irish Travellers. It was a full language in its own right, and classed as one of the 'secret' languages of Ireland. It is certainly extremely ancient, and is probably linked to the language used by the ancient Celtic bards. It consists of Gaelic words which have been amended or backslanged, and words from cant and Romani which have been similarly treated. I made several attempted to learn it from books, but never succeeded.

Some Shelta words are still known amongst Irish Travellers but it is difficult to assess how much. Since the 1960s, I have never found evidence of its still being spoken as a full language. I have collected samples in various parts of the country, but Dick's is the fullest list of recent years.

Shelta

The following list of Shelta is in Richard Wade's own hand. The list is reproduced as he wrote it, including the Greek letter ,which here represents the sound 'ch' as in the Scottish word 'loch'. An apostrophe after a letter indicates that the letter is aspirated.

a – his, her, of, in
a (before participle) – at (eg a kraydi, standing)
a – interrogative prefix
aburt – at all
agratis – afraid
agraisya – back, backwards
a – oh! Alas!
Aχaram – tomorrow
aχair – last night
aχim – out, outside
aχiver – before, ever
aχonsyuk – tonight
ala – another
analt – to wash
ar – on, after
arirt – again
aspra – sixpence
awast – away
avali; elum – town

balast – hair
bilsag – mouth, lips
been – great, good, grand
blatchi – coal
bladhunk – prison
blaiky – metal pot, kettle
blanag – cow
bleater – sheep
blinkie – window
blinklum – light
bog – get, find, take
bord; bunk – table
browan – corn, grain
braas – food
brassi – top feed, dine
brikler – bowl, cup
brod – house
brogies – trousers
bug – give
bulskur – wire

buri – great, fine
bwikad – to hold, keep, contain
byayg – to steal
byinyi – little
byinyan – a little
byewer – woman

chaulra – knife
charp – true, real, excellent
chigger – door
chimmel – stick
chonawdu – to go
chumik – to swear
chiuχ – *not translated*

darlyan – God
dartair – father
dunnik – cow
doora – bread
dyarelallen – eye
dyarp – true
dyigger – door
dyimmer – stick
dyonadu – to go
dyumikm – to swear
dyooχ – clothes

elima – milk
enaχ – *not translated*
eerpa – another

fay – meat
faytyerp – pan
feen – man
fogus, fungari – tobacco
furrus – Fair

gaffa – lame
garro – bull
gasal – donkey
garter – beer, drink

garter, dart'air – father
gaverog – goat
gawp – kiss
gawt – young
gawtner – young person
gawterin – child
gen – bog
ghesti – magistrate
get – to leave, cease, wait
getool – to shake, tremble, fear
getya – hot
gitan – horse
giligoppa – teapot
glader – to swindle
glodaχ – dirt, dirty
gloχ – man
gloori – to hear
glooroag – ear
glyeet – mountain
goiχil – all, every
goithean – dog
goχyi – leave, put, place
gop – poor
goppa – pot
gored– money, coin
gori; goti – put, give
goshta – plenty, many
gopa –pocket
gradum – life
graχu – hurry
gramail – like, as
grani – to know, want
granlesk – green
granta – aunt
grasano – Scotland, England
grat – smoke
grata, gruti – hot
gratya – a place, to watch
growra – summer
gradna – nail
gradni – Saturday
graskal – to open
grarg – street
grarlta – welcome
gransha – stranger
granya – ring
graak – field
graw – to love
graw – luck

grawkin – boy, lad
grawser – saucer
grawsi – to please
grawt – gold
grentya – quick
grespan – to show
gray – to rise
graidan – face
graidi – to make, do
graidya – hair
gary-ed – bridge
graiχol – tooth
graisub – pan
graityin – bird, chicken
grifi – mare,.female animal
grifin – coat, skirt
grimsher – month, year, time, weather
gris – fortune, soul
griso – to tell fortunes
grisoag – beard
grisool – a watch
grityair – dinner
grityoon – onion
greeyed – silk
greenta (-us) – market, fair
greeson – news
greesh – heart
greeto – wind
greetya – sick, ill
greetyath – sickness
greewog – fairy, witch
grolan – noise
grolsa – lazy
growmag – egg
gruber – work, job, to work
grunkel – uncle
gruppawn – cup
grood – feather, tea
grooker – sugar
groola – apple
groona – gown
groosku – whilst
grooti – to shut
gulima; strod – boot
goosh – to sit
goot – black
goot-gloχ – policeman
gootena – blacksmith
gwilyi – to lie down

gwope – cold
gyami – bad
gyamyath – badness
gye – with
gyetyam – gate
gyaig – to ask, beg
gyaigera – beggar
gyiliχon – book, bible
gyoer – penis
gyuk – old man, beggar, vagrant

hal – across
harvari – home
hawrum – morning
hawsk – across
hoo – thou, you

i – in, a
in – the
inoχ – thing (or a stop-gap word

kadyoag – stone
kyhed – chair
kam – son
kraudug; kamag – hen
kamererm – dog
kamrailid – quarrel
kara – boat
karb – to kill, strike, steal
kari – to buy, pay
karib – to kill, strike, steal
karnish – meat
kartson – needle
kowvis – testicles
kawb – cabbage
kay – where?
klyton – ditch, wall
klisp – to break
kleetug – sheep
klush – easy
kon – night
korib – to warm
koori – foot
loorig – vulva
kradyl – to stop, stay, wait
krowder – string
krimasht – parson
krish – old
krishena – the elder, the eldest

kreepuχ – cat
kroaker – doctor
krolusk – hungry
kuldrum – to sleep; asleep
kunya – excreta
kuri – horse, mule, donkey
kurlim – to close
kyen – house
kyerp – to tell a lie
kyerpa – liar
kyima – stick

Labairt – to swop
laburt – to curse, a curse
ladyeram – soap
ladu – earth, dirt, dirty
ladneach – daughter
lampa – bag
lampeid – blanket
laprog – duck, goose
laskon – salt
lashul – nice, pretty, flower
labi – to hide
lakin – girl
lyedoag – lady
liba – blood
lee – bed
lispa – dish, basin
lobarn – cabin, tent
lod – white
lodaχ – mud, dirt
lork – car, cart
lober – hit, strike, beat
losp – marry
lospo – married
lub – hole
luba – word
ludni – haste
lugil – cry out
luryan – shoes
lush – eat, drink, smoke
looke – corner
lurke – eye
ly – queer
lyag – lose, forget
lyart – mind
lyey – white
lyesk – tell
lyeskjo – story

lyibis – sweet
lyim – side, edge
lyiten – people
lyiman – mile, year
lyirk – wit, sense
lyogaχ – small boy

maksti – cat
maχal – church
maχon – cup
mankerso – handkerchief *(In brackets,*
Wade notes, 'English Shelta only')
mantri – soup, broth
mootog – stocking
miltog – shirt
mark – bone
masheen – goose
mashoor – hammer
mawlya – hand, arm, to handle
medyeri – to carry
mary – stairs
maryo – nose
midyog – shilling
milk – bit, piece
minkyer – tinker
minyurt – now, today
misla-in – raining
misler – doctor
misli – go, walk, depart
misli – want
mislier – walker, tramp
mish – hit
meeder – devil
meershrun – shawl
meeshoag – tongue
meeshur – scissors
mo – my
mong, mugatan – fool
morghen – rabbit
mugel – apple
mukinya – dwelling, habitation
mul – woman
muntyes – tobacco
munyi – good
munyath – goodness
moorin – cow
muskoag – spoon
mwena – last, behind
mwog – pig

myali – sweet
myaunes – decent
mayaur – fat
myausom – dance (n and v), dancer
myiskon – breast

na – in
nadyeram – mother
nalk – to clean
nati – turnip
nap – white
nap – to take off (clothes)
napper – to meddle with
napper – spade
nasdyesh – here
naup – give
ngyaka – tin can
nimpeen – pin
bidya – person
needyesh – no, not, nothing
nolsk – near
nobyeri – peat, bog
nuga – gun
nulsk – when
numpa – pound
nup – back, behind
nuta – hat
noop – to piss
nyakel – to ie, bind
nyark – rogue
nyarka – bucket, can
nyedas – place
nyefin – shame
nyerp – smell, smell (v and n)
nyok – wish, want
nyokalur – chain
nyuk – head, top, penny
nyurt – now

oid – butter
olomi – night
olsk – over, past
parni – hare

peck – bread
pee – mouth
prask – to break wind

rabaid – cap

rablyim – sheet
rawg – car, waggon
rark – way, manner
rarks – without
rawgli – laugh
rengan – kettle, pot
reglum – iron
Rilantu – Ireland
rilu – mad
rirk – comb
reepuχ – whore
reesbat – basket
reespoon – prison
robikin – rain
rodus – door
ruboasg – box
rudyu – sweetheart
rusparn – purse
roomoag – egg

sacarnta – quiet
saiher – chair
salk – to take, arrest
salta – belt
sarkya – field
sgyibowl – barn
sik – some
sinaul – beer
sinta – pint
siskar – sister
skai – water
skait – transported
skaihan – sailor
skaihop – whiskey
skawfer – silver
skev – fish, trout
sklawtaχ – tea
skolya – to know
skobug – ship
skop – to open
skraχo – tree, bush
skurlum – burn
slang – chain
slahog – rat
slarska – belt
slarta, sraskin – plate, dish
sloχa – rotten
slug – to fall
slunya – glass

sloopen – watch (n)
smarag – nose
sprazi – sixpence
spurk – to have intercourse, flirt
sragon – cloth
srarpa – string
sreek – done, finished
srish – basin
srittle – kettle
sreedya – wine
sreelik – wheel
sreepa – button
sroidyan – morning
srotar – key
srug – jug
stafa – long, far, late
stafara – prayer
stama – letter, paper
stameer – money, bank note
stedi – to stand
staish – yes
stoχa – soft
strod – boot
sturt – in, into
styima – pipe, bagpipe
subol – bottle
sudya – to mix
sudyata – conpany
sugoon – bacon
sulyan – baby
sumol – robber
sup – a few
surgon – bargain
surk – to hang
surχa – tired
sushgad – small pot
sublyi; shakr – brother, friend
soolya – around
sooni – to see
swurk – hair
swudal – gentleman
swurk – to sing
swurkin – song
shang – think, understand
shanger – snake, eel
sharag – kiss
sharig – to vex
shark – to cut
sharog – red

shairk – clever
sheb – to call, name
Sheldru – Shelta
shelk – to sell
shade – police
shaikar – sister
shairku – daughter
Shisher – Irish
shaidyog – soldier, policeman
sheerk – grass
sheert – down
shkimis – to booze
shkimishk – drunk
shktrawχ – tree
shkyiblyin – barn
shlawker – coat
shlia – leather
shlug – slow, weak
shlyan – ale
shlyema – frog
shluχ – to read
shluχter – scholar
shluχ – rain
shluχu – wet
shorknes – cursing
shora – wake, funeral
talop – belly
talosk – day
tarsp – to die, dead
taryin – rope
tashi – to read
tardyir – strong, hard
tardyirach – strength
taral – talk, language

tari – to talk
tawn – full, day, small
tawp – alive
tirpog – rag
ta-im – white
tom – big, great, many
topa – brave, fine
tober – road
tori – to come
torog – tramp
tre-nyuk – threepence
treep – sup, drop
treepus – fight
tul – worth, price
too – you
toor – anus
tyal – half
tyelp – to boil
tyera – fire, fuel
tyairp – to cook
tyairpin – finger, toe
tyoli – to follow
tyuk – clothes

uχ – necessity

waddler – duck
wobbler – goat

yar, yor – penis
yeryan – tin
yedug – lady
yeert – again
yui – town

Counting

nyuk; wart – 1
od – 2
shika – 3
shaka – 4
shooka – 5
shay – 6
sheltu – 7

oχt– 8
nee – 9
tyal gyetya – 10
gyetya – 20
od gyetya – 30
shook gyetya – 100

The word oχt *may be a form of the very rare Romani word* oχta, *also mean-ing 8..*

Typed Item From *Leicester Mercury*

Leicester Mercury, Friday December 18th, 1970

£150 stolen goods charges: three are sent for trial

Two scissors grinders, George Henry Sherriff (52) of 102 Sandhurst Road, Leicester and Max Vincent Sheffield (33) of 98 Station Road, Countesthorpe, were committed for trial at Quarter Sessions when they appeared at Lutterworth magistrates court yesterday charged with burglary and the theft of property valued at £150 at Peatling Magna on December 2.

The property included a silver tray and jug, silver teapot and a French wall clock.

Reginald Wallace Dashwood Green (41) of 126 Doncaster Road, Leicester, a second-hand dealer, was also committed for trial to Quarter Sessions, charged with handling stolen goods worth £124 at Leicester on December 2.

All three were given bail in the sum of £50 each.

(This press cutting post-dates Henry's release from prison when he wrote the letters to Dick Wade.)

Appleby Fair, 1964

This document is in Richard Wade's hand and is a summary of a visit he made to the famous fair in June 1964. Dick was instrumental with Gordon Boswell and other Gypsies in saving the Fair, which was due for closure. His part in this is not well known but deserves fuller recognition.

In the 'Monty' Sherriff tape, Henry claims he met Dick at the Fair, but Dick does not accept this statement.

<u>Ned Calladyne</u> Nephew of Bob Calladyne

<u>Bertie Evans</u> Welsh band of the Boswells. He and brother Denny and brother-in-law are partners in painting large buildings. All of us sat chatting in Gordon *(Boswell's)* trailer on Sunday evening after sightseers all gone. Bertie tired of the fuss and delay of scaffolding. With a high building it may take 4 days to erect and 4 days to take down again. So he has bought a second-hand fire engine and before the client has finished explaining what he wants, Bertie and his partners can be soaring aloft and the client can finish his chat through the built-in telephone.

<u>Old Airus Wood (Young)</u> Bertha told us how this old man used to wear one black shoe and one brown. Cleaned both with black polish and while he was

at it, used to brush a bit into his greying hair at the temples. Walking over the moors one day with Bertie and the conversation turned to dogs and coursing. Old Airus derided such footling about. "Don't know what people want greyhounds for to catch hares and rabbits. I've got an Alsatian'll go off and bring me a sheep. Now that is something!"

<u>Santalina Owens</u> Bertie and Denny Evans' sister. Has a very bad heart but a good looking woman and a jolly soul. Husband Tommy Owens a fine boxer who gave up the ring because he feared the consequences of his own strength.

<u>"Mickie"</u> .... (nee Whatnell) Boy-boy's sister. Unruly son Michael whose hair Gordon cut. Played with our children in the field. "Mickie" is very dark.

<u>Carrie Whatnell</u> Mickie's and Boy Boy's mother. Like several of the old dais, had her boards out on Sunday to dukker the Gaujo dupes who came shambling by.

<u>Clifford Lee</u> of Blackpool and his brother William (Ithal) Lee of Morecambe, sons of Julia Boswell (one of old Booi's daughters).

<u>Maria Wharton</u> (nee Lee), sister of Clifford and William, sitting outside her beautiful trailer by a stick fire with large pot of shredded stew hanging from a massive kettle prop. Sitting by the fire with the bubbling old pot suspended from a huge kettle iron and dressed in bright raiment, looked the eternal Gypsy. Painted since by artist with beard.

<u>Adam and Henry Lee</u> (alias Miller). Grandsons of Mammie Louie Lee, a noted old fighter who died not many months ago. Henry's large stock of Romanes, tushni, rainyaw, lalo, konaf, fardom, saster. Adam's Shelta. Applauded the tinkers' song.

Hundreds of trailers with a few little bow tops at intervals all the way up the hill from the railway bridge to the top and beyond – half way to Long Marton. On the Friday night when we arrived they seemed squeezed into every available space, but all day Saturday and Sunday morning more arrived and were fitted in somewhere – even in the dyke bottom where it is wide enough. Most of the bow-tops down by the quarry and up the little road by Gallows Hill but the quarry partly filled with heaps of stones and gravel left by the Council, either thoughtlessly or with deliberate intent to make things difficult. By Gallows Hill was a pretty little spindle-sided wagon.

Young men up at dawn for coursing. Young people in the pub at night would not have been allowed years ago. "Here's the muskras. We'll get lelled if we don't jul avree."

Scotch Corner blocked off with stones, fences. Planted with orderly rows of little trees – all looking rather like the corner of a Corporation park dropped in the open county of Yorkshire.

Did not stay for Fair Day but Gordon tells me:-

Best fair for horses for years, although not much dealing to start with. Two spotted stallions – one sold for £550. Gordon sold 4 and bought 2 more. Bad weather spoilt the trotting.

Coming back a week later, the hill all deserted.

(At the bottom of the description of Appleby, appears the following, though it is unclear to whom it refers, as the star does not also appear anywhere in the text:)

* Widow of old Bertie Evans. Gordon Boswell says these Evanses are most likely the descendants of old Byram Boswell (son of old Wester) who disappeared into Wales early in his life and lost touch with the rest of the family. Sentibel died at Carlisle (?) in October 1964. Big funeral at Lancaster. Many tales told. One of these, she smacked the bare bottom of another Gypsy woman in the main street of Lancaster. After old Bertie died, she and her family went to Australia, but came back because they missed the social life of the English Travellers and the fairs.

(Additional note on a separate page:)

Sydney Kidd (nephew of Moti Harris, a relative of Rhoda Stubley) sold one of the Smiths a chipped 5s piece for £55 in a pub, the Smith having just been saying he would like to get one, and Syd merely showing the coin without making any description. "How much would you give for this?" The Smith did not realise he had been had until next morning and then demanded his money back, but Syd wouldn't part. A lawsuit followed and Syd lost. (Related by Bill Stubley.)

Romani Words of H.C. (Koorin mush) West

Collected 1965

Bori – great
Rye – (Gypsy) gentleman
Pukker – speak, ask
Pukker Romany kushti
Pukkerd to dik mandi
Kushti – well, good
Ticknoes – children
Dik – see
Aatch – stop, sit, stand
Kekaubi sastra – kettle iron
Mandis – my
Musher – man
Gaffer – man
Aki – here
Loring – stealing
Sturabin – prison
Yek – one
Dui – two
Trin – three
Covells – year
Waffati – bad
Livenor-mengris – hops, hop fields
Lil – book
Boc – luck
Rawnie – lady
Rarti – night
Poggered – broke
Prasti – running
Duveleskoe – God
Thanks to duvuleska
Jall – go
Sumner – sack
Chats – letters
Rokki – say
diniloes – fools
prala – brother
puv – field
yog – fire
cooring – fighting
vasts – hands
vaster – hand

jin – know
dud – light
monashin- wife, woman
divvus – day
tosaulo – tomorrow
dadrus – father
dia – mother
grai – horse
kisterin-vardes – trailer caravans
hobbin – food
tuvvler – tobacco
tuv – smoke
lel – take
Yorals – *(nothing written)*
Jog – shilling
budras – bed
dukkerin – fortune telling
prastimengro – policeman
sastramengro – blacksmith
sapmengro – *(nothing written)*
kitchemer – inn
sonakei – gold
pani shock – cabbage
muller – ghost
cawlo chirclo – blackbird
pawni chiriclo – swan
Matchago – *(nothing written)*
Grasne – mare
swegler – pipe
poshero – half penny
scruner – *(nothing written)*
yasher – *(nothing written)*
pobble – apple
puvangro – potato
monguangro – beggar
chochnas – shoes
gad – shirt
milltog – shirt
glade – *(nothing written)*
lovvel – money

A Final Letter About Henry

Wootton Bassett, Near Swindon, Wilts

Dear Mr. Wade

Many thanks for your letter.

Speaking of marriage pictures, I should like to get a reproduction of "The Storm". It shows Fountain Page (Shrimp) riding a white Welsh mare, rounding up a bunch of loose horses before a storm.

Have you ever heard of a painter of Gypsies named Oakley? I believe he is mentioned in Groome's *"In Gypsy Tents"* but I have never seen any of his pictures. I wondered if you had come across any of his pictures or heard his name.

I think we now know all there is to be known of Sam Price and his waggon, but Tootsy Joe Price is still a mystery, but I do not put much faith in the Joe Taylor theory, I feel sure that he is a Price, and if he is not, why are the Prices so cagey about discussing him. Hodgon told me once he was asking John (his brother in law) what Tootsy had done to get into trouble in Ireland and John at once changed the subject

I have never heard of Gordon's "Abe Ashton Pot Cart". A builder's name I would say. Like a "Bill Wright Pot Trolley". There is a Potter family in the North. I believe Ashton is a Derbyshire name.

I had a very nice photo sent me recently of a two-wheeled grinding forge with a smart pony in the shafts; a horse-drawn grinding machine, whether two- or four-wheeled, is always called a "Forge". This photo came out in *The Birmingham Sunday Mercury*, a few weeks ago, and was sent in by a Mr. Green of 27, Beech Road, Bourneville, Birmingham a retired Shipping Clerk of 70 years of age, who is interested in obsolete horse drawn vehicles of all sorts. I wrote to him and asked him if he would sell me a copy of the original photo, and he sent me a small photo of it, and no charge.

The grinding forge travelled the Birmingham district about 25 years ago and belonged to a man named White. The newspaper photo was a bit cloudy, but the small photo was clear to good.

I heard from Henry about a week ago that he was being transferred to Ashwell Piro – Stiriben *(open prison)*. He somehow missed the last draft, but is expecting to go any day now.

I sent a few of Henry's best words to Gilliatt Smith to analyse, not mentioning any names of course.

Kuknida = a stinging nettle. This is a variant of the Czech Romane word Cuknida, the form ending in – "dka"is a Slavic diminutive ending that has been tacked on to it, actually it is a loan-word borrowed from the Greek word Tsuknida meaning a stinging nettle.

Nilo = blue. This is not a Romani word; it is a Romanified rendering of a very well known word in the Near East meaning blue dark blue. Indigo blue, it is used in Turkish and in the Bagdad dialect of Arabia. But is in origin an Old Persian word Nila meaning Indigo – blue.

Jelto = yellow is a Slavic word which the Romani folki picked up when they were in South East Europe.

Shulavka = shovel. In most Romani dialects across Europe this unoubtedly Romani word means a broom or besom and I think English Gypsies have muddled its meaning (broom) because of its similarity in sound to the English word shovell also the Welsh Rom Shuvla = a shovel which is only English Shovel + a , and I think has caused a confusion of meanings

Hulum = mushroom is a corruption of the Welsh Rom Xuxuni (huhum) and South European Rom "Khukhunr" and Hindustani "Khukh".

Mirima = Unclean, is coppersmith Romani marime.

I picked out these words as I have never heard any other Romani use them and never seen any of them in any vocabs, except marima which appears in the Coppersmith Roma in the *Journal* as marime, some of the old South Eastern European loan words are much more interesting than these compounded words in – engero like drabengero = man of the medicine = doctor.

That Stiriben Rai *(prison governor)* who is soon retiring must be a Kushko mush *(good man)*, and I would think he was interested in Romani folki, did you know there is a member of the G.L.S. who is a moskero of some sort. Miss Yates told me this once but never told me his name. I would like to know his name. Do you know the name of the Stiriben Rai (as Henry calls him)?

You no doubt read the newspaper account of the proposed Challenge to Fight by a rag and bone man with Hughie. I had the cutting sent me by a friend but sent it to Henry or I could have told you the paper it was in, however I am told that – "The next week Hughie Burton denied that anyone wanted to fight him, he said I am a peaceful man, and want to be left so. As for being King of the Gypsies, that is a load of rubbish, there are no Gypsy Kings".

My friend goes on to say, "I meant to send you that cutting also, but I have mislaid it. It is a good thing that everything went off peaceably at Doncaster, otherwise there might have been a lot of summonses for breaking the peace and a few broken heads."

I am having my kitchen and back kitchen knocked into one big kitchen, and fitted with the modern kitchen units, round the walls. We are in a proper old muddle, brick-dust and plaster flying everywhere. They reckon to have it finished in another couple of weeks.

Hoping you are keeping well and kind regards to Mrs Wade and the children.

And the best of luck
From Fred Huth

Editorial note: Additional pages of Henry's, but all taken from other sources (and therefore inauthentic), are available from Derbyshire Gypsy Liaison Group. Write for details.

BIBLIOGRAPHY

BORROW, George Henry. Romano Lavo Lil. London, Murray, 1907.

BORROW, George Henry. Lavengro. London, John Murray 1900.

BOSWELL, Sylvester. The Book of Boswell. London, Gollancz, 1970.

CAREW, F.W. No. 747, Being the Autobiography of a Gypsy. Bristol, Arrow-smiths, c 1890.

CAREW, Bampfylde Moore. Life and Adventures of Bampfylde Moore Carew, King of the Beggars. London, Buckland, Bathurst and Davies, 1793 (1st ed.).

DAWSON, Robert M. The Genealogy of the Romany Boswells. Unpublished MS, 1997.

DAWSON, Robert. Gypsy Wayside Burials. Blackwell, Derbyshire, Robert Dawson Publisher, 2000.

GROOME, F.H.. In Gipsy Tents. Wakefield, EP Publishing, 1973.

LELAND, C.G., TUCKEY and PALMER. Gypsy Songs in Romany. London, Trubner and Co, 1875.

MACALISTER, RAS. The Secret Languages of Ireland. Cambridge, The University Press, 1937.

MACCOLL, Ewan, and Seeger, Peggy. Travellers' Songs from England and Scotland. London, Routledge and Kegan Paul, 1977.

PETULENGRO, Gipsy (Xavier). A Romany Life. London, Methuen, 1937.

SAMPSON, John. The Dialect of the Gypsies of Wales. Oxford, The Claren-don Press, 1926.

SMART, B.C. and CROFTON, H.T. The Dialect of the English Gypsies. London, Asher and Co, 1975. Note: My copy of the book, having been owned by F.G. Huth, contains many additional notes in Huth's hand.

SMITH, Cornelius. The Life Story of Gipsy Cornelius Smith. London, John Heywood. C 1850.

SMITH, Rodney. Gipsy (Rodney) Smith. Various papers given to me by the family.

SMITH, Gipsy. Gipsy Smith: His Life and Work. London, National Council of the Evangelical Free Churches, 1901.

SMITH, Hubert. Tent Life with the English Gypsies in Norway. London, 1873.

STANLEY, Denise, and BURKE, Rosy. Assisted by Thomas Acton, Donald Kenrick and Bernard Hurley. The Romano Drom Song Book. Brentwwood, Essex, Romanestan Publications, 1971.

STEGGALL, John H. The Suffolk Gipsy. London, Ward Lock and Tyler, c 1857.

WADE, Richard. Mentions and articles about Henry Sherriff and by Richard Wade appeared in the following Journals of the Gypsy Lore Society (3rd Series) beginning in 1963:
    Vol XLIV, p.101, 147
    Vol XLVI, 123 ff
    Vol XLVIII, 24 ff
    Vol XLVIII, 83 ff

YATES, Dora E. My Gypsy Days. London, Phoenix, 1953.

INDICES

Index of Places

Index of People

General Index